Remarkable Stories
of Newfoundland

Other Jack Fitzgerald books

Crimes That Shocked Newfoundland
The Jack Ford Story – Newfoundland's POW in Nagasaki
Legacy of Laughter
Newfoundland Adventures – In Air, On Land, At Sea
Ten Steps to the Gallows (2 Editions)
Treasure Island Revisited – A True Newfoundland Adventure Story
Newfoundland Disasters (2 Editions)
Untold Stories of Newfoundland
Ghosts and Oddities
A Day at the Races – The Story of the St. John's Regatta
Beyond the Grave
Jack Fitzgerald's Notebook
Beyond Belief
The Hangman is Never Late
Another Time, Another Place
Where Angels Fear to Tread
Newfoundland Fireside Stories
Strange but True Newfoundland Stories
Amazing Newfoundland Stories
Up the Pond
Stroke of Champions
Too Many Parties, Too Many Pals
Convicted
Rogues and Branding Irons

Ask your favourite bookstore or order directly from the publisher.

Creative Book Publishing
430 Topsail Rd.,
St. John's, NL
A1E 4N1

Tel: (709) 748-0813
Fax: (709) 579-6511
E-mail: nl.books@transcontinental.ca
www.creativebookpublishing.ca

Please add $4.00 Canadian for shipping and handling and taxes on single book orders and $1.00 for each additional book.

Remarkable Stories
of Newfoundland

Jack Fitzgerald

St. John's, Newfoundland and Labrador
2009

© 2009, Jack Fitzgerald

Canada

We gratefully acknowledge the financial support of the Canada Council for the Arts, the Government of Canada through the Book Publishing Industry Development Program (BPIDP), and the Government of Newfoundland and Labrador through the Department of Tourism, Culture and Recreation for our publishing program.

Layout by Todd Manning and Joanne Snook-Hann
Cover design by Maurice Fitzgerald
Printed on acid-free paper

Published by
CREATIVE PUBLISHERS
an imprint of CREATIVE BOOK PUBLISHING
a Transcontinental Inc. associated company
P.O. Box 8660, Stn. A
St. John's, Newfoundland and Labrador A1B 3T7

Printed in Canada by:
TRANSCONTINENTAL INC.

Library and Archives Canada Cataloguing in Publication

Fitzgerald, Jack, 1945-
   Remarkable stories of Newfoundland / Jack Fitzgerald.

ISBN 978-1-897174-49-4

   1. Newfoundland and Labrador–History–Anecdotes.
I. Title.

FC2161.8.F597 2009   971.8   C2009-904670-9

TABLE OF CONTENTS

Dedication

I am pleased to dedicate this book to the late Michael Cahill who passed away in 2009. Mike was a long time personal friend and a well-known and respected coxswain of the Royal St. John's Regatta. He was also a source of some wonderful stories of old-time St. John's, and the Royal St. John's Regatta. Mike will be missed by all who knew him.

CHAPTER 1

FASCINATING NEWFOUNDLAND STORIES

NEWFOUNDLAND'S PINK, WHITE AND GREEN
IS BEING FLOWN BACKWARDS

Although the pink, white and green flag flown by thousands of Newfoundlanders today is believed by many to be the old Newfoundland flag, it has no official status in Newfoundland history, yet it does have international recognition.

Dr. Whitney Smith, the world's leading authority on flags and author of twenty-seven books on this subject, has displayed the Pink, White and Green in his book *Flags – Through the Ages and Across the World* published by McGrath-Hill Books, London and New York in 1975. The Pink, White and Green is displayed in his book with the caption "Newfies' Flag," and it is included in a section entitled "Ethnic and Cultural Minorities."

Dr. Smith honoured this old Native Flag in the same year by including it in a collection of silver ingots of flags produced by the Franklin Mint. He explained that he selected the Pink, White and Green of Newfoundland because of its long history of fact and legend which has made it unique among Canadian flags.

Today, the resurgence of the old flag's popularity is due to a growing feeling among Newfoundlanders that this province is not getting its fair share within the Canadian Federation. However, the flag being flown throughout the province today is being flown contrary to recognized flag protocol. According to that protocol, the colours of a flag read from the mast out. The flag should be flown with pink nearest the mast, followed by the white and green.

Not only is this confirmed in Dr. Smith's books, it was also mentioned in an editorial in the *Evening Telegram* on June 18, 1920 which stated:

> The well-known Pink, White and Green flag has no official status. It was, we believe, the flag used by some Native Society[1] back in the early days of our history, and in that way has by some become regarded as the official flag of Newfoundland. It may not be out of place to remark here that even this flag is, in the vast majority of cases, flown incorrectly. The colours of a flag read from

the mast out. The pink, therefore, should be nearest the mast. Instead, it is more often oft the mast.

– Editor, *Evening Telegram*

The flag is shown flying correctly on the cover of Fred Adams' book *Potpourri of Old St. John's* published by Creative Publishers in 1991.

THE TRADITIONAL STORY OF THE NATIVE FLAG

The story of the Pink, White and Green Newfoundland flag has its roots deep in Newfoundland history. In his book *The Paths to Yesterday*, published in 1931, John Maclay Byrnes recorded the story which he asserted was based on the best authorities.

Byrnes noted that the Native Society of Newfoundland was formed in 1840 as a protest against alleged favouritism shown to the foreign-born residents of this colony over those born in Newfoundland.

He explained:

> The flag of the Society was originally all pink, with two clasped hands extending to the elbow and a spruce tree in the centre. This tree was held in the joined palms, and underneath was the word 'Philanthropy.' The arms and the tree were green, the letters white.
>
> A great deal of ill-feeling was engendered by the Society, and bad language and rows were of frequent occurrence. The culmination point was reached in February 1843 during a big haul of wood for Bishop Fleming. There was considerable rivalry for the biggest load, and each slide bore distinctive colours.
>
> The 'Bush Borns' and the 'Old Country' people had a difference of opinion as to which had the larger load, and a row ensued in which a good many heads were broken. When Bishop Fleming heard of it, he called the ringleaders together, gave them a bit of advice, and induced them to join the Pink and Green together. This they did by inserting a piece of neutral White between, and thus was born the flag as we have it today.
>
> A few of the founders stuck to the plain pink for two or three years, but after the death of Richard Barns, the

Native Society's leader, and the blowing down of the Native Hall in 1834, the Pink, White and Green became the recognized Native Flag.

LOGAN STONE FOUND AT PETTY HARBOUR
A curiosity at Petty Harbour attracted the attention of a visitor in 1857. It was a large several ton stone on a hill opposite the Anglican Church on the south side of the harbour. What made this stone unusual was that it sometimes rocked back and forth without any apparent outside force being applied. Yet, it was impossible for several men to dislodge it. One could imagine the superstition and beliefs that the stone inspired.

In 1857, Reverend William Grey was visiting Petty Harbour as part of his project to publish a book of coloured pencil sketches of communities along the Newfoundland and Labrador coasts. Upon returning to England, he completed his book and gave it the title *Sketches of Newfoundland and Labrador* which was published in 1858 at Ipswich by S. B. Cowell, Anastatic Press.[2]

Referring to the Petty Harbour curiosity, Grey explained, "This rock is what Druidical antiquaries would call a Logan Stone. The Druids were the priests and learned classes of the ancient Celts in Britain prior to the Roman invasions."

RARE STONE

Although rare, Logan Stones are found in many places around the world. England has its famous Men Amber and Pendower Logan Stones while Scotland boasts of the Coylton, and the Samnox Logan Stones. Perhaps the world's largest Logan Stone is the one in Burma on which the famous religious shrine Kyaiktiyo Pagoda is built.

Thanks to Reverend Grey's mid-nineteenth century book, Petty Harbour can now be added to any list of Logan Stones found around the world.

The strange nature of Logan Stones caused many to associate them with witchcraft or the Druids. For example, it is claimed that a Logan Stone in Cornwall, England could only be moved by a witch at midnight. The stones are also associated with being used to cure childhood diseases. A sick child rocked on a Logan Stone would be cured of his illness.

Incredible as it may sound, the several ton rock shown in this picture had the power to move apparently unaided by any outside physical force, and may still have it. It was identified as a Logan Stone in 1857 by author Reverend William Grey. The stone is known at Petty Harbour as Indian Rock. This picture was taken between 1895 and the early 1900s.

WHAT IS A LOGAN STONE?

A Logan Stone is one left by nature to be so balanced that a wisp of wind can move it. Among the lore surrounding Logan Stones is the claim, "A wisp of wind can move it, but sixty men could not dislodge one." Little wonder, then, that a wide variety of beliefs associated with them have developed over the centuries.

GOOD FORTUNE FOR PETTY HARBOUR

Besides witchcraft, Logan Stones are associated with ancient law practices, religious ceremonies and superstitions. One such superstition is that they bring good fortune to communities where they are found and to honest people who touch them.

Sometimes superstitions worked against the Logan Stone as was the case in Cornwall, England in 1650. This stone was described as being a very sensitive rocking stone and was named 'Men Amber.' During the Cromwell era it was dislodged because of a prophecy of Merlin. Merlin claimed that the Men Amber would stand until the monarchy in England came to an end.

USED IN ANCIENT LAW

In Scotland, the stones, sometimes called 'Judgement Stones,' were once part of the justice system and open air courts were held around them. If the stone moved during a statement being made by an accused person, he was deemed an innocent man and allowed to go free. T. Lowndes wrote in his book *The History and Antiquities of the Parish of Halifax* in Yorkshire in 1775, "The Brimham Logan Stone in Yorkshire is said to rock only for the efforts of an honest man."

USED IN ANCIENT LAW

Grey's discovery is long forgotten in Petty Harbour as was any knowledge of a Logan Stone or what it represented. Yet generations of Petty Harbour people found something special about this stone. They chose the name 'Indian Rock' for this wonder which is edged on a hill that is passed by thousands of visitors each year.

Once moved by a wisp of wind, the Petty Harbour 'Indian' Logan Stone remains where it stood in 1857. Perhaps the wonderstone still moves on its own, and in this modern world where everyone is in a hurry to get some place or another, the curiosity goes unnoticed. Maybe the passing of over 150 years has taken its toll or interfered in some way with its curious nature. Regardless, we do know that it once attracted the attention of a well known clergyman and author during the summer of 1857.

UNIQUE WHISTLE OF FIRST NEWFIE BULLET TRAINS

The Newfie Bullet was once described as probably the only railway in the world whose engines have been charged head-on more than fifty times by bull moose. J. Wentroth Day in his book *Newfoundland, the Fortress Isle* said there was a good reason for this. He explained, "There were problems with moose because the original train whistle sounded like a moose's mating call. They eventually changed the note of the whistle."

Also, there were frequent occasions when the train was held up by vast herds of caribou on the track.

Jack Fitzgerald photo
The Newfie Bullet was a name describing the Newfoundland cross-country train system. It was attributed to movie star Joan Blondahl when she sang the song in a live broadcast to the American troops around the world in February 1943. It was part of a show called *Command Performance* which was broadcast from Carnegie Hall in New York City. See *Newfoundland Adventures: In Air, On Land, At Sea,* by Jack Fitzgerald.

THE ACTUAL OLDEST CITY IN NORTH AMERICA

Although St. John's is promoted as the oldest city in North America and Water Street the oldest street, neither claim is historically correct. The claim ignores that Mexico City was a metropolis before Cabot discovered Newfoundland and even before Columbus discovered America. At the time of the Spanish conquest, Mexico City was one of the greatest cities in the world. Its main drag, the Passeo de la Reforma, had eight lanes and was constructed by order of Emperor Montezuma long before Water Street was a pathway. St. John's may correctly claim to be the oldest city in Canada.

MYSTERY OBJECT MAY HAVE BEEN
SIR HUMPHREY GILBERT'S

Twenty-five years ago I came across a newspaper clipping, dry and yellowing with age, stuck to another item and filed among a stack of about sixty or seventy clippings in the offices of the Newfoundland Historical Society. After reading it, I was amazed at its contents. It told the story of the discovery on September 23, 1943, of an ancient, mysterious object in the harbour at Bay Bulls. The find attracted a great deal of public attention and, if speculation as to its origins could be proven, it would have an effect on a major event in Newfoundland history.

National Archives Canada
An artifact believed to be connected to Sir Humphrey Gilbert's visit to Newfoundland in 1583 has been missing since 1943. Jack Fitzgerald's attempt to trace the item turned up this picture which was taken at Canada House on Circular Road in 1943. Hon. C.J. Burchill, Canada's High Commissioner to Newfoundland, is shown examining what was described as "A relic of Sir Humphrey Gilbert's sojourn in Newfoundland in 1583." Its amazing story is told below.

This discovery took place during WWII when the Royal Canadian Navy was operating a repair and supply base at Bay Bulls. During the dredging of the Bay Bulls Harbour by the Cape Shore Construction Company to accommodate navy needs, one of its steam shovels picked up a piece of metal that caused excitement throughout Newfoundland.

The engineer on the job, a man named Jenkins, reported that the object was found in about four feet of silt, fifty feet from the shore. It was made of lead and measured eighteen inches long, four inches wide and two inches deep. The item was a hollow, oblong object which at one time was affixed to a staff or post. It was flattened on both ends and seemed to have been hacked by some rough implement.

One side had carved into it what seemed to be the copy of a seal in oval form, with a face in bold relief, surrounded by a scroll of possibly flowers or leaves. There was no lettering on the object, but a series of undecipherable numbers appeared on top.

On September 24, members of the press joined Dr. Vincent Burke, President of the Newfoundland Historical Society, at Bay Bulls to inspect the discovery. Some people suggested the item was the Royal Arms used by Sir Humphrey Gilbert to claim Newfoundland for England in 1583. Gilbert's Royal Arms were cut in lead and affixed to a pillar which he put into the earth when he made his historic claim. That event was described in Moses Harvey's *History of Newfoundland* which states, "The Banner of England was hoisted on a flagstaff. The Royal Arms, cut in lead, was affixed to a pillar near the water's edge to mark the ceremony."

If the mystery item was Gilbert's Royal Arms, the question arises as to how it got into Bay Bulls Harbour. Hon. H. A. Winter, Commissioner for Home Affairs and Education, accepted the artifact which he intended to send to the College of Heralds in London for assessment and identification. The article has since disappeared.

Several years ago, I made an inquiry to the College of Heralds, London, England, requesting information on the item with a recommendation that it be returned to Newfoundland. I was informed that they had no record of ever having received the item. Neither could I find any record of the item being stored at the Newfoundland Museum or Archives.

It is possible that the item was stored in some government building during the era of Commission of Government. I was able to determine that, at one time, it had been held by the Canadian High Commissioner in Newfoundland, C. H. Burchill, at Canada House on Circular Road. I have previously written about fossils and mineral samples which were stored by the Commission of Government, and mistakenly crushed into stone and used to construct a floor in the old Sanatorium on Topsail Road. Perhaps the mystery article met a similar fate.

UNKNOWINGLY DESTROYED PIECE OF HISTORY

An even more incredible story regarding the loss of an historic item occurred in 1926. When Old Day's Pond, Bonavista Bay, was drained in 1926, a group of fishermen unearthed an object from the bottom which had a connection with one of the best-known events in Newfoundland history. Unfortunately, the men had no idea of its value. They destroyed it.[3]

The item recovered was the remains of a black oak lifeboat, of the type used by the English during the reign of Queen Elizabeth I. The timbers and planking were still intact and the measurements and identifying material were easily obtainable.

The craft had a brass disk fixed to it showing the date 1583. On the disk was displayed an emblem, the heads of a double eagle with the letter G in between. A French coin from the time of Louis XIII of France was found jammed in the boat's timber.

The men felt the boat was of no special value. They simply broke up the wood and divided it among themselves. Some dried the wood and used it as firewood. The others made oak walking sticks from their shares.

Meanwhile, the brass disk passed from family to family until, in 1930, it fell into the hands of the Anglican clergyman, Reverend Canon Boyle. Boyle was curious as to where the boat came from and what the emblem represented. Through study and research, he learned the boat had been twenty-five feet long and the date on the plate coincided with the year Sir Humphrey Gilbert had claimed Newfoundland. Gilbert was the only one known to hold a patent for Newfoundland at that period. The Reverend concluded that the emblem was Sir Humphrey Gilbert's, and the boat had once belonged to him.

This team of hockey players sporting sweaters displaying the Nazi swastika, the symbol of the Third Reich, played in a hockey tournament in St. John's in 1911. These players, however, had no connection with the Third Reich, but were a team from Windsor, Nova Scotia, who visited St. John's to compete in a three-game series with local teams. St. John's won the first game 5-4, with Windsor winning the second game 4-3. It was a close and exciting tournament with the third game ending in a two-all draw. In the final game, St. John's scored the winning goal to take the tournament.

THE SWASTIKA TEAM

The late Frank Graham, Newfoundland Sports Archivist, noted:

> The series was not without significance inasmuch as a native-born Newfoundlander, Jack McGrath, (In picture seated on floor at the left) played with the visitors. McGrath was studying at Dalhousie University in 1911 and joined the visitors on the trip to Newfoundland. Jack distinguished himself at Dalhousie. On graduating in law from that university he emigrated to the United States and ultimately became secretary to Theodore Roosevelt, President of the United States. In the early 1920s, he was one of the prime movers responsible for introducing professional hockey (NHL) to the United States.

PRESIDENT HOOVER'S ADVISER A NEWFOUNDLANDER

During the term of United States President Herbert Hoover, his right-hand man in Europe was a Newfoundlander named William Goode who became Sir William. In a book on Newfoundland, written by Premier J. R. Smallwood in 1937, the author wrote, "The name may not convey much to American readers, but in certain parts of Europe Sir William Goode's personality loomed for awhile in large proportions. He was born in Newfoundland, the son of the Reverend T. A. Goode. He served as purser in the British Merchant Marines, then for awhile in 1894 in the 4th US Cavalry. When he left the cavalry, he became night city editor of the *New York Recorder*, and in 1895 he was made city editor of the *New York Mercury*. Later he was employed by the Associated Press and represented them on Admiral Sampson's flagship throughout the Spanish-American War. After the war, he was sent to England for six years. Eventually, having left the Associated Press, he became news editor, and then managing editor, of *The Daily Mail*.

He was unofficial advisor to the Government of Hungary. During the war, he was liaison officer of the Ministry of Food with the US and Canadian Food Administrations. He was organizer of the National Committee for Relief in Belgium and in that connection became the right-hand man in Europe to Hoover. He was President of, and British representative on the Austrian section of the Reparation Commission."[4]

THE SCALPING AT CAVENDISH SQUARE

As barbaric as it sounds, an inhabitant of St. John's was scalped in a most brutal fashion in the area of Cavendish Square. The incident took place during a French invasion of St. John's in November 1696.

One hundred and eighty men, women and children from the town of St. John's sought refuge inside Fort William during the French attack upon the town. Fort William was located in the area known today as Cavendish Square.

The soldiers inside the fort held off the French for three days. On the third day, the French brought forward one of their prisoners, a St. John's man named William Drew. Viciously, they began the scalping process on Drew. The attack was described in *A History of Newfoundland*[5], "Drew was cut all around his scalp and then, by the strength of hand, stripped of his skin from the forehead to the crown."

The French sent their victim, covered in blood, inside the fort with the message that if those inside did not surrender, all of them would be inflicted with the same brutal treatment. A surrender was arranged, and soldiers and private citizens were taken prisoner by the French.

STRANGEST BIRTHPLACE

Perhaps the strangest birthplace known to Newfoundlanders was the birthplace of Michael McNamara of Murphy's Cove, Catalina, Trinity Bay. McNamara was born on a pan of ice in April of 1862. In that month, a schooner left Catalina for St. John's carrying a small crew, and several men and women passengers. Among the passengers was a Mrs. McNamara, who was pregnant. During the trip a sudden storm struck and the little schooner became trapped in the ice. The storm continued, and the pressure of the ice crushed and sank the schooner. Fortunately, all hands were able to escape onto a large pan of ice and they succeeded in taking a supply of food and some tarpaulins. Soon after the men had constructed a shelter from the tarpaulins, Mrs. McNamara gave birth to a baby boy. It was believed that this was the one and only case of its kind in the history of Newfoundland or any other country. Several days passed before the stranded people were rescued by a passing steamer which brought them to St. John's. Michael McNamara passed away in 1942 at the age of 80 years.

INCREDIBLE AIRLINE ACCIDENT

One of the rarest of accidents to occur on an airplane took place in the skies over Newfoundland in March of 1947, and made front page news around the world.

The incident took place at exactly 9:05 p.m. on March 14, 1947, in a Trans-World Airlines Constellation which was flying south of Newfoundland. When word of the tragedy reached TWA officials, they immediately issued an order that all Constellations in service adjust their maximum height to 12,000 feet.

The flight had been operating normally at the time, and was cruising at 19,000 feet. Navigator George H. Hart, thirty-five years old and of Stag Harbour, New York, was taking a navigation shot of the stars. Without warning, the Plexiglas astrodome broke away from the plane. The pressurization of the cabin carried Hart through the dome hatch. Immediately, the co-captains of the plane, J. T. Miller and O. S. Hamilton, changed course and landed at Gander, Newfoundland. They had been en route to Geneva via Santa Maria in the Azores and Paris, France. The plane had been carrying eighteen passengers.

As a result of the tragedy, the airline ordered that all their aircraft be equipped with a harness in the astrodome to protect the navigator. Also, the dome itself was redesigned and made safer.

WORLD FAMOUS PILOT VISITS ST. JOHN'S

An American Overseas Airliner which was en route from Shannon, Ireland to New York City made an unscheduled landing at Torbay Airport in St. John's on January 3, 1947. Its pilot made world history just seventeen months earlier as co-pilot of the *Enola Gay*, the B29 bomber which dropped the atomic bomb on Hiroshima on August 6, 1945. The co-pilot's name was Robert A. Lewis.

During his stay he visited with Brendan Devine, a well-known citizen of St. John's with whom he had attended school in New Jersey.

A CURIOSITY IN AN OLD ST. JOHN'S CANDY SHOP

During the month of July 1922, there was much excitement and curiosity around St. John's which was caused by a very unusual item on display in Mrs. Poole's Candy Store, which was located at the western corner of New Gower and Springdale Streets.

The item was described in newspapers as, "A freak of nature." It was part of the left claw of a lobster and a little larger than a walnut. *The Evening Telegram* of July 16, 1922 described what made it so unique:

> The item exhibits plainly the features of a human face and when viewed sideways has the characteristic features of the late Queen Victoria. (Seen from other angles of the curio, it shows the head of an elephant and a bulldog.) The lobster from which the exhibit was taken was caught about two years ago in Notre Dame Bay by Mr.

Absalom Solomon Burton, who has exhibited it in over 180 places around Newfoundland. It shows no sign of touching up and is simply mounted on a small shield.

The lobster from which the claw was taken was boiled, and the teeth and wrinkles in the shell make the representations realistic.

(Above item was found in The Evening Telegram, *July 16, 1947, p6 in column entitled* From The Telegram Files.*)*

STRANGE FISH IN NEWFOUNDLAND WATERS!

Occasionally, while researching old newspapers, I have come across items that remind me of the saying, "Truth is stranger than fiction." The following item which I found in *The Daily News* on August 16, 1909 is such an item. The headline read, "STRANGE FISH– WHAT IS IT?"

The article reads:

Captain Fitzpatrick of the coastal steamer *Portia* brings news this trip of a peculiar fish recently captured in Fortune Bay. About two weeks ago, fishermen overhauling their salmon nets found the strange monster rolled up in the twine at Point Rosey.

The fish measured about twenty-five feet in length and was about twenty feet around the body. There were two forelegs measuring five feet each in length, while the tail fin held a perpendicular position when the fish swam.

Having been captured, it was taken ashore and the liver, which filled eight barrels, yielded a rich, brown looking oil when melted by the sun, closely resembling seal oil in smell. A portion of the bone as well as the gill was brought here by Captain Fitzpatrick, and may be seen by those interested at the coastal office of Messrs. Bowring Bros, Ltd.

No person on the coast has ever seen any product of the sea like this latest find, and, there is naturally much speculation as to what it is. A small quantity of the oil has been brought here with a view of determining its value.

Reproduced from
The Evening
Telegram,
November 1904
One of the strangest sea craft ever to visit Newfoundland was the egg shaped one shown in this photograph taken November 15, 1904 and described as a "Marine Wonder."

THE *URAD*: MARINE WONDER IN ST. JOHN'S HARBOUR

Newfoundlanders were in awe over the arrival in Petty Harbour on November 15, 1904, of a craft described by *The Evening Telegram* as, "The greatest marine wonder ever devised in the way of a lifeboat." Even the most experienced seamen watching the craft tie up at Petty Harbour were amazed by what they were viewing.

The *Urad* was in the shape of an egg with a signal mast near the pointed nose. When the vessel was closed with its crew inside, it was considered the most bizarre object to meet at sea. It measured eighteen feet long, about twenty-four feet in circumference, eight feet high and eight feet wide. *The Evening Telegram* noted, "The people of Petty Harbour were absolutely astounded at this peculiar object entering port."

Captain O. Brude was accompanied on his cross-Atlantic adventure by a three-man crew which included Iver Thorsen, Karl

Johannsen and Lars Madsen. The boat was designed and built in Norway by Captain Brude, who sailed it successfully across the Atlantic. Brude was believed to be about twenty-two years old at the time. His interest in the project was sparked by an offer by the Government of France of a large cash prize to the person who could develop the safest lifeboat, and demonstrate its safety at sea.

It took 100 days to cross the Atlantic. The *Urad* left Alesund, Norway, on August 6, 1904. Brude told reporters they could not have picked a better period of time to test the safety and reliability of the vessel. The *Urad* ran into frequent storms and hurricanes, and the Captain and crew were forced to remain inside the egg-shaped vessel for the entire trip. During the storms, the single wing was folded and the vessel allowed to drift. Most of the time, the *Urad* was beneath the surface. The experience proved it to be waterproof, and the ventilation system worked perfectly. The bottom of the vessel was double with a water tank for ballast. A small skig, which contained a rudder, extended astern. If this was destroyed, or torn from the ship, the *Urad* would remain watertight. Even the breaking of the outer shell by collision would not endanger the lives of those on board. The steering gear was inside the hull and from there it was navigated across the ocean.

After arriving at Petty Harbour, Captain Brude went to St. John's and stayed the night at the Crosbie Hotel where he met with the press to talk about his invention and adventure. He returned to Petty Harbour on the tugboat *Ingraham* the next day and returned to St. John's with the egg-shaped vessel.

Thousands of people visited the little marine wonder at the wharf of C.F. Bennett & Company. While in St. John's, the *Urad* was fitted with a new iron spar and a fresh supply of water and provisions were taken on board. Improvements were made inside the hull for the crew.

The public was invited to visit inside the *Urad* for a fee of ten cents. Hundreds availed of the opportunity. They found the hull very comfortable, the lockers were upholstered in leather and the vessel carried an adequate supply of specially designed lifebelts. *The Evening Telegram* noted, "She is the most novel thing in the way of a boat ever seen inside this harbour and is well-worth ten cents for inspection."

The *Urad* was driven ashore at Gloucester, Maine, on January 10, 1905.

WHO WAS PETER THE BONESETTER?

A high vertical tombstone standing inside Belvedere Cemetery bears the inscription, "Peter Brennan Who Died a Celibate." In nineteenth century St. John's, Brennan was a famous and wealthy citizen who many believed was a true saint, and he was respectfully called "Peter the Bonesetter." He helped those in need of his special gift without charge, and traveled in winter over difficult roads in storms, at risk to his own life.

When he passed away, he left a fortune behind, with most of it being distributed to Catholic Churches around the Avalon Peninsula, including an amount to improve the Catholic Church at Petty Harbour. He also left large amounts of money to Catholic Churches in his home city in Ireland. Some of his wealth went into perpetual funds which are still being used today for charitable purposes.

The following item recorded from *The Newfoundlander* of February 13, 1845, will give the reader an idea of the type of person Peter was. It stated:

> As I have been called upon from time to time during the last 24 years by those who have unfortunately met with dislocated and fractured limbs, some of which have been of long standing when placed under my care, and which were before in the hands of gentlemen, who pretend to understand the art of Bone Setting, and who left them in a worse condition than at first, and as my chief reward has been traveling far and near, through frost and snow and unbroken paths, I beg of those who may unfortunately receive such injury to let me know in time.

> There are six now labouring under different cases these three or four months and who are in a more dangerous state than when they received the injury. I will take any one of these six and with God's assistance put his limb beyond danger in twenty minutes. At the same time I will wager two hundred pounds in money to be staked with Ambrose Shea, Esq., with any man that he will not make a cure of either of the six cases.

THE BONESETTER BECOMES POLITICIAN

In 1866, Peter Brennan was elected to the Newfoundland

Carter-Fitzgerald Photography

Tombstone of Peter the Bonesetter.

Parliament for the district of St. John's West as an anti-confederate. He defeated the popular John Casey. In 1869, he stood again
as an anti-confederate and won the district by acclamation.
He was also mentioned in a popular political song of the
1870s called *The Bennett Government*. The song describes the scene
in the Speaker's Room at the Colonial Building immediately after
the closing of the 1871 Assembly. In the last stanza of a seven
stanza song, it states:

"Maister Sphaker," quoted Brennan, "Oh hone and
Oh hone,"
Why didn't the Major just fracture a bone.
I'd have set it as nately-ome, shut up, says Glen,
Here's the Premier's good health, Mr. Speaker, say when.
Come gentlemen all, 'tis the session's last day,
Let us all liquor up, and the country shall pay.
Then fill high the bowl, with champagne fill the cup,
We've all sacked our tin, and the session is up.

Peter Brennan passed away on Friday, April 15, 1887, at the
age of 98. Peter the Bonesetter was born at County Kilkenny,
Ireland and moved to St. John's with several of his brothers at an
early age. He lived on Monday's Pond Road (Mundy Pond Road)
on the part which has since been renamed St. Clare Ave.

ASTOUNDING INCIDENT

In the year 1761, one of the most astonishing events ever to
occur at sea took place on an English ship taking passengers to
St. John's, Newfoundland. According to *The Newfoundlander* of
June 1848:

The accident sounds incredible, but it is sober history, for it is recorded in the 1761 edition of "The Annual
Register," an old annual publication which published all
the main events in English history from year to year during a period of almost a century.
The English vessel was the *Tuscany*, hailing from
Bristol in command of Captain Edward Power. She left
Bristol late in April 1761, and evidently was carrying a
number of crews to engage in the Newfoundland fishery.

On the first day, they encountered the French Duke de Biron's privateer which immediately opened fire on them. The *Tuscany*, in those wartimes, was obviously carrying some explosives, for the account says that when the French privateer's shots struck her, she blew up.

Out of 211 people aboard, only the captain and four or five others were saved. Among those saved was an infant. When the explosion occurred, this infant was blown completely away from the *Tuscany*, and landed on the deck of the Frenchman completely unhurt!

FATHER AND SON FROZEN TO DEATH IN EACH OTHER'S ARMS

The tragic deaths of Reuben and Albert John Crew at the 1914 seal hunt were considered to be among the most pathetic tragedies to occur in Newfoundland in three hundred years. Reuben Crew and his son Albert John were natives of Elliston, Trinity Bay. At the time of the sad event, Reuben was forty-nine years old and had been going to the seal hunt since he was a young boy.

He gave up the hunt in 1911, but when he learned that his sixteen-year-old son Albert had secured a berth on the SS *Newfoundland* and was determined to go to the 'ice' for the first time, Reuben decided to go with him. According to Joseph R. Smallwood, the Barrelman, "Reuben went to help initiate his son, but principally to keep a protective fatherly eye on him out there where hundreds of Newfoundlanders have met their end."

In a 1946 broadcast, Smallwood said:

The rest is quickly told. That was the year of the Newfoundland disaster when scores of her sealers were caught out in a howling storm and perished. Both Reuben and Albert Crew were found on a pan of ice, both frozen to death. They were found frozen together with the boy's head inside his father's blue guernsey where the father had tried to protect him from the fury of the blizzard, while his own life ebbed away. They were brought to their home in Elliston, and buried without being separated. Truly, may the fishermen and seal hunters of Newfoundland exclaim, 'If blood be the price of glory, we have paid in full!'

HYPNOTIST PULLS STUNT ON
BOWRING BROTHERS' ROOF

In 1954, hypnotist 'Uncanny Barardo' hit St. John's with his famous act days after the arrest of Dr. Alfred Valdmanis, who was at the centre of one of Newfoundland's most famous political scandals. Cars jammed the Torbay Airport area to get a glimpse of Valdmanis under RCMP escort after being arrested in New Brunswick. Newspapers ran banner headlines, and hundreds turned up at the Duckworth Street courthouse to get a glimpse of the man at the centre of the nationwide news story.

With such strong competition for media attention, Barardo came up with a daring stunt to divert some of the attention from Valdmanis to himself. He announced that he would walk blindfolded along the parapet of the roof of Bowring Brothers' Department Store on Water Street.

On the same day that newsmen flocked to the courthouse to cover an appearance by Valdmanis, the Uncanny Barardo was on top of Bowring's roof. After explaining his stunt to the hundreds of citizens who had turned out, he had an attendant tightly blindfold him and had two witnesses to verify it.

As Barardo edged his way along the edge of the roof with both hands extended to provide balance, many spectators gasped. According to *The Evening Telegram*:

> The most exciting moments came as he mounted the raised buttresses on the roof, and crossed them. Many times it appeared he would fall, but with his uncanny sense of balance, he accomplished the feat and received the thunderous plaudits of the crowds below.
>
> The great Uncanny Barardo was brought to St. John's by the Canadian Legion and he performed a series of shows at their hall.

THE STRANGER AT GLEESON'S BOARDING HOUSE

Gleeson's Boarding House was a popular establishment in St. John's during the nineteenth century. It was located on Carter's Hill near the property of Nancy Coyle[6], an area believed to be haunted for more than a century. One of the interesting stories associated with Gleeson's is that of a tenant she had between 1876 and 1880. His death is a mystery that has never been solved.

There was no reason to have any suspicions about the man, until after his death on Thursday, December 23, 1880. He was known at the boarding house as a real gentleman, and he sometimes left the city for weeks to visit the outports. His frequent departures from the city were not questioned because it was known that he had worked as steward on a vessel owned by John Munn and Company. However, after his death some interesting facts came to light that shocked the Gleesons and those few who knew him in St. John's. For example, in Carbonear he was believed to be a Professor Hubbard, and accorded a great deal of respect during his visits.

Stranger still is that at Change Island, Herring Neck, and along the French Shore, he was a welcome visitor at any time. In those communities, he was known and respected as Dr. Sheppard, and tended to the medical needs in those communities.

On June 25, 1880, there was a diphtheria epidemic at Joe Batt's Arm and Barr'd Island. When Mr. Sheppard heard of this, he bade farewell to his friends at Gleeson's and days later was treating the sick at Joe Batt's Arm as Dr. Sheppard. In addition to caring for those afflicted with diphtheria, the saintly Dr. Sheppard cured several people suffering from erysipelas, a skin infection. He then moved on to Barr'd Island to deal with a diphtheria epidemic and contracted the disease himself. He passed away on December 23, 1880. He was buried at the Church of England Cemetery on Barr'd Island. While his body was being prepared for burial, another mystery was noticed. On his arm, the name Thomas Davis was marked in India ink. Who Mr. Sheppard really was has never been determined. However, it was said that he was a native of Florida before coming to Newfoundland.

Other than the above, nothing was known of him. Whether or not he was truly a doctor mattered little to the many people he nursed back to health. Nobody had anything unkind to say about him, and the fact that he lived several lives while in Newfoundland didn't change Mrs. Gleeson's opinion that he was always a fine Christian gentleman.

THE FLOATING BOARDING HOUSE

During the early 1890s, people from the outports visiting St. John's to do business or seek work could avail of cheap rates at the city's only floating boarding house, the *Devon*. The *Devon* was anchored at Rogerson's Wharf (opposite Queen Street).

In July 1894, the *Devon* sprung a leak and sank at Rogerson's Cove. To the delight of its patrons, the *Devon* was refloated and reopened. *The Daily News* reported on August 1, 1894, "It was resurrected by the skillful management of Mr. Joseph Tuff, Mr. Rogerson's wharfinger. The job was done with the aid of a Spanish windlass; the *Devon* is now afloat and the interior of the ship has been thoroughly cleansed."

THE BRIGUS MONSTER

One evening some citizens of Brigus were passing along the home of Captain Bob Bartlett when they heard a loud grunting and snorting in a nearby garden. They never heard the like of it before and were frightened. They dared not go near to investigate and one of them suggested it might be a mad bull. However, they were certain that neither Bartlett nor anyone else in the immediate area owned a bull, and this thought terrified them more than ever. The citizens told others, and in a short time a crowd had gathered near the Bartlett home. All heard the same furious grunting and general uproar as if some giant creature was tearing up the ground and uprooting the trees and bushes. People became convinced that there was some kind of monster on the Bartlett property. In daylight the next day, the people of Brigus were relieved, and many had a good laugh when they learned that the monster was a creature brought back to Brigus by Captain Bartlett on his recent Arctic expedition. Bartlett had taken some animals from the arctic which he was delivering to a Zoo in New York. The 'Monster,' which people had feared the night before, was actually a full-grown walrus which the Captain had let loose in his garden.

MILES OF SLEEPWALKING

In the early twentieth century, a lady who lived at New Chelsea, Trinity Bay, was known as the woman with Newfoundland's sleepwalking record. She was known simply as 'Granny Harris.' Just four miles from New Chelsea was the settlement of New Melbourne where one of Granny Harris's daughters lived.

One hot summer's night, Granny Harris got up out of bed while still sleeping, and walked the entire four miles to New Melbourne, and another quarter of a mile to her daughter's home. She entered the home, got in bed with her daughter, and did not awake until daylight the next day. This was not the only sleepwalking experience of Granny Harris, but it was her longest.

PUNCH, A WONDER DOG

Punch was the pet dog of a Mr. A. Goodyear of Trinity Bay, Newfoundland, during the 1940s. Punch amazed his owners and their neighbours by a practice he developed while eating hot food. When the Goodyears first got Punch, they used to feed him the pot liquor in which dinner had been boiled, with added leftovers from dinner. The pot liquor was usually too hot for Punch to poke his nose and mouth down to get at it. When Mr. Goodyear saw this, he helped the dog by picking up a few lumps of ice from a nearby snowbank and dropping them into the feeding tub to cool it down. The amazing thing about this dog was that he quickly caught on to the practice. Afterwards, whenever the pot liquor was poured into his feeding tub, Punch would first fetch a couple of lumps of ice with his mouth and then drop them into the meal and wait a few minutes for it to cool before he started to eat it. When ice was not available, Punch would use mouthfuls of snow.

ANOTHER AMAZING DOG

How long can a dog survive on a pan of ice in the Atlantic without food? This story answers the question. In 1888, the Newfoundland schooner *Willie R* sailed to the ice fields in the Gulf. She was somewhere off Cape Anguille, at the southern mouth of St. George's Bay, when the skipper's dog, Knotty, strayed away from the schooner and became lost.

Fifty-four days later, a North Sydney schooner was sailing along about seventy-five miles from Prince Edward Island, and came upon Knotty on the ice. The poor dog was pretty miserable, but very much alive. Knotty was taken on board the vessel, given water and food and taken to North Sydney. Weeks later, the Newfoundland captain who owned the dog heard of the rescue of a dog at sea and went to North Sydney to investigate. There was no doubt the survivor was Knotty. When he saw his master, his tail wagged and he rushed to greet the Captain.

NOT READY FOR WOMEN DOCTORS

The following story provides some insight into conditions in old-time Newfoundland. In 1802, the doctor at Ferryland District was Dr. Michael Davenport Dutton. That same year, Dutton came up against competition, not from a man, but from a woman. However, she was not a certified doctor, and according to court records for 1802, the following letter was issued by Dr. Dutton:

> Notice to Margaret Curry ordering her to desist from practicing as a doctress at Trepassey or any other place in the Island of Newfoundland, and if I find upon my return you continue to follow this practice, I will cause your house to be pulled down and have you conveyed out of the island.
>
> *Signed - Dr. Michael Davenport Dutton*

That was the last ever heard of Margaret Curry as a medical practitioner in Newfoundland.

UNUSUAL FORCES HELPED FIND MISSING CHILD

A little girl lost for a week in the countryside near British Harbour, Trinity Bay, was located and returned home safely due to two strange happenings. In 1947, Mrs. Robert Rodgers of St. John's confirmed her story, which happened when she was five years old and living at British Harbour.

One day she went berry-picking with her aunt and they were accompanied by the family dog. The little girl wandered into the woods and became lost. Following a frantic search for the child, the aunt returned home and reported her missing. The response to a call for help was immediate. The whole population of the settlement joined in the search, but without success. Exactly one week later to the day, the little girl was found in a very unusual way.

First, the child's grandfather, a Mr. Leonard, dreamed one night where the girl would be found and that she would be found alive and in good health. He told the child's parents of his dream and they told neighbours participating in the search. It didn't take long for the searchers to arrive at the place described in Mr. Leonard's dream, and sure enough, the child was there as he predicted she would be.

While her grandfather's dream led to her rescue, another unusual thing happened. After talking to the child, searchers learned that her dog had helped her survive. From the first moment she had been lost, the dog had remained with her. After the first night in the woods, the dog went into the settlement and stole a large meat bone and carried it back to the child.

Each day afterwards, the dog returned to the settlement, sometimes two and three times, and returned with food for the little girl. The faithful dog had protected and fed the little girl for an entire week while her grandfather's psychic experience led to her rescue and safe return home.

MOSES CUTLER'S FRIDAY

Moses Cutler, one of the first settlers in Fair Island, Bonavista Bay, always believed Friday was a special day in his life. Here's why he was partial to Friday. He was born on a Friday. He joined the British Navy on a Friday. He left the navy on a Friday. He arrived in Newfoundland on a Friday and arrived at Fair Island on a Friday. However, while Friday was a significant day in Cutler's life, his good fortune changed when on a Friday he got badly frostbitten and became crippled for life. Moses Cutler passed away on a Friday.

NEWFOUNDLAND'S MOST UNUSUAL WEDDING

Perhaps the most unusual wedding ever to take place in Newfoundland and Labrador was the marriage of B.C. Bailey to a Miss Shave at Nipper's Harbour, Notre Dame Bay. Mr. Bailey was the telegraph operator at Nipper's Harbour. When Miss Shave said, "Yes" to his marriage proposal, the two made a visit to the local clergyman to schedule the marriage ceremony. Yet, this wedding was not to be like any other wedding.

The couple decided to wait until the end of 1899 to get married so they could celebrate the coming in of the New Year, and the new century. On New Year's Eve, December 31st, the church at Nipper's Harbour was filled. Mr. Bailey and his soon-to-be bride came into the church just a few minutes before the stroke of the hour. While the minister pronounced the words, the groom held an open watch in his palm to make sure that he was being married both on the last day of the nineteenth century and the first day of the twentieth century. It worked out perfectly. The Bailey's marriage ceremony took place in both centuries.

BELIEVE IT OR NOT!

During the twentieth century, a St. John's man named Moses O'Neill had the distinction of being a stepbrother to a man who had died over 150 years before. This was believed to be the only such case in the entire world and some kind of world record. Here's how it happened. Moses O'Neill was ninety years old at the time his story became known. O'Neill's father was married twice. His first son died, and sixty-five years later, when he was married again, at the age of over eighty, his other son, Moses O'Neill, was born. Thus it came about that Moses O'Neill could say that his stepbrother died over 150 years ago.

LOST AND FOUND RINGS

This is the story of a woman who lost her gold wedding ring and found it fifty years later! In 1892, at Foxtrap, Conception Bay, a Mrs. Elizabeth Rideout was married. A year after being married, Elizabeth was working in her potato garden when her ring slipped off her finger, unknown to her, and was lost. Later, when she realized that she didn't have it, with the help of family and friends, she searched her house and property without success.

In 1943, fifty years later, Elizabeth was in the same potato garden, and while turning over some clay, noticed something projecting from it. She picked the object up, cleaned it off and was overjoyed to find that it was the wedding ring she lost in 1892.

This story involving a lost ring took place during the 1930s. Thomas Noseworthy and his son Gordon, of Markland, Newfoundland, were fishing along the southside of Junction Pond near the community. Trout were plentiful and the two men were having a successful day. Gordon had been wearing a gold ring on his finger which was a little too large. Near the waterfall there, Gordon reached down to adjust his hook and line when the gold ring slipped from his finger. The two searched, as best they could, but without success. The water was really too deep to do little more than look for something shining from below. Gordon returned to his home that evening convinced he would never see his ring again. A year passed. The loss of the ring was forgotten when Gordon and his son returned to Junction Pond and were fishing on the northside directly opposite the waterfall. After about an hour of fishing, Gordon heard his son call out, "Dad, I've got the breeder," and sure enough the boy had a beautiful trout about fourteen inches long and weighing about three pounds. Later, when they cleaned their catch, Gordon opened the trout caught by his son and was amazed to find a gold ring in its stomach. It was the same gold ring he had lost a year before.

JUST HOW IMPORTANT A COLONY WAS NEWFOUNDLAND?

The *British Annual Register* for 1769, according to *The Newfoundlander*, also published a table of figures showing the total number of vessels that had sailed from England for the previous twelve months to the British colonies in North America. It also listed the number of seamen aboard the vessels.

The numbers are extraordinarily interesting because they show the immense importance of the colony of Newfoundland at a time when the American colonies were very prosperous. The Register showed:

The total for the year was 1078 ships. Over one-third of them to Newfoundland. The total number of seamen aboard the ships was 29,000, and, of those, 20,560 came to Newfoundland. Others sailed to Nova Scotia, Canada, New England, South Carolina, New York, Virginia and Maryland. Approximately 6000 seamen landed in the American colonies.

It is little wonder, in later years, that the Newfoundland fishery was described as the nursery of the British Navy.

HARD TACK TOWED 150 MILES

Hard bread, better known throughout Newfoundland history as hard tack, was used mostly for fish and brewis. Purity Factories in St. John's supplies Newfoundland's modern day demand for the popular hard tack, but in the nineteenth century all hard tack on the Newfoundland market was imported from Hamburg, Germany and was known as "Hamburg Bread." This German-made bread was a lot harder than the modern day article as the following story will illustrate.

A coastal captain took a cake of Hamburg Bread, bored a hole through it, inserted a line through the hole, tied a knot, and let the cake of bread down over the stern of his vessel into the water just before sailing from St. John's. He towed the hard bread for 150 miles, all the way to Seldom Come By in Fogo district before it melted enough to break clear of the line.

THE BALLOT ACT

An important date in Newfoundland political history is April 27th. It was on that date in 1887 that the Newfoundland Government passed the Secret Ballot Act. Up to that time, voting in elections was done openly and everyone knew for whom the other fellow had voted. This, of course, led to much dissatisfaction and kept many people away from the polls. On April 27th, 1887, there came into effect what is now known in history as the Secret Ballot Act by which a man could cast his vote and no one on earth know after whom he put his X.

TRIED RENAMING NEWFOUNDLAND

A serious effort was made in 1829 to change the name Newfoundland to *King George IV Island*. At the time there was a strong movement towards obtaining Representative Government for the colony, and some leaders of the movement felt it would help to flatter the reigning monarch of England, George the Fourth, by calling this country after him. Although the idea was not adopted, it took a long time in dying. Even after Representative Government was granted to Newfoundland in 1832, a bill was introduced in the legislature to rename the colony to *King George IV Island*. The bill was defeated and the name Newfoundland remained.

OLD JUSTICE CRUEL

One of the last homes of the Great Auk, which is now extinct, was the Funk Islands. During the late eighteenth century, the taking of the eggs of the Great Auk was forbidden by proclamation. In 1794, several fishermen were arrested, tried and found guilty of taking Great Auk eggs at The Funks. According to historian Judge D. Prowse, Chief Justice Reeves who tried the men was a just and impartial man, "...but in this case might have tempered justice with a little more mercy."

The fishermen were sentenced to be publicly whipped. However, the trial revealed that a man named Clarke of Greenspond, Bonavista Bay, had taken the eggs only as food for his wife and family who were in need. The Chief Justice weighed this factor and solemnly ordered that while the other fishermen should be publicly whipped as decreed, Mr. Clarke should only be flogged in private.

Prowse felt this was a backhanded method of showing clemency and commented, "We do not think this unfortunate victim of a cruel law appreciated the distinction."

LAW DEMANDED SEALERS BE SERVED FIGGY DUFF
A law was passed in Newfoundland in 1916 that specified exactly what meals were to be served at the annual seal hunt and on what days specified foods were to be served. This law was one of twenty-six different sections covering penalties and punishments on the owners and officers regarding the 'limitations of catch, load line, carrying guns, killing hood seals, bonuses to cooks, compensation for injury and conveyance home of any dead sealer.' There were also eleven pages of printed reference material included.

Some of the items required to be served at meal times were: potatoes, turnips, beans, soft bread, figgy duff, and fish and brewis. The law demanded that figgy duff be served three times a week, whilst Sunday morning's breakfast was to be the well-known fish and brewis.

Also, there was a law that forbade seals to be killed on Sunday. That particular law was in effect as early as 1840. These laws were repealed in the early twentieth century.

AN UNUSUAL SEALING CUSTOM
When the sealing vessel *Ellen* arrived in St. John's in 1838, she had six thousand seals on board. Unknown to the people on shore most of them were 'cats', young small seals. Competition to buy the catch was strong and hopeful buyers lined up to have a look at the pelts. They were unaware that Skipper Bob Purcell had put a few older and much bigger seals on top. The firm of Tobin and Bland, owners of the *Ellen*, sold the entire catch to the firm of Bennett and Morgan. A legal agreement was signed by both company owners and the sale was finalized.

When the large seals were unloaded and the 'cats' began to appear, the buyers realized that they had made a bad bargain and offered Tobin and Bland one thousand dollars to get out of the agreement. The sellers would not agree and they insisted the deal was legally binding.

After all the seals were unloaded, Bennett and Morgan discovered what they thought was a fatal flaw that could lead to the reopening of the contract. The perceived flaw was as follows:

When workers finished unloading the seals and signed forms that the cargo purchased had been delivered to the buyers, the buyers discovered that one seal, a large one, had been left aboard, and not unloaded with the remainder of the load. The buyers wasted no time in launching court action against the owners of the *Ellen*. They claimed that all the cargo of seals had not been delivered as per the agreement.

They were shocked when Tobin and Bland argued that they had a legal right to keep one seal from the cargo sold. They brought in a dozen witnesses to support their claim that it was a long tradition in unloading seals to leave one seal aboard to be run into oil for the vessel's use during the ensuing summer!

After hearing the evidence in the case, the judge found that it was indeed the old custom of the Newfoundland seal hunt to leave one seal aboard when unloading. He dismissed the case.

FIRST CLERGYMEN TO ARRIVE IN NEWFOUNDLAND

The first clergymen to visit Newfoundland were the Augustinian or Black Friars who accompanied John Cabot on his discovery voyage in 1497. After this, the Reverend Erasmus Stourton arrived here in 1611 with John Guy's Colony at Cupids and remained in Newfoundland until 1628. The first Roman Catholic priests were Fathers Smith, Hackett and Longville who were at Ferryland with Lord Baltimore in 1622. The first Methodist clergyman was the Reverend Lawrence Coughlin who came to Harbour Grace in 1765.

SELL NEWFOUNDLAND

The prestigious London, England newspaper, the *Times*, once advocated that England sell its oldest colony, Newfoundland, to France. Had they succeeded, Newfoundland today would be a colony of France. The famous editorial making the suggestion appeared in the *Times* on December 17, 1890. At the time, the French Shore question was a hot political issue in England, France and Newfoundland. The newspaper stated that some solution to the problem had to be found, and as France would not consider selling her claims, then England should sell all Newfoundland to France as the easiest and quickest way to settle the matter once and for all. The matter was eventually settled with Newfoundland's colonial status remaining unchanged.

AMAZING PROJECT

It was described by newspapers as, "One of the most fantastic projects ever associated with Newfoundland." This praise was lavished on a proposal made in the early twentieth century to dam up the Straits of Belle Isle. There were two motives behind the project. One was connected to Newfoundland, the other was not. The Newfoundland part involved the construction of a dam across the Straits of Belle Isle. A railway track was to be built across the dam which would connect Quebec with the northern peninsula of Newfoundland and give it access to Green Bay. At Green Bay, there was to be a great transatlantic passenger and freight ship ocean terminal.

Passengers and freight would be taken by rail from Montreal down along the shore of Quebec and Labrador, across the dam, and on to the terminal, where they would join the large cross-Atlantic boats. The other motive was to change the Maritime Provinces of Canada, and the Northern Atlantic Seaboard States of America. The theory was that by damming the Straits of Belle Isle, they would shut off the branch of the Arctic Stream that flowed through the Straits, down through the Gulf of St. Lawrence, past the Maritimes, and on to the United States coast. This current carried icebergs and floes and was itself icy cold, and if it could be diverted by means of the dam, the climate of all that territory would be made much milder. The western coast of Newfoundland, all the way from northern St. Barbe to Port aux Basques, would be a different country altogether, insofar as climate was concerned. However, the scheme was abandoned due to the gigantic cost. And in any case, it was later established that there is no branch of the Arctic current running through the Straits at all. It was nothing, more or less, than tides which flowed one day into the Straits and out the other day.

– *The Newfoundlander*, July 1945

NO OFFER MADE TO BUY LABRADOR

Another revealing news item in *The Telegram* on January 17, 1948, was related to the long-standing claim that the Newfoundland Government once seriously considered selling Labrador. The item read:

In response to an enquiry by *The Telegram*, it is learned that the reported offer to buy Labrador for one hundred and fifty million dollars has no foundation in fact. *The Telegram* is informed that the Commissioner for Natural Resources had received a letter in which the suggestion was made if Labrador could be sold for one hundred and fifty million dollars, all Newfoundland's troubles would be over. The writer did not make any definite offer nor suggestion who the purchaser might be. The suggestion was not taken seriously and the matter was not pursued any further as far as the Commissioner was concerned. It was, however, taken up in the National Convention by Mr. Pierce Fudge on Friday last when he directed a question to the Department. During Tuesday night's proceedings, Mr. Fudge reported that he had received a reply, and press and radio reports have made it appear that an offer was received.

That instead of an offer it was only a suggestion may be gleaned from the letter from the Secretary of the Department of Natural Resources to Mr. Fudge. The letter reads as follows:

13th January, 1948

Sir,

With reference to your letter of the 9th of January, 1948, I am directed to inform you that in a letter to the Department of Natural Resources dated the 15th of October, 1947, the suggestion was made that Labrador should be sold for one hundred and fifty million dollars. The letter did not indicate who was the prospective purchaser and there were no further developments.

Sgd. K.J. Carter, Secretary for Natural Resources. The Secretary National Convention, Colonial Building, St. John's

FROGS!

In the early nineteenth century, Newfoundland was known outside the colony as the Ireland of the New World because it had no reptiles, toads, or frogs. The first record of frogs in Newfoundland is dated 1864. Newspapers reported that a frog had been found on a wharf in St. John's. It was believed it had been brought here on a schooner that was in port from Nova Scotia with a load of hay. The next record of a frog is dated 1889. At this time, a workman, digging a ditch or drain in one of the streets in St. John's, found a frog. Both findings created a lot of interest and excitement in the colony. Frogs made their way to Newfoundland by way of the vessels from Nova Scotia and Prince Edward Island that frequented our ports.

FALKLAND ISLANDS HONOUR NEWFOUNDLAND

In 1955, the Falkland Islands issued two stamps to individually honour two Newfoundland ships for their participation in several Antarctic Exploration expeditions. The *Eagle* stopped at the Falklands on each of its trips to the Antarctic in 1944 and 1945. The *Eagle* was sunk ceremoniously in 1952 off St. John's Harbour. The *Eagle*'s captain was Captain Robert Sheppard, MBE of St. John's.[7] Jimmy Hearn of St. John's was a crewman on the historic trip.[8] The *Trepassey* stopped at the Falkland Islands on its adventure to the Antarctic between 1945 and 1947. A cove discovered near the South Pole during the *Eagle*'s Expedition was named Sheppard's Cove in honour of Captain Robert Sheppard MBE. Captain Sheppard's story could fill volumes.

OLD TIME HEALTH CARE

The following story is true, and while describing a hardship in the way of life in pre-Confederation Newfoundland, appears humourous in today's world.

This story of the olden days was told in 1954 by John and Patrick Dower of Conche in White Bay.

This woman (the mid-wife) was called to Crouse three miles distant. She had to go over the ice and the weather was very stormy, drifting heavily. After three days at Crouse, she was called back to Conche. Now there were no dogs at Conche, and it was too stormy for the woman to walk. So the owner of the house had a dried seal-skin in his store and he decided to lace the old woman up in the sealskin and haul her over the three miles of ice. He made record-time with her and she was ready for her next call without mishap.

DOLE DAYS

In 1949, when Newfoundlanders bid farewell to the old independent Newfoundland, many Newfoundlanders had lived little better than those in third world countries.

Prior to becoming a province of Canada three thousand people were collecting Old Age Pensions. To qualify for Newfoundland's Old Age Pension Program, one had to be seventy-five years old. However, just reaching the seventy-five year mark did not guarantee one a pension. Whether one was added to the roles of pensioners to receive payment depended on whether the Government had enough money to pay out.

It was not at all uncommon for people to wait until the age of seventy-eight to receive their first pension cheque, and it was not retroactive. If the Government couldn't pay it, you didn't get it.

Once a senior qualified for the Newfoundland Old Age Pension Program, he or she could not expect to receive a monthly payment. The pension was paid quarterly. Husband and wife received a combined cheque of thirty-six dollars. When one partner died, the other's pension was reduced to eighteen dollars paid quarterly.

Immediately upon Newfoundland becoming a province of Canada, the age for old age assistance was reduced to seventy and thirty dollars was paid per person on a monthly basis. For a husband and wife this meant a yearly jump in income from one hundred and twenty dollars to seven hundred and twenty. A single person's pension jumped from seventy-two dollars yearly to three hundred and sixty dollars. Over the years the monthly pension continued to increase and the qualifying age was dropped to sixty-five years.

In 1949, the Newfoundland Government paid out $264,000 to just 3000 people. In 1969, twenty years later, thirty-six million was paid out and twenty-eight thousand Newfoundlanders were receiving OAS.

NEWFOUNDLANDER DISAPPEARED SEARCHING FOR CAPTAIN KIDD'S TREASURE

While researching the story of Captain John Keating, the Newfoundlander who found treasure on Cocos Island in 1841, and again in 1845, I came across an intriguing item in an old book on pirates written almost one hundred years ago. The book was called, *The Book of Buried Treasure* written by Ralph D. Paine. The item involved a man from St. John's, Newfoundland, who visited a Captain Jonathan Chase in Casco Bay on the coast of Maine. It is important to know that part of the tradition of treasure stories in that area is that Captain Kidd had buried treasure on Jewell Island in Casco Bay.

Paine quotes from the story told by a gray-bearded, God-fearing clam-digger of Jewell's Island in Casco Bay. The quote stated:

> I can't remember when the treasure hunters first began coming to this island, but as long ago as my father's earliest memories, they used to dig for gold up and down the shore. The biggest mystery, though, of all the queer things that have happened here in the last hundred years was the arrival of the man from St. John's when I was a youngster. He claimed to have the very chart showing the exact spot where Kidd's gold was buried. He said he had got it from an old negro in St. John's who was with Captain Kidd when he was coasting the islands in this bay. He showed up here when old Captain Chase that lived here then was off to sea in a vessel. So, he waited around a few days till the captain returned, for he wanted to use a mariner's compass to locate the spot according to the directions on the chart.

> When Captain Chase came ashore the two went off up the beach together, and the man from St. John's was never seen again, neither hide nor hair of him, and it is plumb certain that he wasn't set off in a boat from Jewell's Island.

> The folks here found a great hole dug on the southeast shore which looked as if a large chest had been lifted out of it. Of course, conclusions were drawn, but nobody got at the truth. Four years ago someone found a skeleton in the woods, unburied, simply dropped into a crevice in the rocks with a few stones thrown over it. No one knows whose body it was, although some say - but never mind about that.

> This old Captain Jonathan Chase was said to have been a pirate, and his house was full of underground passages and sliding panels and queer contraptions, such as no honest, law-abiding man could have any use for.

THE PIRATE FROM TORBAY

Captain John Nutt, who deserted a British Naval vessel in Newfoundland waters, lived for years in Torbay with his wife and family. He turned to piracy to make a living and did very well. Nutt's first victims included a French ship, an English ship and a Flemish vessel. From these he went on to plunder the fishing fleets on the Grand Banks.

In three years, he amassed a fortune and buried much of it around Newfoundland. Although considered by authorities to be a bloodthirsty pirate, there was a humane side to John Nutt. He paid his crew good wages on a regular basis. The pirate looked after his wife and family in Torbay, and once saved Ferryland. When other pirates attempted to attack and plunder the settlement at Ferryland, Nutt came to its rescue. He successfully fought off the attackers. In May 1623, he wrote to a Lt. Eliot in London who had been ordered to arrest him. Nutt offered Eliot three hundred pounds sterling in return for a pardon. When he upped the offer to five hundred, Eliot accepted. Nutt buried some in secret hiding places around Newfoundland and then took the rest back to England.

However, by the time Captain Nutt arrived in England, his period of grace had run out and he was arrested. The penalty for piracy at the time was to tie the victim's hands and feet, cut his throat and pull out his tongue, then, at low water mark, his body would be tossed into the sea. This method was eventually replaced with death by hanging.

Lt. Eliot was on the verge of issuing the execution order when Sir George Calvert, who later became Lord Baltimore, intervened. Remembering Nutt's valiant deed in defending the settlers at Ferryland, Calvert ordered Captain Nutt's release and had Eliot arrested.

Calvert said he had pardoned Captain John Nutt once, and he would do it again. He commented, "I have no other end but to be grateful to a man that had been ready to do me and my associates courtesies in a plantation which we had begun in Newfoundland by defending us from others."

In addition to pardoning Captain Nutt, Calvert awarded him one hundred pounds sterling.

FIRST NEWFOUNDLAND ESKIMOS IN LONDON

George Cartwright, one of Labrador's first businessmen, sometimes took groups of Eskimos with him on his visits to England. Describing one such visit, Cartwright wrote:

> Although the Eskimos had often passed St. Paul's Cathedral without betraying any great astonishment, yet when I took them to the top of St. Paul's and convinced them it was built by the hands of men - a circumstance which had not entered into their heads before, for they had supposed it a natural production - they were quite lost in amazement.

When Cartwright asked how they would describe it to their countrymen on their return, they replied with a look of utmost expression that they would neither mention it, nor mention many of the other things they had seen, lest they be called liars.

THE STRANGE GRAVE IN FOREST ROAD CEMETERY

The badly decaying grave adjoining the grave of Tasker Cook, a former Mayor of St. John's, hides one of the amazing stories from old St. John's. The gravestone and the walnut casket buried below it were designed by the man buried in the grave.

Carter-Fitzgerald Photography
This grave along with the marble vault and casket inside were designed by the grave's occupant, the famous Professor Charles H. Danielle.

A visiting journalist to St. John's for *The Scenic Magazine* around 1902 described it as the most elaborate casket he had ever seen. Having viewed it at the Octagon Castle, he wrote:

> This casket is covered with black satin beautifully embroidered with gold, while the interior is upholstered with seven thousand and eight hundred white satin shells. A fluted satin pillow filled with eider down is at the head, while a white satin shroud and golden slippers lay within, ready for the body of this strange man. All this burial outfit is the individual work of the man it is waiting for. At the head of the casket, hanging upon the wall, is a gilt frame encircling a sheet of paper on which is written, 'In the back of this frame will be found full instructions to be followed immediately after my death.'
>
> – C.H. Danielle

The casket had a glass lid and at the time of the Professor's burial in May 1902, it was placed in a marble vault. *The Evening Telegram* described it as, "The most elaborate casket that was ever seen in these parts."

The writer for *The Scenic Magazine* described the Octagon Castle as follows:

> The main building is a large eight-sided, four-story structure with wings running east, west and south. The interior is elaborately designed. On entering the front portals, visitors are fairly dazzled. A large rotunda, the full size of the Octagon part of the building, with a thirty-foot ceiling, serves as a reception room and reading room; there also is stationed a band which discourses excellent music during the open season, for the Octagon Castle is a summer resort hotel. Around this rotunda runs a gallery, the face of which is hung with paintings and satin banners, embroidered with gold and silver in designs and with artistic skill that almost passes human conception. From this floor runs winding stairways in full view leading to the upper floors, the wings being entered from the gallery.
>
> The reading room and the ladies' parlor, approached through a high archway, are hung with elaborate satin

and plush draperies, embroidered in gold and bespangled, and must have cost many hundreds of dollars.

The bridal chambers is a bower of satin, lace and plush, all dazzling in gold and silver, while on the bed is a quilt composed of small shells of satin of every imaginable color, adroitly put together, each shell overlapping the other like the scales of a fish, and not a stitch is visible. It took two years and a half to complete this quilt; it contains eighty-five yards of satin and is valued at seven hundred dollars.

On the third floor is a large square room that is kept locked; it is called the mortuary chamber. It is draped in black velvet embroidered in gold. In the centre of this room is a catafalque, covered with black velvet trimmed in white satin on which rests the most elaborate casket the writer has ever seen.

Any guest or visitor to Octagon Castle will be shown through it on application to the head butler or any of the servants or the proprietor himself.

The writer suggested that no one should visit Newfoundland and leave before seeing Octagon Castle and talking with its entertaining and witty proprietor.

Professor Charles Danielle was very prominent in old St. John's and is remembered as perhaps one of the most outstanding characters of this province's history. The magazine article noted, "Charles H. Danielle is eccentric in many respects but immensely popular with all classes of the people of Newfoundland. He is a retired ex-dancing professor and theatrical costumer, hence his taste in the decorations which are all the work of his own hands."

Charles H. Danielle

Danielle built his famous Castle with wood and materials taken from his famous Royal Pavilion, also known as the Oriental Pavilion which he had built in 1893 on the banks of Quidi Vidi Lake. The entire disassembled pavilion was placed on a freight train at the old Fort William (Cavendish Square-Plymouth Road area) and unloaded nine miles from St. John's at Octagon Pond for the Professor's Octagon project.

THE DUMBBELL GOVERNOR

Sir Charles Alex Harris served as Governor of Newfoundland from 1918 to 1922. He was a familiar sight around the city and always carried two official leather pouches. Those who encountered him always tipped their hat and showed the courtesy and respect that was so common in those years. However, the townspeople always believed that his pouches contained important state papers, but they didn't.

Governor Harris, sixty-two years old at the time, was a keen physical fitness enthusiast. He worked out on the weights several hours each day and practiced boxing. In each of those leather pouches he carried was a twenty-eight pound dumbbell.

Harris was known for his knowledge of Newfoundland history. He was author of *Newfoundland 1783-1867* and *Newfoundland 1867-1921* which were published in the *Cambridge History of the British Empire* in 1930.

GIFTS FROM SIR ROBERT BOND

On October 7, 1927, a series of what are described as presentation caskets made of gold and silver were bequeathed to the Newfoundland Museum by Sir Robert Bond. Each casket measured twelve by eighteen inches. The gold one contained the Freedom of the City of London. The silver casket held the Freedom of Edinburgh, and the silver-gold casket contained the Freedom of the City of Bristol. There was another silver-plated casket with the Freedom of the City of Manchester.

Bond also gave the museum a piece of the old Roman Bridge which existed at Rochester, England in the year 80 A.D.

At the expense of the Bond Estate, a special display case to show the collection was constructed in England. Unfortunately, the Bond gifts disappeared along with other items during the Commission of Government days in Newfoundland.

40

THE JUDGE WHO WOULDN'T GO

When Newfoundland Supreme Court Justice Sir Brian Dunfield turned seventy-five on April 10, 1963, he refused to retire. The Federal Government's legislation required that judges retire at age seventy-five. Dunfield's argument was that in 1939 the Commission of Government in Newfoundland had appointed him for life and he felt perfectly able to continue in his work.

It took an amendment to a section of the British North American Act to force Dunfield's retirement. The Judge was not pleased with the action and said that he felt he could go on serving in the position until he was eighty.

NOTED NEWFOUNDLAND HISTORIANS WRONG

Several early Newfoundland history books have recorded the accomplishments of Sir Thomas Hampshire during the sixteenth century. However, it was later discovered that Sir Thomas never existed and his reported activities were nothing more than figments of somebody's imagination.

Historian L.A. Anspach and later Judge D.W. Prowse credit Hampshire with having succeeded in securing permanent wharves, flakes and settlements in Newfoundland. However, Premier J.R. Smallwood, also a noted historian, was one of those who, through research, determined that Sir Thomas Hampshire never existed.[9]

HE GREW A SECOND CROP OF HAIR

Peter Murphy of Net Cove in the Codroy Valley on Newfoundland's west coast amazed his friends and neighbours by growing a second crop of hair. While Peter was a young man, he came down with scarlet fever which caused him to lose all his hair. This did not prevent him from growing a beard, which grew long and turned white as Peter grew older.

At age seventy-five people began to notice a reddish fuzz on the top of Peter Murphy's head. He was growing a second crop of hair. Many a doubting Thomas proved for himself that the hair was genuine. Proud of his red curls, Peter refused to have them cut. He carved a comb to groom them with, and woe betide the one who used that comb. These curls never changed their color, and before he died at the age of eighty-seven, they were long enough to tangle with his beard.

HARBOUR GRACE HAD NO SMOKING LAWS IN 1813

The 1813 records of the Newfoundland Grand Jury record that the following law was drawn up for the town of Harbour Grace. It read:

> That no person shall smoke pipes of tobacco in the open paths of this town between the first of April and the last of October, under the penalty of twenty shillings for each offence; and all persons that shall be convicted of carrying fire from one house to another without a covering shall be fined ten shillings for such offence.

The regulation was not a recognition of the health hazards of pipe smoking. It was passed as a fire prevention measure. The mention of "carrying fire from one house to another" referred to a practice common in Newfoundland of neighbours carrying hot cinders to each other's homes to help start the fireplace in the morning each day. These cinders, dropping to the ground, often ignited grass and other material and was responsible for many fires, both in St. John's and the outport communities.

AMAZING FACTS

• A William Ledrew of Cupids, Conception Bay, found a curious object on the bank of a river near his home around 1880. It was believed to be a petrified pig which had drowned when John Guy had his colony at Cupids in 1610. Ledrew passed away during May 1882.

• The largest Union Jack in the world is the one which is flown over the Parliament Building in London on special occasions. The community of Cupids has a Union Jack which is the second largest in the world. The Cupids flag measures forty by thirty-two feet. It was presented to the people of Cupids by Newfoundlanders living in Toronto in 1910, at the time of the 300th anniversary of the founding of Cupids by John Guy. It has become a tradition to raise the flag annually on Canada Day.

• A technicolour movie was shown in St. John's long before technicolour became a trade name, and years before sound pictures were shown. The movie was featured at the Nickel Theatre during the winter of 1908. It was a version of a famous play of the time called the Passion Play. The film was made by a French film company called Messrs. Pathe which later became famous worldwide for Pathe News.

• One of the most amazing instances of a ship being saved from a watery grave occurred in the year 1879. Just off the Newfoundland coast, the United States ship, *Arizona*, rammed an iceberg, gouging a huge hole in her bow. A huge chunk of the berg wedged in the hole, plugging it like a cork in a bottle. The *Arizona* limped into St. John's, repairs were made, and she continued her voyage as good as new.

• In 1917, Patrick Timmons was buried in his native village of Holyrood, Conception Bay. He was a veteran of four wars: the Spanish American War of 1898, the Boxer Rebellion in China in 1900, the Boer War in Africa in 1902 and World War I, 1914.

• Here is an amazing fact that is almost unbelievable, but was well-known in pre-confederation Newfoundland. In 1829, a man shot and killed a wolf on Water Street, St. John's. John Ennis put it on display and charged a small fee to those who wanted to view it.

• The little community of Old Perlican, Trinity Bay, Newfoundland, experienced one of the most amazing storms ever to strike the province. In August 1861, blocks of solid ice fell on Old Perlican for fifteen minutes, causing tremendous damage. Then, an amazing thing happened. When the ice melted, millions of caterpillars which had been enclosed in the ice covered the ground, moving on the vegetable fields, and eating everything in their path.

• In August 1877, another strange weather event occurred at Smith Sound, Trinity Bay. During a terrific summer gale pieces of ice four inches square fell from the sky and caused extensive damage to trees and crops.

• During the trip to the seal fishery in 1911, the SS *Kite*, a Newfoundland sealing vessel, had more stowaways than crew. The *Kite*'s crew totaled twelve while there were seventeen stowaways.

• The first sealing captain to be fined for taking seals on a Sunday was Captain Arthur Jackman of St. John's. This event took place in 1907. Captain Jackman was fined $2000.

• The first long distance wireless voice communication in the world took place in July 1920 between Signal Hill and the SS *Victoria*, which was 1200 miles at sea.

• The town of Bay Bulls, about twenty miles southwest of St. John's, got its name from the bull walrus which were plentiful there during the early days of settlement in Newfoundland. They were sought after by hunters and, in time, they could no longer be found except in the far north of Newfoundland and Labrador. According to author Harold Horwood, Bay Bulls was the site of the last French attack on Newfoundland during the wars of Napoleon.

• The community of Kelligrews, made famous in Johnny Burke's *Kelligrews Soiree*, got its name from the great Cornish family, the Killigrews,[10] remembered in history as "the robber barrons" of Land's End, England. They used their large castle at Falmouth, called Pendennis as a refuge place for pirates. It was the Killigrews who helped the notorious pirate Peter Easton build a fleet of forty armed ships. Easton fortified Harbour Grace, and later set up a stronghold on Kelly's Island on the other side of Conception Bay, where Kelligrews was named for his English patrons.

INCREDIBLE BUT TRUE

This story involves a fisherman-planter who lived near Port Saunders around 1910. It's one of many incredible, but true stories from Newfoundland's past. This fisherman-planter's home was a remarkable structure. Records show that it was finished with mahogany timbers that had drifted ashore from a wreck in the Straits of Belle Isle.

The man had enjoyed a successful life in his profession and had managed to save over ten thousand dollars, a tidy sum in those days. From time to time, he would convert his money into gold sovereigns which he hid somewhere inside his home, as was common in that era, as most people did not trust banks because of the bank crash of the 1890s, which wiped out people's savings.

The man was a simple hard-working individual who was a good friend to neighbours and trusting towards others.

One night, a severe storm struck and a bolt of lightning hit his house, causing it to catch fire. Despite his strongest efforts, the house burnt to the ground. By morning, the embers were cooling off and he searched for his golden hoard amid the ruins.

He was horrified to discover that the heat from the fire had melted down and welded his gold coins into a nugget of gold weighing about forty pounds. The poor man was convinced that the coins were now useless. The following day a well-known peddler who had been traveling up and down the coast came to visit him. The man was not a Newfoundlander. After chatting with the fishermen and hearing his story, he confirmed that the gold coins were now worthless. However, the peddler said he could use the gold to make cheap trinkets and he would be happy to purchase the nugget. He quickly added, "Of course, I wouldn't pay anymore than a hundred dollars for it." The fishermen accepted the deal. With the gold in his possession, the peddler bade farewell to the fishermen and wished him good luck.

The swindler later sold the nugget for more than nine thousand dollars and used the money to start up a business in St. John's. By the time the poor fisherman learned what had happened, he felt it was too late and there was nothing he could do.

WHAT WOULD SMALLWOOD SAY?

If Joey Smallwood was around today, and if asked, "Was Confederation brought about through a conspiracy?" how would he answer?

Well, the allegation of conspiracy did not originate in the past decade, but was made by opponents of Confederation in 1949. In those days, Smallwood often answered, "I wish there had been a conspiracy, my job would have been a lot easier."

Smallwood replied to the accusation which was made by Peter Cashin during the first session of the Newfoundland Legislature as a province of Canada.

Nothing was brought about more democratically in Newfoundland than the bringing about of Confederation. If Great Britain was so very anxious to have Newfoundland join Canada, she could really have

45

done something which would further that end a great deal. She could simply have told Newfoundlanders that as far as she was concerned, her aid to Newfoundland was finished. She could have said that she was facing the present dollar shortage, and would no longer be able to help Newfoundland. She could have told Newfoundlanders then, that if she voted for the Commission of Government, they would in effect, be voting Responsible Government, for the country would be entirely on her own under a continued Commission.

The 22,000 votes that went for Commission of Government would have then gone for Confederation, and the Confederates would have won in the first Referendum. No, they didn't do that! It was as fair as fair can be. Even suppose that Churchill and Mackenzie King were plotting to put Newfoundland into Confederation. After all their conniving, they only managed to have Confederation put on the ballot paper, they only managed to get to the point where Confederation was com-

Joseph R. Smallwood

peting, that's all! Why would I have to fight if it was cut and dried by these great men and their Governments.

Smallwood caused laughter in the House when he added, "It's like this Mr. Cashin - 'This is my story, that is my song. Talking of plots all day long.'"

When Cashin responded with a laugh, Joey commented, "That's a politically infectious laugh, worth over a thousand votes any day." The Premier continued, saying that he would rather see all his colleagues go rather than Mr. Cashin. He explained that he and Cashin could make a House of Assembly between them, "Mr. Cashin is worthy of Gilbert and Sullivan sometimes with his Cashinistic arguments."

LEGISLATURE JULY 30, 1949

Commenting on the quality of politicians in Newfoundland's past, Smallwood said, "There were great men. Men like Whiteway, Bond, Morris, Squires, Coaker, Alderdice and Monroe, but there were also some ignoramuses and illiterates.... the best thing they ever did for Newfoundland was to die."

TOO RISKY FOR LLOYDS OF LONDON

Lloyds of London, the world's oldest and best known insurers, were known to insure just about anything. A three story house east of the Hill o' Chips on Duckworth Street, St. John's, was one of their few exceptions. Lloyds had refused to insure the house while Smallwood lived there.

During the political battle for Confederation, there was widespread anger throughout St. John's against Joey Smallwood who was the leading spokesman for the Confederate Movement. One of the most serious incidents of the Confederation campaign erupted and was over before Smallwood knew anything about it. He was broadcasting from radio station VOCM on Parade Street when a large mob of angry anti-confederates turned up at the door with a rope and threatened to lynch Smallwood.

Unaware of the danger lurking outside, Smallwood was delivering one of his famous speeches in support of Confederation inside. The station's owner, Joe Butler, saw the mob and called in the Newfoundland Constabulary who quickly succeeded in dispersing them.

Jack Fitzgerald photo
Even Lloyds of London would not insure this house occupied by Smallwood on the east end of Duckworth Street during the battle for Confederation in 1948.

At the time, Smallwood was renting the bottom two flats in the Duckworth Street home shown above. According to the former Premier, "Friends of the landlord used to say that a mob would tear the house down and that he was foolish to let Smallwood live there. But the house owner merely smiled. He had, he thought, neatly provided against any such possibility for he had contacted the great Lloyds of London Insurance people and asked for a policy to fully insure against riot and civil commotion."

In fact, a crowd of 1500 anti-confederates who were angry at Smallwood did gather outside the house on one occasion and threatened to tear it down.

Ten years later, Joey Smallwood, then Premier of Canada's newest province, recalled, "Imagine the landlord's chagrin, after it was all over. He discovered that Lloyds had said they would not insure the house while Joe Smallwood lived there. And the local agent forgot to tell the landlord that Lloyds would not accept the policy."

Years later Smallwood said that all the opposition he encountered during the battle for Confederation never once made him nervous.

KENTUCKY DERBY RACER
DELIVERED BREAD IN ST. JOHN'S

Skipper Mike Walsh, owner of Central Bakeries, better known in old St. John's as Walsh's Bakery on Central Street, played a prominent role in horse racing in and around St. John's from the early 1930s until the late 1950s. In addition to the Bella Vista Horse Track, there were the winter derbys on Quidi Vidi Lake held between January and March with special races for St. Paddy's Day. Walsh dazzled local horse race enthusiasts in 1935 when he added to his stable of delivery horses on Flower Hill the once famous Kentucky Derby racer Moses H.

Moses H. was bred at the Fair Field Farms in Lexington, Kentucky. His sire was Belwin-Darn Olliwood, a famous trotter himself. Although Moses H. was retired from the big time racing circuit, he still bore the look and the style of the champion he once was.

James Walsh photo

Moses H., with his owner Skipper Mike Walsh, was a famous Kentucky race horse before coming to Newfoundland in the 1940s.

In fact, Moses H. was a true delight to fans at the Bella Vista track and the Quidi Vidi Lake races and went from 1926 to 1935 without ever being defeated. He was treated like royalty by Skipper Walsh, and only went on deliveries when really needed by the bakery. He was twenty-two years old when he was put down.

FIRE-EATER

Stan Short, who lived at 254 New Gower Street in the 1930s and 1940s, was capable of a remarkable feat that was in the true category of Believe It Or Not. Short possessed the remarkable ability to be able to lick a red-hot piece of iron with his tongue!

In November 1938, after newspapers reported on a man in the United States who could lick a red-hot iron with his tongue without injury to himself, Joseph R. Smallwood, later to become Premier of Newfoundland, received a telephone call claiming that Stan Short of St. John's could do the same thing.

Smallwood, then popular throughout Newfoundland and Labrador as the famous host of the radio broadcast *The Barrelman*, invited Short to his office to demonstrate this amazing feat.

Smallwood described what he witnessed in one of his November 1938 broadcasts. He said:

> When I expressed absolute disbelief in his willingness and ability to perform this wonder, Stanley Short didn't attempt to argue the point, or to try by word-of-mouth to convince me.
>
> He just asked very simply, 'Have you got a poker or lifter?'
>
> I gave him a short thick stove-lifter, and he poked one end in through the bars of the grate. In less than ten minutes, this lifter was blood-red hot on one end, so hot that even the outside end couldn't be gripped until two handkerchiefs were wrapped around it. There was no fake about it – I saw it with my own eyes and another gentleman was in the office at the time and saw it with his own eyes.
>
> Deliberately and slowly, while this gentleman and I watched in fascinated amazement, and a bit white about the gills, deliberately and slowly Stanley Short licked this glowing, blood-red hot lifter with his tongue, not once, not twice, but no less than four separate times within quarter of a minute.
>
> You could hear his tongue sizzle every time he licked it. This other gentleman and myself were absolutely paralyzed with astonishment, and when I regained sufficient strength to ask him if his tongue were burned, he replied, 'No, not hurt at all – here I'll do it again.'

All of which goes to show you once again, ladies and gentlemen, that Newfoundlanders can lick anything that comes up against them.[11]

CAPTAIN BEN TAVENOR'S PSYCHIC EXPERIENCES

In September 1927, the American monoplane *Old Glory* was lost in the Atlantic with its three-man crew while trying to improve on the non-stop record set the previous May by Charles Lindberg on his historic flight from New York to Paris.

No one had the slightest idea where the monoplane might have gone down. While authorities on both sides of the Atlantic tried to figure out where to search, the lost plane was located by Captain Ben Tavenor, a Newfoundland sea captain. The discovery made news around the world, and what led Tavenor to the tragic site turned out to be incredible. But before I disclose that, let me continue with the story.

Upon learning of the Tavenor finding, the New York *Daily Mirror* sent the following cable to the St. John's *Evening Telegram*: "We wish to know more about the man who performed the remarkable feat of going halfway across the Atlantic and finding the *Old Glory*."

The Evening Telegram provided some biographical background on the Newfoundland Captain who was then centre of world attention. It told of Tavenor as a boy running away to sea on a foreign vessel. Eventually, after many adventures at sea and traveling around the world, he earned his master's certificate. Members of his crew agreed, upon returning from finding the monoplane, that their Captain was endowed with a sixth sense.

CHILDHOOD EXPERIENCE

Evidence of this was shown at an early age when the Tavenor family lived in Trinity. On Christmas Eve 1887, when Ben was just seven years old, he had a vision after he had gone to sleep. Not at all like a dream, it was as though he was witnessing something that was happening then. He saw an old lady who lived in a small cottage some distance from the Tavenor's. She was wearing a thin bright-coloured cotton dress. There was much snow on the ground and the old lady left her cottage and began walking through the snow. He watched as she walked towards the beach. When she reached a fishing stage, she suddenly fell into the icy water.

51

This frightened Ben and he awoke from his sleep. There were many people in his house but Ben did not tell anyone because he felt they would say it was just a dream. "It was so real," he thought, as he dozed off asleep.

The next morning, neighbours came knocking on the door of the Tavenor house asking if they had seen Mrs. Coombs who had gone missing. The old lady had poor vision, and they feared that she might have fallen over a cliff while out to visit friends.

Ben heard the conversation and spoke up, "Mrs. Coombs is in the water near the fishing stage." Little attention was paid to Ben, and his parents ordered him to go back to bed. As the search continued, one man went to the fishing stage and was astounded to find the lifeless body of Mrs. Coombs.

The story of Ben's vision spread quickly and brought a policeman to the Tavenor home to interview Ben. He told them of his dream and brought the police to the old lady's footprints as he had seen them in his vision. When found, she was wearing the dress described by the seven-year-old boy. Ben's parents confirmed that he had not left the house since supper the night before.

After World War II broke out, Ben Tavenor became Captain of the *Caribou* which ferried passengers between Port aux Basques and North Sydney. In October 1942, the *Caribou* was torpedoed by a German U-boat and sunk. Of the 237 people on board, 136 men, women, and children died in tragedy. Among the dead was Captain Ben Tavenor. The story of the *Caribou* is told in Jack Fitzgerald's book *Newfoundland Disasters*.

BACK TO *OLD GLORY*

Concerning the monoplane mystery, neither Tavenor nor any of his crew were aware that the plane had crashed. Captain Tavenor was troubled by a recurring vision of a sea gull in the distance. He had no idea of its meaning. Just before taking a rest, he told his first mate, "I'm going to lie down for an hour or so. But if you happen to see something like a sea gull floating around, I want you to call me."

Less than an hour later, the wheelsman reported seeing what he thought looked like a giant sea gull tossing around on the waves ahead of them. It was the wreckage of *Old Glory*.

AN INCREDIBLE JUDGE

Throughout the history of justice in Newfoundland, I doubt if any judge has ever made the same decision as did a judge in Harbour Main in the late seventeenth century. When faced with making a judgement on a dispute between a fisherman and his master, the judge made an extraordinarily unorthodox decision.

A fishing master named Edward Fahey was a bully who abused Tim O'Rourke, a young Irishman employed by him during Tim's first season of work in Newfoundland. As was the practice at the time, employees were paid at the end of the season. When it came time to make payment, Fahey deliberately picked a fight with young Tim to avoid having to pay him for his season's work.

Tim O'Rourke took his complaint to the local judge and explained what had happened. He said he was going back to fight Mr. Fahey and to get his just pay. He said, "I ask ye'r honour's permission to defend meself?"

The judge, who was outraged by what Fahey had done, gave O'Rourke permission to defend himself and added, "Go out and give him a taste of his own medicine. Kick the stuffings out of him."

Tim took a few days to train himself for the fight. When ready, he marched straight down to the wharf, followed by a few curious villagers, and went unannounced aboard Fahey's boat. "I wants me pay right now. I worked for it," Tim told Fahey.

Fahey raised his fist to strike Tim and said, "There's no pay here for troublemakers."

This was just what Tim O'Rourke was expecting to hear. The fight was on. Fahey had never had an employee fight back before and he proved to be no match for the angry Irishman. Tim made good on the judge's instruction and he beat Fahey from one end of the boat to the other. When Fahey couldn't take anymore, he gave up. He paid Tim his wages and said, "Let by-gone's be by-gones. I'd be happy to have you work for me again."

Tim accepted the offer and the two became longtime friends.

THE TREATMENT FOR GREAT
WHITE PLAGUE IN NEWFOUNDLAND

Tuberculosis was also known in Newfoundland as the great white plague. Every family was touched by it and thousands died from the disease. It was in St. John's in 1911 that doctors accidentally discovered the benefit of 'the open air method' on those suffering from the dreaded disease. The breakthrough was made during a period when doctors treating TB patients were trying to make it through a tough winter under very difficult circumstances.

This episode in our history began when a volunteer ladies' group set out to raise money for the construction of a building to be used as a small summer camp for TB sufferers in their neighbourhood. The ladies collected funds for the project, and when W.D. Reid of the Newfoundland Railway learned of their effort, he offered to pay for the cost of the buildings and the MacPherson family made land available for the project in the Mundy Pond area at a nominal rental rate.

Dr. H. Rendell who was involved in the treatment of these patients at the time recalled in an interview a few years later with the magazine *Cadet*:

> Three modest shacks were built and, in this manner, a great impetus was given to the campaign against consumption (TB). Of these shacks, one accommodated the nurse and servant, and the other two provided beds each for three patients. The buildings were of the frailest construction, as no one dreamed they would be used except during the warmer summer months.

This was the first experiment in sanatorium treatment in Newfoundland and many challenges were encountered. Dr. Rendell explained:

> Not the least of these drawbacks was the lack of knowledge on the part of the physician in charge of the finer points in this method (open-air-treatment) of dealing with the disease. Yet, their attempts proved so successful that all concerned were encouraged to repeat it during the following summer and also to keep the camps open later in the autumn months.
>
> As the autumn gradually passed into winter, patients, nurse and physician often looked and asked the question, 'Shall we close up now or keep open a little longer?' and the answer from one and all was always the same, 'Let us

try a little longer,' and so day by day, week by week, and month by month, the time passed by, until to our surprise and joy we found we had successfully weathered the winter, and, so far from being any the worse for our rather trying experience, we were one and all feeling much better.

In this manner was it demonstrated that consumption (TB) could be successfully treated in Newfoundland by the open-air method all the year round.

The success of treating TB at this camp, (Jensen Camp) led to the opening up of the sanatorium on Topsail Road in St. John's which for decades treated thousands of Newfoundlanders suffering from TB.

FIRST MEDICARE IN CANADA

Canada's first medicare program was introduced, not in Saskatchewan as most people believe, but in the province of Newfoundland by Premier Joey Smallwood during the first years of his administration.

Noted Newfoundland author, the late Harold Horwood wrote in his book *Joey*[12] published in 1989:

> Joey felt that all medical services ought to be provided without cost to the consumer, but after a committee presented the projected costs of such a service if the provincial government shouldered the burden alone, he backed off, temporized and introduced medicare for everyone up to the age of sixteen. Even this step had been taken by no other province, and it happened years before medicare was introduced with much fanfare and struggle in Saskatchewan. Newfoundland doctors never uttered a peep against it. After Joey's plan was introduced, a national survey showed that Newfoundland doctors had the highest incomes in Canada, although they served the province with the lowest per capita income.

THE ST. JOHN'S K OF C DISASTER 1942
Did Doors Open Inward or Outward?

In the Dunfield Enquiry into the destruction of the Knights of Columbus Hostel and the loss of ninety-nine lives, there was a difference of opinion between witnesses who had been trapped inside the hall during the fire and the builders of the hostel over whether the front doors opened inwards or outwards. Witnesses insisted the front doors opened inwards. After considering the evidence before him, Sir Brian Dunfield concluded in his report, "On the whole I think both doors opened outwards."

After his report had been completed and published, Dunfield obtained new evidence which provided him with a definitive answer to the issue. Too late to include the material in his report, he submitted the following letter to the press. I came across the information during recent research on the matter.

The letter was published in *The Evening Telegram* on February 25, 1943, as follows:

RE: K OF C FIRE

Dear Sir, In paragraph 11 of the report in referring to the front doors of the K of C Hut I said, "Opinions differ as to the outer pair of doors. They were supposed to open outwards, and the builders say they did, but some witnesses say unequivocally that they opened inwards. The inner pair of doors undoubtedly opened outwards. On the whole I think both doors opened outwards."

Since the publication of the report, a citizen has shown me a private snapshot taken of friends standing in the front door which shows beyond doubt that these outer doors did open outwards.

No doubt, those who were in charge of the building will be glad to know that this is proved.

Yours truly,
Brian Dunfield

WHO REALLY DISCOVERED NEWFOUNDLAND?

For many decades, the claim by some historians that Newfoundland was discovered by John Cabot in 1497 has been disputed by other historians who argue that Cabot's first landing in North America was in *Nova Scotia*. Neither side may be correct in this dispute. Why? Because there are documents in the British and Spanish archives that precisely state that Newfoundland was discovered in 1494 by two British merchants.

According to the late author and historian, Harold Horwood[13], there are 16th century chronicles and letters in British and Spanish archives that claim *Newfoundland* was discovered by two Bristol fish merchants, Robert Thorne and Hughe Elliott. Included in these records is a written account by Thorne's son Robert Jr. in 1527 in which he states his father was the true discoverer of New Found Land.

A letter written by a John Day in 1498 to the Spanish ambassador to London and mistakenly filed under Brasil (sic) in the Spanish archives was discovered by researchers in 1956. This letter also casts doubt on claims that John Cabot discovered Newfoundland. In the letter, Day informed the ambassador that for the previous seven years 1491 to 1497, merchants from Bristol had been sending two to four ships annually into the western Atlantic. He wrote, "We begin to see the Cabot voyage in its true perspective, as an official follow-up to earlier discoveries by the Bristol merchants."

The Isle of Brasil was the name given to Newfoundland by the Bristol merchants who discovered it. In Spain, the John Day document was mistakenly filed under Brasil (sic) and the error escaped notice for almost five hundred years.

MOST FAMOUS PUBLICITY STUNT OF 19TH CENTURY

A feat performed in New York City in 1876 was described in later years as the most incredible publicity stunt of the nineteenth century. The man who carried out the daring and perilous act was Newfoundland-born Henry Supple Jr. who was born and grew up at 78 Gower Street in St. John's and, as a young adult, moved to New York City to find work. Henry was the son of Henry Supple Sr.[14] who was a well-known advocate for fishermen's rights in Newfoundland in the 1850s.

GREAT PUBLICITY STUNT

In New York, Henry Jr. was employed as a master mechanic with an engineering firm owned by John Roebling and his son, Washington Roebling. John Roebling developed a great engineering program to design and construct a bridge across the East River to connect Manhattan and Brooklyn. John did not live to see his dream fulfilled. Completion of the project was taken over by Washington Roebling and by August 1876, twin towers, 278 feet high, rose in the air on both sides of the East River. On August 14, the first strand of steel wire was raised to connect both twin towers.

On August 25th, Henry Supple, with the entire New York press and thousands of spectators assembled nearby, climbed one of the towers and began his death-defying walk across the steel wire connecting the towers on each side of the river. Cautiously, Henry inched his way across the 1600 feet of wire. On several occasions it appeared that the wind swaying the wire would cause the Newfoundlander to fall to his death. When he reached the Manhattan side, there were thunderous cheers from both sides of the East River. Henry Supple's stunt received national attention and he was the toast of New York. He is the only person ever to cross the Brooklyn Bridge on a wire.

[1] The Native Society was an association of long-term settlers in Newfoundland, sometimes called bush borns, founded by Richard Barnes in 1840 to protect their rights and interests against loss to new immigrants to Newfoundland. The Society had a building inside what today is known as Bannerman Park which was blown down in a September windstorm in 1846.

[2] A rare copy of Grey's book is preserved at Memorial University's Centre of Newfoundland Studies.

[3] This story is told in *Strange But True Newfoundland Stories*, Jack Fitzgerald, Creative Publishers, 1989.

[4] *The New Newfoundland*, J.R. Smallwood, The Macmillan Company, New York, 1931.

[5] *A History of Newfoundland*, D.W. Prowse. Boulder Press 2002, NL.

[6] Coyle's, a three-story house with a working shed in its back garden, was located on James Street at the eastern corner of James and Queen's Road. The Nancy Coyle story is told in *Beyond Belief* by Jack Fitzgerald, Creative Publishers, 2001.

[7] MBE stands for the coveted honour of Member of the British Empire.

[8] Jimmy Hearn was married to Rose Cahill also of St. John's. Both have since passed away.

[9] Encyclopedia of Newfoundland, Vol. II, Joseph R. Smallwood, Newfoundland Book Publishers (1967) Limited. 1981.

[10] The family spelled their name Killigrews. In Newfoundland this became Kelligrews.

[11] *The Best of the Barrelman (1938-1940)*, edited by William Connors, Creative Publishers, 1998.

[12] Published by Stoddart Publishing of Toronto, Ontario in 1989.

[13] *Newfoundland*, Harold Horwood, The Macmillan Company of Canada Limited, Toronto, Ontario, 1969.

[14] His sister Mary married a Henry Oldridge and they operated the Devonshire Inn at 120 Water Street, which was one of the city's popular public houses of that era. The Inn was located near Keating's Corner (eastern corner of Prescott and Water Streets) where the famous Captain John Keating of Cocos Island fame lived. The Inn's name may be more than a coincidence because of Keating's fame for having found the Lost Treasure of Lima and a ship named the *Devonshire* was part of that story.

CHAPTER 2

NEWFOUNDLAND OFFBEAT

NEWFOUNDLAND'S OLDEST BARBERSHOP

The Harris Barbershop on Casey Street in St. John's is the oldest barbershop in continuous operation in Newfoundland, and perhaps all of Canada. Its founder, Richard 'Dick' Harris, was born in 1887 and became an apprentice barber in 1902 with one of the city's most popular hairdressers at the time, Henry V. Tuff. Tuff's Hair Salon was located next door on the east side of the now famous O'Brien's Music Store.

Three years later, Dick Harris opened his own barbershop at 178 New Gower Street. Several civic developments in the downtown area forced Harris to move his shop twice: first to Brazil Square and then to its present site on Casey Street, and the customers followed.

Dick Harris worked as a barber until 1983, the year he died, and just four years short of reaching his 100th birthday. By the time he passed away, his youngest son Rick Harris had taken over the family business. Rick was born in 1948 when his father was fifty-eight years old, which accounts for a second generation Harris still operating a business founded over 100 years ago.

Most customers remember having the elder Dick Harris cut their hair, some even remember playing chess with him. Yet, there is more than the human connection and traditions of the store that remind people of its long history. The store's strong connection with the past can be seen among some of the furnishings still there after 100 years of service.

THE CASH REGISTER

The cash register which Rick's father purchased in 1910, quite remarkable in its time, is still used in the Harris Barbershop. It adds, counts the sales, counts how many times the cash drawer is opened, records the daily number of customers and keeps an account of the money in the till. An indication of the value of money in those days is that the register is limited to ringing up only $3.99 per customer. Rick Harris still has the receipt his father received when he purchased the cash register.

Cash register purchased in 1910 is still in use at the Harris Barbershop.

Carter-Fitzgerald Photography
The cabinet in the corner came from the home of Prime Minister Sir Robert Bond.

A Connection with Sir Robert Bond

When Mr. Harris purchased a corner cabinet from the estate of Sir Robert Bond, who passed away on March 16, 1927, it became the centre of attention in the store until memories of the famous Newfoundland Prime Minister had faded. Most customers today are not even aware of the historic past of the old cabinet which now displays magazines and the latest *Telegram* and *Newfoundland Herald* for customers to read while waiting to be served.

The Stands

Today the barber's work station, referring to the cabinet along the wall that holds all of the barber's supplies and work tools, is also from the original store. These were handcrafted, at the Horwood Lumber Company on Water St., St. John's, in 1910.

THE HORNED OWL AND THE CHESS BOARD

The two things that made the Harris Barbershop famous in old St. John's was the shop's reputation as the chess and checker centre of the City, and the stuffed owl on display in its window.

In the 1920s, a regular patron of the barbershop, who was from Witless Bay, shot and killed a great horned owl. When Mr. Harris expressed an interest in having the owl, the customer brought it to Ewing's Furriers on Pleasant Street and had it stuffed and mounted. Harris put it on display in the store window and it soon became known around the neighbourhood and eventually throughout St. John's. Like Cash's wooden Indian on Water Street east, the owl in the barbershop window became a point of reference, particularly during the war years in the 1940s. When giving instructions on where a location could be found, people would say, "Go west on New Gower Street until you come to the barbershop with the horned owl in the window and from there....." The owl lasted throughout the dirty thirties, the war years, the referendum, and the first couple of decades of Confederation. Unfortunately, in the mid-1970s, a thief broke the store window and stole the owl. It marked the first time in the shop's history that anyone had broken the store's window.

Checkers was a popular game in the 1920s and Mr. Harris once won the title of Newfoundland Champion Checker Player. The title attracted many challengers to the barbershop. Harris was also one of the city's top chess players and had a chess-checker board made locally to satisfy his favorite pastimes. Rick Harris, his son, commented as he placed the chess pieces on the board in preparation for a game, "This board and table were made by Jack Hackett, Elsie Power's grandfather. Elsie married Jack Power and lived on Flower Hill before moving to Stephen Street. She passed away some years ago."[1] The board is still in use in the shop to this day.

The popularity of checkers at the Harris Barbershop led to trouble. It seemed that everybody wanted to be a winner and there were many sore losers. Rick Harris recalled:

> People would come from everywhere to challenge my father to a game and he would accommodate them when time allowed. Often, they played for hours after the store closed. But when they lost, they would argue and even

Rick Harris photo
L-R: R. (Dick) Harris, Mr. Wadden, Pat Hunt, Roy Barnes and J. Murphy.

some challenged him to a fight. He was a powerful man and he brooked no nonsense. He wouldn't hesitate in tossing a troublemaker out the door. He began playing chess in the store and in no time, checkers took a back seat, and there was a big following for chess. During the 1940s, he had soldiers from the American and Canadian bases come to the store to challenge him.

Yes, when father had five barbers working for him with each chair filled and another crowd seated and waiting their turn, the chess games would go on. If my father was cutting hair, he was also watching the game. While giving a customer a shave or a haircut, he would direct comments at the players like, 'Ah, you made a wrong move there!' or 'You'll never get out of the fix you're in. Checkmate is only a few moves away.' He would go on with his work and he was usually right about the play.

WAR YEARS

During the war years of the 1940s, New Gower Street was a rough place. Soldiers from many nations frequented the many businesses in the area and there were often donnybrooks between them and the locals, and sometimes even among themselves. The son recalls:

> The hard crowd never troubled our shop. We never had a window broken, which might have been some kind of record in the downtown of that era. There were some famous local characters who brought trouble everywhere they went, but they never bothered my father. The only trouble he had was over a bottle of rum. He settled that quickly by hitting the fellow and blackening his eye. Buddy had come up banging on the door several times. We lived over the store then. When skipper answered the door, buddy mentioned he was trying to get enough money together for a bottle of rum and it got hot from there. He was refusing to take no for an answer, so skipper decked him.
>
> Buddy came into the store the next day with his black eye showing and said, 'Skipper, look what you did to me last night.'
>
> Skipper said, 'You're lucky I didn't blacken two of them because you were told twice.'
>
> As hard as New Gower Street was we never lost a window until we lost the owl. I think the tough characters respected dad. Fellows knew that if you started trouble with him, he'd end it.

Barbering in the early years was very different than it is today. Rick Harris explained:

> Barbers worked six days a week, from Monday to Saturday. The Saturday night business usually ran into early Sunday morning. The working day started at 8:00 a.m. and continued to 7 or 8 p.m., depending on the customers. On Saturday night everyone wanted to get cleaned up for church on Sunday. Usually they wanted a cut and a shave. My father often worked until 1:00 a.m. Sunday morning. Even City Council workers would clean up the streets on Saturday for Sunday.
>
> In the summertime, there were lineups waiting, and those who couldn't get a chair in the store waited outside

on the window ledge for their turns. They were all regulars who came two and three times a week. Each person had his own mug, which was numbered, and a brush. I still have one here in the store. Some customers even had their own razors.

All the mugs were kept on a shelf in the store. If a fellow passed away, his mug would be given to someone else. At one time we had over 100 mugs on our shelves.

At the peak of operation, we had five barbers working in the store which meant we were handling a few hundred customers on a weekly basis. I estimate that over a half a million haircuts were given in our shop since it was opened and that's not counting the walk-ins.

In those days, nobody shaved himself. The shave cost seven cents and you could get three a week for fifteen cents. Haircuts were ten cents.

My father never took any holidays. Even in 1982, when he became sick, he continued to work. I remember I had an injured hand at the time, and was looking for a way to keep him out of the shop. I went in and would whisper to customers to come back and see me on Tuesday. He over-

Carter-Fitzgerald Photography

Author Jack Fitzgerald playing chess with Rick Harris on the same board used so many years ago.

heard me and said, 'It's just as well that you get out of here now, cause you're only fooling up my business.'

Today, Rick Harris Jr. has maintained the atmosphere and flavour of the barbershop of his father. It's a place to relax, enjoy the humour and keep up with the news of the day. If you have forgotten the feeling of getting a good haircut in the company of good natured customers, you haven't visited Harris Barbershop lately.

HOW NEWFOUNDLANDERS BECAME PUDDING AND DUMPLING EATERS!

Dumplings and puddings have been enjoyed by Newfoundlanders for centuries and no authentic 'True-Newfoundland Scoff' is complete without one or the other. However, the origins of these favoured dishes go back to ancient times. It was Julius Caesar who brought the dumpling into Britain. These were simple concoctions of flour and water, but, in time, the dumpling became a pudding.

In the beginning, they resembled pancakes, without eggs, milk or lard. Then some housewife somewhere used milk instead of water, another captain of the kitchen introduced butter or some other fat, and in time, sugar and fruit were added.

The addition of eggs to puddings was purely accidental. A housewife was making a pudding, and just above where she stood mixing it, there was a shelf containing some eggs. Suddenly, some disturbance caused two or three of the eggs to roll off the shelf, and they fell into the pudding. The woman decided to chance whether the pudding was spoiled or not, and she left the eggs in, after having carefully picked out all broken shells. She felt that if the eggs did not improve her pudding, they would certainly do no harm, and when the pudding was cooked and tasted, she discovered she had a pudding superior to all other puddings.

The idea spread. King John had heard all about the woman's accidental 'eggs periment' and sent for her to cook such puddings for the royal household. Thus, the making of her puddings for royalty enhanced her reputation and her product was in great demand.

The making of dumplings and puddings spread throughout England, Scotland and Ireland with each developing its own recipes. In time, settlers from all three countries brought their recipes to Newfoundland where variations to the recipes created the Newfoundland dumplings and puddings like figgy duff, blueberry, and many others.

FIRST MOOSE IN NEWFOUNDLAND

Wm. Earle photo

A moose at the intersection of Monroe and Casey Streets as seen from Haley's Pharmacy.

In 1946, a man who was a witness to the first moose being introduced to Newfoundland wrote a letter which was published in the newspaper, the *Newfoundlander*. The letter made interesting reading at the time and is presented here in its entirety.

Dear Editor:

I am writing you with reference to the first moose ever landed in Newfoundland. I can remember the event very well. They were landed at Harris Point, South Gander, a cow and a bull. The party who put them ashore fired powder guns to drive them into the forest. They were gone 10 to 12 days when they returned. The moose swam across Gander Bay to the North Side and became so tame they would not leave the settlement. The Magistrate of that day was authorized by the government to hire a man to attend to them. Richard Bursey was appointed, and he built a shelter and hauled birch boughs all through the winter months. The next year the bull moose was found dead on the bank at the mouth of Gander River. The cow moose now became very annoying after the loss of her mate, and would travel long distances in the country, and whatever she came across such as trapper's camps, saw pits, etc., she would level to the ground. Many trappers were put to their wits ends by her. The year after the death of the bull, she disappeared. There was no increase from these two moose. They were different in colour from the moose of these days, very gray, and altogether different in habits. I was born in 1863, and these moose referred to appeared some time in the 1870s.[2] I am the only person here in Gander Bay who can remember anything about the first moose ever landed in Newfoundland. About 40 years ago, I caught a fawn caribou, got permission from the Game Board to keep it, and she became very tame. I made a harness and sleigh for her and believe me, I could go places in record time. I would let her go out of my garden and she would go for miles and for days at a time. Finally she went away and never returned.

– John Gillingham

A VISITOR'S DESCRIPTION OF THE ST. JOHN'S OF 1872
In 1872, a visitor to St. John's named David Kennedy kept a written record of his impressions of the city. He wrote:

Let us see what kind of place we have been cast upon while awaiting the next Allen Line boat. St. John's town has a population of twenty-three thousand. A queer place it is with one really good street a mile and a half long following the water frontage at the back of the wharves. Higher up on the hill is another street, less regular, full of heights and hollows, corners and angles and not substantial of its buildings.

The rest of the town is composed of by-streets and lanes and a nebulous collection of wooden huts perched higgley-piggley upon stony braces. The better class of houses are of brick, some faced with plaster, too many with an old, unwashed appearance. If the folks here used whitewash or paint on their houses, it would wonderfully brighten up the town. The larger shops are very respectable and do much business, St. John's being the emporium of the whole island. You will see one shop ornamented with the sign of a white polar bear, another with a big black seal, here a dog over a door, there a golden codfish. One noticeable thing is the startling frequency of drinking shops. Very often there are two together, sometimes there are actually four.

Through the streets drive little fish carts drawn by diminutive shaggy horses. Burly, red-whiskered men in blue guernseys walk along, trailing heavy cod in their hands. A knot of bulky black dogs are snarling over some fish refuse. There are scores of dogs. You see them prowling around the streets, romping with the children or sunning themselves in the doorways.

No matter where you go, you are always knocking against a bass-voiced dog. Everybody owns one. 'Half of the poor brutes are muzzled to keep them from fighting with the other half,' an Irishman tells me. Every second or third dog has its coat frayed across the back and loins from having to haul firewood.

You walk on rough cobbled pavements and climb steep, foul byways with rocks cropping up in the middle of them. You see rickety houses all out of the straight shored up by long poles, and at one part enclosed with high palisades like Maori pahs.[3]

You come upon narrow rows of squalid dwellings, the narrow doors cut in half with only the lower part left shut. No matter how decayed or wretched the house, it possesses a little shop for the sale of confectionery and taye (tea). Hens dance in and out behind the counter. Pigs, goats and scraggy cows dispute supremacy with bare-legged, bare-head children who play at 'ringba jing' and other games in the middle of the street.

And down by the shore, the fishermen are drying and mending their nets and at wooden stands erected on the wharves people are buying and selling cod, haddock and salmon.

INVENTOR ALEXANDER GRAHAM BELL'S LETTER
On September 2, 1885, Alexander Graham Bell, the world famous inventor, along with his wife and two children were passengers on the *Hanoverian* on a trip from Halifax to Liverpool, England. While it neared Trepassey, a heavy fog moved in rapidly along the southern shore of Newfoundland. While entering Portugal Cove South, the blinding fog caused the *Hanoverian* to hit a rock and she became a total loss.

Fortunately, all on board survived, as did much of the cargo. The survivors were taken to St. John's on board the *Miranda* where they were housed at the Atlantic Hotel. Just before departing from the city to continue his trip to Liverpool, Bell penned the following letter to *The Terra Nova Advocate*. It read:

Sir,

The appeal to the inhabitants of St. John's for aid to the steerage passengers of the *Hanoverian* has been most liberally responded to by donations both of clothing and of money.

As many of these donations were addressed to my care, I feel that the duty devolves upon me of thanking the donors for their generosity, which I do most heartily, and of explaining the manner in which the gifts have been applied.

A number of the ladies of St. John's kindly volunteered to act as a committee to investigate the needs of the various passengers, and to distribute the clothing and money as required. The self-denying and arduous efforts of these ladies have happily been successful in accomplishing the relief of all ascertained cases of distress. The proprietor of the Atlantic House[4] promptly granted the committee the use of one of the rooms in his hotel, and Mr. Fred Smith of St. John's undertook the collection and care of the cash contributions which amounted to upwards of forty pounds.

I am sure that the unfortunate passengers of the *Hanoverian* will ever remember with gratitude the timely aid that has been so cordially extended to them. The generosity of the people of St. John's has been so great that there will probably be a surplus which will be available for the poor of this city.

Yours truly,
Alexander Graham Bell,
St. John's, September 8, 1885

According to the late historian, P. K. Devine, the famous inventor had another connection with Newfoundland. His father had worked as a chemist with McMurdo's Pharmacy on Water Street in St. John's before Alexander Graham Bell was born.

THE 1892 FIRE CLOCK
Not everyone carried a watch in old St. John's. After several public buildings that had displayed clocks as a public service were destroyed in the Great Fire of 1892, it presented a problem. Henry Norman, a watchmaker at the corner of Holdsworth and New Gower Streets, came to the rescue. He placed a large clock outside his door when he opened in the morning, and took it back in at closing time. This served the public well for some time after.

NEWFOUNDLAND DIMES
During April 1945, the Royal Canadian Mint manufactured 170,000 Newfoundland dimes for the Government of Newfoundland. A shortage of dimes during WWII made it necessary to order additional coins.

LAST MAN ELECTED IN
RESPONSIBLE GOVERNMENT DAYS
The last person elected to the Newfoundland Legislature when Newfoundland was a Dominion was Ernest Gear. Gear, who was born in St. John's in 1914, was elected in a by-election under the leadership of Prime Minister Frederick C. Alderdice on March 21, 1933. The following year Newfoundland's constitution was suspended and Commission of Government was introduced.

ST. JOHN'S LIFE IN 1840s

The following excerpt from a letter written by John Pearson, son of a St. John's Merchant, to a friend in England in 1844 describes the climate and how people spent their time in St. John's. Pearson wrote:

The climate differs some little from that you have, by being almost the two extremes - either very warm or very cold. In summer the heat is at times almost suffocating, and were it not that the town is open to the breezes of the Atlantic, would be very bad to bear. What adds to the warmth is the houses being chiefly built of wood, which is more susceptible of heat than brick and stone would be.

The streets are also paved with wood in parts, but that is rarely found, except opposite the various places of business. It is not an uncommon thing to see the thrermometer between 80 and 90, (fahrenheit)[5] at eight o'clock in the morning, so you may judge how it will feel at noon. This is in the months of June, July, and August.

In addition to this, if you go a short distance into the country, you have the satisfaction of allowing the musquitoes [sic] to make a meal upon the blood they draw from your face and hands. They are very troublesome, and unless you are prepared for them, by having your face rubbed with a preventive, they will bite you desperately.

Perhaps you will not credit it, when I inform you that I have in about six hours took thirty dozen trout with rod and line. There is also any quantity of shooting, and no Game Laws here - knock down anything you come across. Partridges are very plentiful, also snipe. You may sometimes get a chance of a shot at a fox or bear, both of which are found in the woods at no great distance from the town. These are the only amusements you have with the exception of boating.

Winter is the time of year when the most enjoyment is to be found. After the first of January we have nothing to do but to think of passing our time in the best and merriest way we can until the middle of April, at which period the spring goods arrive from England.

You can form no idea of a Newfoundland winter - for months nothing to be seen but frost and snow. We have usually a heavy fall of snow early in January, which will lie on the ground until spring. This becomes frozen and is as hard as ice. You will see as much snow fall in an hour as will lie six to seven feet deep, and often after a few hours snowing, you will require to dig yourself out of doors. Then is the time for fun in sleighing, the favourite amusement of the country.

You may go for miles and miles over fields of frozen snow, across the ponds and rivers in your sleigh without the least fear of danger. The sleighs are drawn by dogs and horses, around the necks of which are hung bells as a preventive for running foul of each other, as they make not the least noise in moving along, and travel at a very rapid rate.

The sleighs are usually painted in very gaudy colours, and are covered with furs of various descriptions. The horses are dressed in like manner. You will see vast numbers of these vehicles running in procession, each one armed with an immense ring of bells, as before named, which to a stranger has a very strange appearance.

At this period, it is customary for the poorer classes to go into the woods and cut timber which is drawn over the snow by dogs. This is used for ship-building, also for firewood, as they have little or no coal to burn, and unless they lay in a large stock at this season, they will not be able to procure any during the summer, owing to the access being so difficult into the woods.

You have no doubt heard and read of the prairies in America and were you here you would be able to form an idea of what they are. You will see vast extents of fine land covered for miles with forests of wood, the greater part of which is spruce, or what we call in England fir. It is such places as these that hundreds of the poor seek their livelihood, depending chiefly upon what they procure by fishing, shooting and taking furs of various kinds, these they bring to St. John's, and sell or barter for articles of clothing etc.

It is not an uncommon thing during the summer to witness fires of an alarming extent, which take place in the woods, and are occasioned by parties kindling fire for the purpose of cooking which they often leave burning, and there by tending to the brushwood, and so on to trees.

I was witness to one of these terrible conflagrations this summer. The fire was about four miles out of the town, and it was considered by persons who were able to judge, that it covered a space of not less than six or seven miles. This was one mass of burning trees, the sight it would be impossible to describe, and may be more easily imagined. The heat given to the atmosphere was intense, and was almost unbearable at many miles distance.

FAMOUS NAME

While researching the burial records for the old cemetery adjacent to the Anglican Cathedral in St. John's, I noted an unusual name entered in the register on December 3, 1843. On that date, in the presence of mourners and a Church of England clergyman, Eugenie Louis Napoleon Le Chaudelac was laid to rest. Was the first name of the child chosen because of the father's admiration for the Emperor Napoleon and his wife, or did it reflect a Le Chaudelac family connection to the Emperor's family?

The only other reference I could find of the name Le Chaudelac was contained in a newspaper record of September 3, 1840 which reported that M. Peter Louis Le Chaudelac had married Maria Tarahan in St. John's, Newfoundland.

[1] 2008 interview with author Jack Fitzgerald at the Harris Barbershop.

[2] Moose were introduced to Newfoundland in 1878 and were landed at Gander Bay. The second release was 1905. *Newfoundland and Labrador Who's Who-Centennial Edition 1967-68.*

[3] Huts or houses built by Maoris.

[4] Atlantic Hotel was located on the site now occupied by the Sir Humphrey Gilbert Building.

[5] A measure of temperature in which water freezes at 32 degrees and boils at 212 degrees.

CHAPTER 3

TALES OF THE GHOSTLY
AND GHASTLY

A SPIRIT, AN ENERGY AND A SECRET

During the 1980s, three St. John's businessmen purchased a house on Queen's Road to renovate and divide into apartments. During the renovations, they encountered unexplainable happenings that led to a confrontation with an entity and the discovery of a secret about the house that added to the mystery.

There was nothing strange about the house until one day Roy and Ed, two of the three new owners, began discussing what to do with the boxes and containers stored in an attic room. The discussion brought out two different views on what to do with the stored material.

Roy took a quick look around the room and suggested they simply take it, as is, and bring it directly to the dump. Ed held a more considerate view of the problem and protested, "We can't just toss everything away without looking through it. There could be things stored here that might have special meaning to the former owners, or whoever lived here over the years."

"Have it your way," commented Roy, "but it's going to make our job a lot longer."

Later that day, Ed returned to the attic room to begin the clean-up process. When he reached towards the doorknob to open the door, he was literally shocked. He described it:

> Something, some kind of force, was between my hand and the doorknob and whatever it was, I felt a slight shock go up my arm. It was strange but it did not deter me or cause me any concern. I made another reach for the knob, and this time, I had no trouble opening the door. I began checking the boxes and bags. I had totally dismissed from my thoughts the episode with the doorknob when I sensed that someone else was in the room with me. I turned around but there was nobody there. Yet, I had felt the presence so strongly that I thought that

either Roy or Paddy had come up from downstairs, so I went out into the hall looking for them. The hall was empty. I searched the other rooms which were also empty. Again, I dismissed it as nothing more than my imagination and I went on with my work.

That afternoon I was talking with Roy in the downstairs kitchen when we heard Paddy running down over the stairs. He was visibly upset and shaking. You could see in his face that something had scared the daylights out of him. Before we could ask any questions, Paddy said, 'This place is haunted. I went up to clear the attic room, and something was stopping my hand from touching the doorknob. When I pushed hard against whatever the force was, I got an awful jolt, like an electric shock right up my arm.'

Well, all three of us went up. By this time I was a little more concerned because I had a similar, but less frightening experience with the doorknob. When we got to the door, neither Paddy nor Roy would touch the doorknob. Although a little reluctantly, I reached out and grabbed the knob, turned it and opened the door without anything happening. We went inside and searched around, we even checked the door to see if there had been any exposed wire affecting it but there was no explanation. For a few days things were quiet.

But then one night when all three of us were together in the downstairs living room, we experienced a feeling that we were not alone in the house. The sense was so strong that to satisfy ourselves, we did a floor by floor search of the house from basement to attic. Only in the attic rooms did we get the feeling that someone was watching us.

We returned to watching television and it wasn't long before we began hearing someone walking around upstairs. Doors were opening and closing, then there was a creaking sound as though someone was coming down the stairs. It was scary and we didn't know what to make of it. Then the noise stopped and things returned to normal.

In the days that followed, it seemed that the haunting spirit or spirits showed more anger towards Roy than it did towards Ed and Paddy, perhaps because Roy wanted to make quick work of the home's memories.

The most frightening experience of the whole episode, according to Ed, took place on a Monday night when all three were just relaxing and chatting in the living room. Ed remembered:

> Once again we heard the creaking sound like someone coming down the stairs. But unlike the first time, on this occasion the sound stopped when it got down to our floor and we looked over towards the stairs. There was something hovering around there. At first glance it was like cigarette smoke, then we could see it was more bluish, and although not a solid form, it hovered there as though it was some kind of entity.
>
> I said to the boys, 'We got to have a closer look at this.' We got up and walked towards it. It did not move at first, but when we got close, it moved up the stairways and continued back to the attic. I said, 'That's it! We got to tear that room apart. There has got be some explanation.'
>
> Then the next day we cleared the room and moved everything out. We started to tear apart one of the walls. We found something that stunned us just as much as the haunting that we were experiencing. We could not understand the meaning of it at the time, and only now I have a small suspicion of what it could have been.
>
> Yes, we stopped in our tracks when we found a hidden room behind the wall. A hidden, pad-locked room with bars on the only window. It was obviously a place where someone had been locked up, perhaps for short times, or perhaps a lifetime. Maybe it was the spirit of the victim pushing us to keep on. We made enquires about the house and were told that the family that originally owned it had a mentally ill child and built the room to keep the child in when she became a threat to herself or others. Who knows? In old St. John's there were practically no services to help the mentally ill except confinement.

The tenant before us had not experienced anything unusual and heard nothing from others about the house being haunted. Perhaps, it was the conversation between myself and Roy in that attic room when Roy wanted to quickly dispose of everything that sparked the weird happenings that led us to the hidden room?

We completed our renovations without disturbing the hidden room and we replaced the wall that concealed it. Soon after we sold the house.

Ed never went back to the Queen's Road house. He still lives and operates a business in St. John's and whenever he passes the house, especially at night, he always slows down a little and glances towards the attic windows, wondering if the spirit he had encountered had found peace.

PHANTOM DRUMMER AT BRIGUS GRAVEYARD

During the early 1950s, a funeral procession solemnly wended its way to the graveyard at Brigus. Just as some mourners expected, as it neared the cemetery, it happened. Out of nowhere came the sound of the rolling of a drum. It lasted until the cortege arrived at the open grave awaiting the deceased. It was not surprising to some of the mourners who remembered the legend of a faithful English drummer boy who had made good his promise to an old Brigus settler. He made the promise over two hundred years before. "I'll drum you to your grave, Sir," he told the old settler, "and I'll also drum every direct descendant of yours to the grave in payment of your kindness to me." The oldest settlers at Brigus knew that he was keeping his promise.

The tale of the phantom drummer of Brigus was passed on to Leo English M.B.E., curator of the Newfoundland Museum and an authority on Newfoundland history and folklore. He was told the story by one of the mourners at the funeral who asked to remain anonymous. In recording the story, Mr. English wrote:

Over two hundred years ago, the fishing fleets that came from West England were convoyed in troubled times by British warships. Some of these warships patrolled the waters of Newfoundland during the fishing season, keeping lawlessness in check. Warships in those days used to have a drummer boy who would perform at certain naval services.

On one of those man-o-wars there was a young drummer lad who was treated rather harshly by the captain and the lad sought the first opportunity to escape. The warship put into Brigus one day and that night, under the cover of darkness, he escaped from the vessel. The warship was scheduled to sail the next morning, and did. The absence of the drummer boy, whom many of the crew suspected escaped from the sadistic captain, didn't cause too much concern. The captain probably laughed heartily over the little fellow running off from his captivity. Besides there were more drummer lads in England who were anxious to come to the New-found-land for adventure.

The drummer lad was befriended by a kindly settler at Brigus. He accepted the boy into his family, and he grew into sturdy manhood. He learned the fishing trade and became a Newfoundlander as many English lads had done before him.

As a reward for the kindness shown to him, the drummer boy made a promise to the old settler. He told him that when he, the settler, died, he would drum him to the grave. And he also promised that he would sound his drum at the funerals of the old man's descendants.

The old man died. And true to his word, the drummer followed the coffin to the grave beating solemnly on his drum. He performed the same ritual for other direct descendants, and then the drummer, by this time an old man himself, passed on to his eternal reward.

Mysteriously, the drumming went on. After the drummer died, one of the fisherman's direct descendants died. On the way to the cemetery, the mourners heard the roll of the drum...this time from a phantom drum...beat by a phantom drummer. And since then in Brigus, whenever a direct descendant of the drummer's benefactor dies, the beating of a drum can be heard while the funeral procession is en route to the graveyard.

MACABRE SIGHT AT BELL ISLAND GRAVEYARD

One of the most bizarre occurrences ever to be witnessed in any cemetery in Newfoundland, and perhaps in all Canada, took place in the cemetery at Bell Island on July 8, 1914. This macabre incident happened in broad daylight and attracted crowds of curious spectators to the area outside the cemetery. Only the presence of police kept them from entering the grounds for a closer look at the extraordinary event in progress. The Inspector General of Police, John Sullivan, had been sent over from St. John's with several police officers to secure the graveyard.

The spectacle, which attracted so much public attention, was what appeared to be a medical operation being performed next to an open grave. Adding to the gravity of the scene was an open, but empty coffin lying nearby the linen-covered operating table. Two doctors and an assistant, all dressed in white, performed their task oblivious to the public interest being shown in their work from outside the cemetery. A stranger arriving on the scene may have thought some kind of supernatural appearance was taking place. However, the incident had nothing at all to do with spectres or the supernatural.

The event in progress had been sparked by another event that happened a few days earlier. The body of Thomas Fitzgerald, a mine worker on Bell Island, had been found near the Whitney Bridge, badly battered about the head and with deep wounds to his face and throat. He died shortly after being found. No sooner had his body been buried in the grave when word reached authorities that foul play had been involved in the man's death.

Police arrested a James Ryan, the last person to see Fitzgerald alive, and then obtained a court order to exhume the body to perform an autopsy. Since there was no morgue on Bell Island, a decision was made to bring the corpse to St. John's. This plan was changed when doctors noticed that the high summer temperatures had already caused some decomposing of the body, and they feared this would be accelerated if the body was transported to St. John's. Preparations were initiated to carry out the autopsy inside the cemetery adjacent to Fitzgerald's grave. Nothing like it had ever been witnessed in Newfoundland. *The Evening Telegram* stated on July 14, 1914, "There, in the graveyard, under a hot sun and blue sky, the gruesome work of post-mortem was conducted."

The magisterial enquiry was held immediately after the autopsy, and it concluded that no foul play was involved. It stated, "Death was caused by injuries suffered by a heavy fall." John Ryan was immediately released by the police.

A CHILLING EXPERIENCE AT GRAND FALLS

The late Michael MacKenzie, author of *Memories Recalled*, published in 1992, told of a chilling experience he had in Grand Falls. He wrote:

It seems that when I was returning westward from St. John's, Newfoundland, one fine June day in 1980, I entered the Mount Peyton Motel in Grand Falls on the Trans Canada Highway. As I approached the desk, I noticed Joe W. MacNeil of Castle Bay and his sister, a Sister of Service, coming out of the dining room, just opposite the reception desk, after finishing his breakfast. There were two others with them.

I warmly shook hands with Joe and his sister, and Joe introduced me to the other two gentlemen travelling with them in the same car. After chatting for a little while with them, the four of them left together to continue westward their trip to the mainland. As this was a 'normal' regular meeting, I thought no more about the chance meeting.

I noticed Joe MacNeil several times in the church that summer on Christmas Island (Nova Scotia). I really didn't get a chance to talk with him about the pleasant surprise I experienced in seeing his group in the motel in June. Two months later, however, Joe died rather suddenly on September 8, 1980. Unfortunately I missed his funeral, for I had to return to school as usual in September.

A little later that fall, when I was again in St. Barra's Church on Christmas Island, I spoke to Joe's brother, Angus, and his only remaining sister, Agnes, about the friendly chat or visit I had with their brother Joe in Grand Falls. I was rather crestfallen when they said, "Oh, Joe was never in Newfoundland."

That new revelation really upset me, for how could that be, I had talked to him for almost ten minutes about three months earlier?

THE CURSED 'PIGGIN' OF TICKLE COVE

A 'piggin' is a homemade wooden dipper used for bailing water out of a boat. There were thousands of them around Newfoundland, but only the 'piggin' of Tickle Cove carried a curse with it. The cursed 'piggin' was owned by Billy Philpott of Tickle Cove who ignored the warnings from fellow fishermen that the item held supernatural powers.

Billy was born at Tickle Cove in the nineteenth century and developed the reputation of the best and roughest fishermen in the area. Billy's knowledge of the sea and his fearless disposition came from the fact that he traveled to the Labrador fishery twice a year. In the summer he participated in the Labrador fishery and in the spring he returned for the seal hunt.

On one of his Labrador adventures he came across the grave of an Eskimo woman and decided to take the skull back on ship with him to use as a 'piggin'. The others pleaded with him to leave the skull where he found it. One fisherman said he was sure that anyone who tampered with an Eskimo grave would be cursed. Billy ignored their warnings and chose to bring the skull home with him. During the return trip, a strange occurrence was witnessed, not by the superstitious crewmen but by the unbeliever Billy. He swore seeing a mysterious figure flitting from deck to deck of the boat. The others believed he was just trying to spook them.

When they arrived home, Billy kept his punt in Otter Gulch near the local fishing grounds. Strange happenings followed the 'piggin'.

On a trip to King's Cove he witnessed a phantom figure beckoning him from a hole in the cliff near his home. He suspected it was his mother calling him but when he arrived at the house it was empty and his mother had gone into Tickle Cove for the day.

John Hamilton, now living in St. John's, but originally from Fortune Harbour, knew the story so well in his youth and recalled:

> Billy set out for King's Cove on a fine spring day to sign up for a berth to the ice. He paid his berth money but disregarded the warnings of his friends who saw signs of a severe storm coming their way. Billy took his package of sugar and tea and began the long, hard tramp to Tickle Cove.
>
> The storm suddenly struck. It snowed intermittently for days, each fresh blizzard worse than the last. When

84

the snow finally ceased, several of Billy's friends organized a search party and set out to look for him. When they got to Tickle Cove, they saw that Billy's boat and 'piggin' had disappeared and only a pair of borrowed oars lay on the ice. They searched for hours but it was useless. Billy's package was discovered, tied to a tree. The searchers grew more hopeful but then, as if signifying a bad omen, a dark cloud hovered above their heads and someone stumbled over Billy's body, lying face down in the snow. The poor fellow was dead.

There are people today who will swear that a strange occurrence happened that night. They insist that witnesses saw a red ball of fire ascending to the heavens with two ghostlike figures clinging to it. And to this very day, that dark hole in the cliff where Billy's vision appeared is called "Billy Philpott's Hole."

KINSELLA PLAYED CARDS WITH THE DEVIL

The story of a man named John Kinsella playing cards with the devil was so well known around Notre Dame Bay in the 1940s that the rock on which the game was alleged to have taken place became a famous monument to the curious event and attracted visitors from around Notre Dame Bay and as far away as St. John's.[1]

The Devil's Rock was located on the property of the family of John Hamilton in Fortune Harbour, a small community in Notre Dame Bay. John's father operated the post office in the area. The most popular pastime in those far-off days was the card game of "forty-fives" and Kinsella would travel miles to find a game, and he thrived on being known as the best player in the bay.

One night he walked from Fortune Harbour to a little place called Webber's Bight, a distance of two and a half miles. As the game unfolded, the other players began kidding him about his zeal for cards and said they felt he would play cards with anyone, anywhere. Jokingly Kinsella replied, "Yes, I would have a game of cards with the devil himself."

Some time after midnight, Kinsella left Webber's Bight to return home. It was a beautiful moonlit night. About halfway home he encountered a strange man who stopped to ask where he was going so late at night.

Courtesy John Hamilton

People still search for the famous rock while visiting Fortune Harbour. This photograph is an actual picture taken of the rock where the alleged card game took place, and though Kinsella is long gone, his renowned encounter with the devil in a card game that night has never been forgotten and the print of the devil's hand remains in the rock.

Kinsella said he was returning from a game of "forty-fives" and told the stranger of his great love for the game. The stranger invited him to have a game there and then. Kinsella enthusiastically accepted. They used the large flat top rock on the Hamilton property for their card table.

The game was going well until the last hand when Kinsella was in sight of winning. The stranger was visibly annoyed at the prospects of being beaten, and only then did Kinsella notice the twitching tail protruding from his back.

Courageously, Kinsella played his final card. It beat the card held by the stranger who became so angry that in laying his card he left the print of his hand in the solid rock table. Kinsella realized then that he had been playing cards with the devil. He rushed to the Hamilton household and told them what had happened. John Hamilton said the story handed down in his family was that whatever happened at the rock that night had an effect on Kinsella because when he arrived at the Hamilton home he was visibly upset.

From there the legend was born that Kinsella was the only man who had played cards with – and had beaten – the devil himself.

STRANGE HEARSE

During July 1907, some citizens in the area of the Anglican Cemetery on Forest Road were puzzled by the sight of an unusual looking hearse leading a funeral towards the cemetery. As was the custom of the time, people stopped when the funeral was passing. Men removed their hats, Catholics made the sign of the cross and all bowed their heads until the funeral passed. In this case, there were many puzzled looks and raised eyebrows. The hearse was unlike any that had been seen in St. John's up to that time. It was completely white and a little smaller than the traditional black hearse.

There was nothing supernatural about this sighting. The white hearse soon became a sad but common sight in the city. It was actually a specially designed hearse exclusively for children's funerals. The Oake Carriage Factory designed and constructed the hearse for the undertaker, J.J. Connolly.

FANNY GOFF

Tryphena Goff died at a young age and was buried on the day she was to be married. She may have been forgotten to history if it had not been for two incredible circumstances in her life.

First, while on her death bed, she made a remarkable prediction of an event that took place days after her own burial. The other circumstance that attributes to her remarkable story is that both her parents had a connection with the Royal Family in England.

Tryphena, whose extraordinary story was recorded by a Mrs. Gordon Miller many years ago, was generally known as Fanny or Pheenie Goff. Fanny was beautiful, charming, congenial and worked in her father's inn at Portugal Cove, north of St. John's. It was a popular watering hole for people traveling to and from villages around Conception Bay. She had many suitors, but the one who won her heart was John Barter, a businessman from Brigus.

It came as no surprise to her family and friends when early in 1823, Fanny accepted John's proposal of marriage and a big wedding was planned for March with the celebration to take place at Goff's Inn. But, this much-anticipated event was not to take place.

Just two weeks before the wedding date, Fanny was stricken with typhoid fever. Although several doctors attended her, the fever worsened. When it became certain to all that death was imminent, Fanny acknowledged her fate and offered encouraging words to her family. A witness said, "She showed a cheerful resignation to the Divine will. Fanny told her family that the Divine Master wanted her for his bride and she was at peace with her fate."

It was at this point that she left a loving message for John Barter. She asked. "Tell John not to grieve for me. It will not be long ere he too will pass behind the veil. John should not mourn, but get ready to meet his God."

Her dying message to her groom-to-be proved to be prophetic. On the day chosen for the wedding, Fanny was buried. John Barter, unaware of her passing, had loaded up his sleigh with gifts for the bride and bridesmaids and, after tackling his horse, set out from Brigus to drive on the ice of Conception Bay to Portugal Cove.

He stopped at the home of his friend William Squires at St. Phillips. He entered the home expressing the sentiment that this was going to be the happiest day of his life. The Squires family was preparing to go to Portugal Cove to attend Fanny's funeral, and it became the sad duty of William Squires to give the heart-breaking news to John.

According to the story, the news struck John like a bolt from heaven. He spoke not a word, just turned and left the house. He harnessed his horse, and returned to his home in Brigus. John quickly settled his affairs and took to bed where he passed away three days later of a broken heart. Fanny's prophesy to him was fulfilled.

Fanny Goff was buried beneath an apple tree in her father's garden where she and John had often sat on summer evenings. The grave is located near a place called *The Gaze,* located on the shore near Cape St. Francis on the northeast side of Portugal Cove. The place got its name from hunters who used the site as a place where they observed and hunted birds. It is said that the headstone erected in her memory is still there, though the inscription is no longer legible.

There were parental secrets on both sides of Fanny's family that remained hidden for decades. Fanny's mother was a daughter of a Mr. and Mrs. Pottle of Bonavista. The Pottles had fled England some years before and their relatives left behind had no knowledge of what became of them.

At the start of the reign of King George III, Mr. Pottle was a Captain in the King's Guards and Mrs. Pottle (nee Jennings) was a great niece of Sarah, first Duchess of Marlborough and a lady-in-waiting to Queen Charlotte.

The couple decided to elope in 1761 but because of both their circumstances, they had to escape England or face the consequences. Captain Pottle had deserted the King's colours and would have been arrested and tried, if caught. Miss Jenning's family would not have approved of her marrying an officer of the Guards.

The two made it to Poole and took a ship headed for Newfoundland. They ended up in Bonavista. The ship which had taken them to Newfoundland was lost on its return trip to England. Their hiding place in Newfoundland remained a mystery.

Mr. Pottle married Miss Jennings and their eldest daughter, Mary, married an Englishman at Bonavista named George Goff who had a secret of his own. Goff was born in England and came out to Newfoundland with his mother at age fifteen to leave behind a family secret. Those who knew him believed the secret he protected was that he was an illegitimate son of a member of the Royal family of England.

George Goff and Mary Pottle married at Bonavista and then moved to Portugal Cove where they opened their famous Inn. Fanny was one of their children.

Captain Pottle's wife passed away at Bonavista and he moved to Portugal Cove and stayed with George and Mary and family.

George Goff passed away on Friday, December 30, 1834 and Mary died on Tuesday, November 25, 1850.

Captain Pottle died in 1826 and was buried near his granddaughter, Fanny Goff.

THE MYSTERY COFFIN

Henry J. Winton, a prominent newspaper editor of the early nineteenth century, lived in a house on Queen's Road located near the western end of the small park which today separates Queen's Road from Gower Street.

Early one morning, while walking to work, he noticed an abandoned coffin inside the cemetery which he identified as, "The Cemetery of the Protestant Establishment," which was located between Court House Lane and Cathedral Street. Since that time, Cathedral Street has been renamed Church Hill and Court House

Lane has become the new Cathedral Street. The cemetery, which was officially named the Established Protestant Cemetery, is remembered today as the old Church of England Cemetery.

Winton went inside the cemetery and determined that the coffin contained a body, but there was no open grave. The newspaper editor spent his day attempting to solve the mystery. Who was in the coffin? Why wasn't there a grave? Could foul play have been involved?

By the end of the day, Winton had unraveled the mystery and pieced together one of the extraordinary stories of old St. John's. He described his findings in his newspaper, "The facts are of a revolting nature, and it becomes our duty to notice them in order to prevent the repetition of such an offensive outrage against public decency and the proper feelings common to humanity."

This strange story began on a day in May 1833 when a man, who was standing on a wharf near Beck's Cove, became suddenly ill with pleurisy. He returned to his boarding home at James Street, which was operated by the widow Gleeson. The man's condition worsened and Mrs. Gleeson sent to the Roman Catholic Chapel on Henry Street for a priest.

It did not take long for Father Troy to arrive at the home. Henry Winton, writing in The Public Ledger on May 17, 1833, reported, "Upon inquiry by the priest, it was discovered that the poor fellow had not been at what are called *Iris deities* for a considerable time." In other words, he had abandoned his church. Father Troy refused to give the dying man the sacrament of *last rights* and also warned those present, "All persons who would convey him to the burial ground for interment should be solemnly denounced."

Soon after the priest left, the man passed away. *The Public Ledger* stated, "A coffin, however, was prepared, and the body deposited therein, but no persons were found to convey the corpse to its last long home." Those present remembered Father Troy's warnings, so they brought the coffin outside and left it on the street. This was an area of what is known today as Queen's Road just west of Carter's Hill.

A Nicholas Croke, well-known builder in St. John's, arrived at the scene and after some enquiry decided that the coffin should be brought to the *Cemetery of the Protestant Establishment*. Such was the strength of the priest's warning that Croke had difficulty in obtaining assistance from his own workmen. An unceremonious funeral took place with Croke and his men depositing the coffin inside the confines of the cemetery.

When word of the incident reached local authorities, the Magistrates ordered that a grave be prepared and the deceased properly buried.

Winton observed in an editorial:

> Our business is not to interfere with the religious ceremonies and observances of any class of Christians among us, but it is our business, as far as possible, to prevent the introduction of a practice which would not only endanger the health of the inhabitants, but which, under any circumstances, would be deeply offensive and revolting to the feelings of the public generally.

He wondered if Father Troy's action was based on an overzealous desire to promote the observance of religious practices, or did he act from an ignorance of the effect which it was calculated to produce.

Church of England burial records for the month of May 1833 record only five burials. Among these, the name Benjamin Chinnick, age thirty-six, stands out, simply because, unlike the others, no information other than the name and age are recorded in the burial register. Each of the other four contained enough information regarding address, cause of death etc. to rule each one out as the man of mystery in this story.

The episode caused a long-lasting rift between Father Troy and Winton which led to the incident recounted below.

WINTON'S HOME ATTACKED

Henry Winton, who lived on Queen's Road next to the old Roman Catholic Cemetery, became the target of a mob of youths on Christmas Eve in 1833 in response to his newspaper's anti-Catholic positions.

The harassment of Winton at his home and office began early in December and became most serious on the evening of December 24, 1833. During the morning and afternoon on that day, crowds of young men assembled about the streets in the lower part of the town and were engaged in "fighting or in very riotous mirth."

As the evening drew on, the mob gathered in front of Winton's house and began terrorizing him and his family. Reporting on the event in *The Public Ledger* on December 27, 1833, Winton stated:

> A drunken fellow, apparently their leader, placed himself before our windows and harangued ourselves as well as the assembled mob. The crowd, as it was fully anticipated, speedily increased, and, of course, the noise and tumult also. In this stage of the proceedings, application was made to the civil power for that protection which it was its duty to afford, and we had very shortly the satisfaction to recognize the magistrates and constables in the melee. The civil force was unequal to the task of restoring order, and it became sufficiently apparent that a resolution had been taken to commit some extraordinary acts of violence.

The mob defied the magistrates and began attacking the Winton property. The magistrates turned to the military for help and requested that they intervene before personal injury was caused. At 5:00 p.m. a Lieutenant Rice from the Royal Veteran Companies led a detachment of eighty men, and formed on three sides of a square in front on the Winton house. The mob refused to move and continued with their rowdy behavior. The military changed their position and formed in lines three deep. Lt. Rice read the riot act and led his soldiers in a march up and down the street to clear it. After partially clearing the street, they moved to the area of the courthouse leaving sentries to guard the Winton house.

Winton described what happened at this time:

> At this stage, the mob again increasing, the sentry beat to arms (called to formation), when the detachment again made its appearance, and the street was again partially cleared. It was about this time (half-past nine) that the Roman Catholic priest, Reverend Troy, of whom we have had repeatedly to make honourable mention, was found exhorting a couple of fellows to retire to their homes, and in about half an hour after this, the town was comparatively quiet.

In an editorial following the incident, Mr. Winton made no apologies for his newspaper's editorial positions:

> We have but few words to waste upon these men. They may destroy our property, but they cannot destroy our principles, and those principles, which are plain and easy of comprehension, and which are for the people's good, shall be inculcated whenever the occasion may require. Still more, if our adversaries have one sincere desire for the restoration of peace in this once peaceful community, the Priesthood must have done with its Priestcraft, at least, in matters of a civil nature, and that political and moral nuisance, *The Patriot* newspaper, must cease to excite to acts of violence, and must have done with its canting hypocrisy. We have no objection to its continuing to be the literary COMMON SEWER, but the nuisance (conduct of the hoodlums) has hither to been too intolerable and must be abated.
>
> – The Public Ledger, December 27, 1833[2]

THE CANDLELIGHT SPIRITS OF QUIDI VIDI

Some years ago while sharing book-signing duties with Newfoundland's great story-teller, Al Clouston, I mentioned to him that in my book *Up The Pond* I had written about a double-tragedy at Quidi Vidi in 1906. Al told me that the story was well-known to him because one of the victims was a close relative. He then went on to relate a bizarre incident preceding the tragedy. The Clouston family lived in a house on Forest Road which, at the time, had an unobstructed view of Quidi Vidi Lake. One night, just before bedtime, Mrs. Clouston looked out the window towards the swimming pool at Quidi Vidi. (The sandy beach east of the present boathouse). It was late at night and the area was usually deserted. However, something strange was happening.

She saw what appeared to be a burning candle, and as she watched, another, then another appeared, so that in a short time, a semi-circle of candlelight lit the night at the swimming pool. She watched the spectacle until the lights suddenly disappeared.

The next day, she mentioned it to the rest of the family, but nobody could offer a satisfactory explanation for the mystery candlelights.

A week later, on August 4, a few days after the St. John's Regatta, Herbert Bancroft and Ted Clouston decided to go for a swim at the Quidi Vidi Pool. A new swimming aid called 'Flying-wings' had been introduced to the market and Herbert and Ted each had purchased one of the new items. They couldn't wait to try them out at Quidi Vidi.

The boys were having a great time when Ted Clouston slipped out of his float and disappeared beneath the water. When he didn't resurface, Bancroft tried desperately to save him. Unfortunately, both boys drowned. When given the sad news of the deaths, Mrs. Clouston felt she had the explanation for the mysterious candles.

This was not the first incident involving mysterious candles at Quidi Vidi Lake. Mike Murphy, author of *Pathways to Yesterday*, often told a story of a candle-carrying spirit boat on Quidi Vidi Lake. In telling the story, he credited the famous Johnny Burke, the Bard of Prescott Street, as his source. Burke had rowed in several Regattas, and for years was an active member of the Regatta Committee. In recalling old-time Regattas, he would often tell of the mysterious boat on Quidi Vidi Lake a week before the 1884 Regatta. According to Murphy, a fellow named Crane from Wexford St. (Now Livingstone Street) had been trouting one night at Quidi Vidi Lake. When darkness began to set in, he packed his belongings and got ready to leave the lake. He had not seen any boats on the pond for nearly an hour and was startled to notice the sudden appearance of a boat on the pond near the northeast shore.

This was no ordinary race-boat. It remained stationary, but the occupants were holding candles. As he walked up the bank to a main path, he occasionally glanced back. By the time he reached the path and looked back again, the boat had disappeared. All the way home, he wondered what he had witnessed.

A week later, during the Young Fishermen's Race, the Torbay crew, rowing in the Terra Nova, got in trouble after taking on water when turning the buoys. Just passed Coaker's River, about forty yards from shore, the Terra Nova went down. Three rowers lost their lives that day.

Crane, after hearing of the tragedy, and that it had occurred in the area where he had seen the candlelights, remained convinced for the rest of his life that he had witnessed an omen of the 1884 Regatta tragedy.

LITTLE WOMEN OF DEVIL'S COVE

Stories of fairies are common throughout Newfoundland, and the one I am about to relate is perhaps a tall tale, but one that was told and retold for over 150 years in the settlement of Job's Cove, once known as Devil's Cove. The story was told in *The Daily News* in 1946. It read:

> In Devil's Cove there was a woman who had a lot of wool to spin, more than she thought she could manage. She remarked to her husband, 'But I'll get it done, even if I have to get the fairies to spin it.'
>
> And no sooner had she spoken than a group of little women, fairies, of course, came rushing down a nearby hill with spinning wheels on their backs. They entered the house and started at once to spin the wool. The poor woman was all worried – she didn't have enough food in the house to feed them all, so she went to her husband and told him all about it.
>
> He advised her to go back to the house, stand near the door and call out that the hill was burning. She did so, and instantly the little women came rushing out with their spinning wheels, and she locked the door behind them. And ever afterwards, when she came to do any wool-spinning, she very carefully plugged up all the key-holes of the house to keep the little women fairies out.
>
> In those days, you know, they believed in fairies as much as we do today in the ability of the weather bureau to forecast the weather.
>
> – Author unknown

DEADMAN'S BIGHT

Deadman's Bight, near the western head of Harbour Breton, is a place that has long been associated with shipwrecks, buried treasures, and ghostly tales. A Jacob Penney of St. Jacques kept many of these tales alive for decades. One of his tales involved a spirit who came to him in a dream on three separate occasions. Each time, he was told to go in a dory to Deadman's Bight on a certain night and take with him a Simon Bunghi.

He was instructed that they were to be at Deadman's Bight at exactly midnight, at which time the door of a cave in the face of a rock would open. Inside there was a great pirate treasure and they could take away as much as they could carry. The spirit in the dream warned that they would have to be absolutely punctual because the door would open precisely at midnight, and it would close again exactly at half past twelve. "If you are not out of the cave by then, neither of you will ever walk this earth again," warned the spirit.

Jacob told Simon of the dreams and the two decided they would go look for the treasure and follow the directions given by the spirit.

The two men planned their adventure very carefully and set out in plenty of time to be in position by midnight. Although the weather was fair, it was a very dark night and they couldn't see through what they thought was the 'spy hole' on Boxy Head. As a matter of fact, there seemed like there were two or three spy holes. This caused them to go aground at Boxy Head and it took half an hour to get back on course.

When they arrived at Deadman's Bight, they were just in time to see the door close-to with a thunderous roar that shook the whole mountain.

They did manage to get a glance at the treasure inside before the door closed and Jacob said, "We were dazzled by the glare of gold and precious stones and nuggets as big as bricks, gems, and gold and silver jewelry. And you can see the door in the face of the cliff to this day, just as if it was made and put together by any carpenter."

[1] Although most articles on this story identify the card player as a man named Kinchler, his name was actually John Kinsella who came over from County Carlow, Ireland in the late nineteenth century and settled at Fortune Harbour.

[2] *The Patriot* was a pro Catholic newspaper in St. John's which was often involved in conflict with *The Public Ledger* over Religion.

CHAPTER 4

Yellow Belly Corner & Other Famous Corners of Old St. John's

The colourful memory of the old Yellow Belly Corner on Water St. has been preserved by the popular St. John's restaurant and brewery known as Yellow Belly Brewery and Public House.

YELLOW BELLY CORNER

In old time St. John's, the eastern corner of Beck's Cove was called 'Yellow Belly Corner.' This was not the place where Irish faction groups regularly brawled, as some have claimed, but it was the place where some of the combatants gathered after a brawl to clean up and wash away the blood of the injured.

Historian Judge David Prowse explained:

> Yellow Belly Corner, on the east side of Beck's Cove, commemorates the spot where the wounded in the melee used to be washed in the little brook flowing into Beck's Cove. The Tipperary Clear Airs, the Waterford Whey Bellies and the Cork Dadyeens were against the Yellow Belly faction of the Doones or Kilkenny Boys and the

97

Wexford Yellow Bellies. These were besides the Young Colts and a number of other names for the factions. They fought with one another 'out of pure divilment and diversion,' as an old Irishman explained to me.

The Yellow Bellies and the Doones were allies and together were called the Yellow Belly Faction. They didn't shy away from fighting either one or all the other faction groups in town. These 'knock 'em down, carry 'em out melees' were frequent events among young Irish immigrants in old-time St. John's and were usually fought in open fields rather than on town streets. History refers to these encounters as 'Faction Fights.' These 'young fellas' delighted in fighting against each other in their Irish towns, a tradition which they brought with them to St. John's where they continued the old country allegiances.

A WITNESS DESCRIBES BATTLE

Faction fighting in old St. John's was a major problem for authorities and often a source of fear for the peaceful inhabitants of the town. Although the faction fighters usually fought among themselves, on at least one occasion it erupted into a citywide riot involving several thousand people.

The most graphic account of such a spectacle was given by an English seaman who witnessed a brawl between Cork and Wexford men on the Barrens, the Fort Townshend-Parade Street area in early St. John's. He told Judge David Prowse:

> The battle raged for over an hour. In the general noise and confusion, and the absence of any distinguishing marks, it was impossible to differentiate between the combatants. But loud hurrahs and yells from the party on my right, and shouts of 'Cork forever' and 'Down with the Yellow Bellies!' quickly enlightened me. Answering shouts of 'murder the Dadyeens' and 'give 'em hell boys for old Wexford!' came from the party on my left, and in a matter of seconds, the din reached a high crescendo and both sides were locked in deadly conflict, deadly, at least, in the sense that heads were being cracked, noses bled profusely and stalwart Cork and Wexford men were apparently doing their utmost to kill one another.

Nearly every man was armed with a stout shillelagh and was using it with dire effect on an opponent's head. Bodies with no apparent life left in them were strewn all over the common and walked on indiscriminately by friend and foe alike. With the groaning, shouting, cursing, and babel of words in which Irish and English were confusedly intermingled, it was a scene to equal Donnybrook Fair or bedlam itself. In such a manner did the hardy, heavy-fisted men from Cork, Wexford, Waterford and Kilkenny and other counties in Ireland divert themselves on the Barrens in years gone by.

According to the seaman's account, the brawl concluded without serious injury being caused and soon afterwards both sides were enjoying a friendly drink at a nearby tavern and swapping reminiscences of the battle.

After the fighting on the Barrens, the combatants went down over the hills of St. John's to one of the streams and rivers running into St. John's Harbour where they bathed and washed the blood from themselves and their clothing. The 'Yellow Belly Faction' favoured Beck's Cove, probably because it was just down over Carter's Hill from the battlefield on the old Parade Grounds.

In 1845, the first water reservoir ever built in St. John's was constructed near Yellow Belly Corner at Beck's Cove. Its capacity was forty puncheons of water. By depressing a brass valve, water was released. A fire plug was connected to the pipes. On June 16, 1862, water was first conveyed from Windsor Lake through pipes to the town of St. John's.

SAWYER'S CORNER

The Clear Airs from Tipperary, the Whey Bellies from Waterford and the Daydeens from Cork favoured another corner along Water Street as their bathing place. They gathered at Sawyer's Corner which was next to the King's Beach. (Where the War Memorial stands today).

At least one of the faction-fights was fought in this part of town during March 1815 when the Clear Air, Whey Bellies and Daydeens squared off against the Yellow Bellies and Doones.

In a letter dated March 21, 1815, to Governor Keats, Chief Justice Ceasar Colclough described the confrontation:

The shameful scene had taken place and continued all day from seven in the morning until nine at night, and wonderful to say, though it raged about the King's Beach, Sawyer's Corner, and the new streets and lanes, neither Magistrate, Sheriff, or Peace Officer knew anything about it.

Colclough, along with the High Constable, went in search of the faction-fighters. By the time they arrived at Sawyer's Corner, it had been deserted. When told the fighters had gone to the Barrens[1], the two officials made their way up to that location and, by the time they arrived there, a large crowd was following in a line behind them. The Judge was infuriated to learn that the brawlers had been warned and had left the scene.

THEY CHALLENGED A GENERAL

Colclough received a report that earlier that day, the day the fighters were supposed to have gone to The Barrens, a group of Irishmen followed their leader to the home of a General Finn and challenged him to a fight in single combat or with him and his troops. The judge responded to the crisis by having sections of the Riot Act printed and posted throughout the city.

This appeared to have worked and for several days there was peace in the town. All this changed on the eve of St. Patrick's Day when a riot erupted, involving over two thousand people. At the time, the population of the town was ten thousand people. This battle involved fighting all over St. John's from Sawyer's Corner up to the Parade Grounds[2] and east to The Barrens. It was a free-for-all for the faction fighters who fought each other and took on all comers, with fists, sticks and anything else they could get their hands on.

The Peace Officers observed the affray from a distance until Major General Charles Campbell, Commander of the Garrison troops, took control and ordered gunfire from Fort Townshend and Signal Hill to place his troops on alert. This action alarmed the rioters, who thought the army was approaching them, so they fled, bringing an end to the fighting. There were many black eyes, bruises and broken bones, but none died from the injuries.

Only a few of the rioters were arrested and the sentences ranged from one week to six months in jail, and for one fighter, a public whipping. Colclough, an Irishman himself, blamed the melee on his hot-headed countrymen.

THE OLD TAVERN

Near the field where much of the faction fighting took place was a place called The Old Tavern, which was a landmark in old St. John's. It was located near the top of Long's Hill and could be entered from either Harvey Road or Long's Hill. Many a racket and brawl started there when opposing factions from around the town confronted each other. Long after the faction fighting died out, the Old Tavern became a popular gathering place for cricket players because of its close proximity to the Parade Grounds, the area where the CLB Armoury stands today. When The Old Tavern was destroyed in the "Great Fire of 1892," *The Daily Tribune* wrote:

> One of the most popular of social resorts, one identified with old time cricketing on the Parade Ground, was The Old Tavern. Memory loves to recall the many enjoyable incidents which transpired within its walls, remembrances of good-fellowship, and of 'the flow of soul,' as rivals at the wickets, victor and vanquished, Bonaventurean and Military, Metropolitan and Amateur, toasted each other and in song and fraternal sentiment speeded the gilded hours of youth and pleasure and hope away.

The building was replaced with a sixty-foot high structure containing twenty-four apartments and described by *The Tribune* as, "One of the finest in the town; of four stories, adorned with a mansard, forty feet breadth by thirty feet depth, and from Long's Hill towers imposingly to the height of some sixty feet."

EAST END VS WEST END GANGS

Journalist and author, Mike Murphy, writing in *The Daily News* in August 1954, compared the faction fighter era with the battles fought between the East and West End gangs of St. John's. He stated:

> The age in which they lived was a brutal one in many respects but courage and a love of freedom and fair play were outstanding characteristics of the rough living, hard-

drinking sons of the 'Auld Sod,' and it was a goodly heritage they left their descendants who have since proven themselves in two world wars and in every phase of our national life. As time went on, bringing with it many changes in manners, morals and customs, the faction fights became only memories of a hard-bitten era. Traces of their influence still lived on, however, in the battles between the East Enders who were referred to as "Down-alongs,' and West Enders who were called 'Up-alongs,' that persisted right up to the time of the First World War. There are many old-timers still living in St. John's who remember, with a touch of nostalgia, no doubt, the furious fights with pickets torn from fences that were waged between the lads from the various sections of the town, and the terror that gripped many an East End or West End boy when he found he had ventured too far into the 'enemy's' territory. But happily, the pugnatown and the competitive spirit displayed by the lads of long ago is today seen chiefly in the field of athletic endeavour and intersection 'warfare' of the type described is practically unknown in our midst today.

PRIZE FIGHTS RARE

Prior to the late nineteenth century, boxing matches and prize fights were rare in St. John's. Yet, records show that Johnny Dwyer, a native of St. John's, won the heavyweight championship of America back in the 1870s. However, Dwyer had moved to the United States at a young age and trained there to become a professional fighter.

Mike Shallow of Fermuse, Newfoundland, gained considerable fame as a professional fighter, and, in the years leading up to Confederation, Frank Stamp, Al Grayson, Don Dwyer and Sammy Lafosse, to name a few, gained notoriety in amateur and professional boxing. In the 1890s, there was at least one newspaper account of a prizefight in St. John's. That event took place on the banks of Quidi Vidi Lake during Regatta Day. An account recalling the event appeared in *The Daily News* of August 1954:

It appears that a Jew, a native of London, England, who claimed to have won several bouts in Old Country rings, arrived in Newfoundland, and, being at the race course on Regatta Day, offered to take on any man present for a certain sum, winner take all. His challenge was accepted by a St. John's man, who did his best to cope with his opponent's hitting power and experience, but was defeated in a couple of rounds.

The next to take up the challenge was an Irishman who managed to last three rounds after receiving a terrific beating. Third on the list of opponents was a native of Torbay who was a left-handed hitter, or, in modern ring parlance, "a southpaw." The Torbay man must have been a born fighter for he punished the Jew severely and knocked him out in two rounds.

After the bout, the victorious Torbay man was carried about on the shoulders of wildly-cheering spectators, and after this demonstration, quietly took his exit from the scene. A potential great fighter, perhaps, born in the wrong day and age.

MORE FAMOUS STREET CORNERS OF OLD ST. JOHN'S

Yellow Belly Corner was not the only famous corner among the streets of old St. John's. Even more notable were:

The Cross Roads at the western end of Water Street where Waterford Bridge Road and Topsail Road branch off, west of Healy's Pharmacy.

Brennan's Corner became Brennan Street and is located east of Hutching's Street east of the Railway Museum.

Rogerson's Corner is today the corner of Queen Street and Water Street now occupied by Dooly's Bar.

The corner of Cochrane and Duckworth Streets which is today occupied by a poolbar.

Queen's Bakery Corner today is the corner of King's Bridge Road and Military Road.

Each of these corners were associated with certain people and groups. Captains Din Mealey and Pat Ryan and their crews were associated with the Cross Roads, Captain Thomas Brennan, William Coady and Thomas Duff were connected with Brennan's Corner and Rogerson's Corner. The harbour pilots were associated with the corner at Cochrane Street and Duckworth Street. The Maggotty Cove men (East end of Water Street area) claimed the corner at the Queen's Bakery.

THE GREAT WOOD HAUL

The one thing that all the previously mentioned people had in common was that they were sealers who participated in the highly anticipated annual wood haul for the Roman Catholic Cathedral and the Presentation Convent. Historian H.F. Shortis described the event as, "One of the greatest annual events in the City of St. John's in the fifties of the past century (1850s)."

Shortis preserved this important part of city history in his December 24, 1921 feature in *The Evening Telegram* entitled, *A Christmas Story of Old St. John's*. He wrote:

> Of course, the most energetic and conspicuous persons amongst the great assemblage were our Vikings – the skippers of our famous Sealing Fleet. They were foremost in every good cause, and were noted for their unostentatious charity and benevolence. Their hospitality was unbounded, and their solicitude for the well-being of their less fortunate neighbours was another of their noble and unselfish characteristics.
>
> Their cheerful fireplace and well-spread table always had a chair or more for the wanderer who might drop in and rarely these chairs were unoccupied. Such were the class of men we had in St. John's in those days of which Captain Din Mealey was a typical specimen. About January, according to the condition of the streets and sufficient snow down, all the great sealing masters, planters and the public generally, of all classes and creeds, assembled in their respective localities. (Referred to on previous page)

Those who could afford to do so, such as the merchants and independent citizens, would purchase loads of wood from the farmers – some five, others two, etc., according to their means. The order was that nothing but large spruce would be accepted. By far, the great majority of the citizens and those of the suburbs would get their dogs and slides, three or four men to each team, and proceed to Deer's Marsh, Topsail Big Pond, Rocky Pond, Neil's Pond, and the East Enders to Twenty Mile Pond (Windsor Lake), each gang having their favourite place to cut the spruce of a specified size.

LOADING THE DRAY

When they returned to town with the wood, each stick of about sixteen feet in length was cut in two parts eight feet long, so that it would fit on the dray.[3] On arrival at the Cross Roads at River Head, Skipper Din Mealey's gang would unload. When they had sufficient wood out to fill the great drays, they started loading up. Each dray was made of eight-inch square timber with three runners bolted together with crossbars sufficient to stand the great weight from 1800 to 2000 sticks.

STYLE IN CONSTRUCTION

There were great long sticks used for "horns," three on each side, to keep the wood in position. As the load was piled up on the dray, every four or five feet of wood was spanned from one horn to the other on each side with chains, topsail, sheets and tacks, borrowed from the merchants and sealing masters to prevent the wood from spreading from the tremendous strain owing to the heavy load. The load would be about twenty-feet high, gradually tapering as it went up, so as to prevent it from 'tilting.'

Captain Din Mealey's big load at the Cross Roads was built wharf-fashion, that is – the lower tier was placed fore-and-aft, the next placed cross-ways and continued so until all was finished. It was built different from the other loads which were built fore-and-aft up to the top. Mealey's method prevented his load from being too high.

When all the loads in the different parts of the town were built up and well secured, the hauling hawsers[4], which were procured from the merchants and sealing masters, were placed in position for the grand 'tow.'

There were two six-inch icelines, which were used for moving the sealing vessels at the fishery, fastened to each load, sufficient to bear the tremendous pulling of two thousand men, and there were three strong guy ropes with twenty-five men on each side, who were picked men and knew what to do to prevent the loads from toppling over.

DECORATED LOADS

The great loads were decorated with numerous flags of the different merchants such as: Baine Johnston & Co., P. Rogerson & Sons, P&L Tessier, J&W Stewart, Bowring Brothers, McBride &

Kerr, W.H. Thomas & Co, Lawrence O'Brien, Brooking, Barnes & Co., Kavanagh, Cusick, etc. In fact, the flag of every merchant in the city was present. The late Hon. J.J. Rogerson, father of the genial W.P. Rogerson of the Government's Lighthouse Department, took the deepest interest in the load of wood built up at the foot of Rogerson's Corner and left an open order with his employees to give all the line, ropes, chains etc. that were required to any sensible person connected with the great haul of wood.

FULL SPEED AHEAD
When all was ready, the order was thundered forth to 'Man the ropes' and off they went. This scene was repeated at street corners around town. Each group was led by a band. There was Bennett's Band, the most famous in town, and other bands which discoursed good, lively, old-time airs, supplemented by the old chanty songs of *Haul on the Bowline; Good-bye, fare ye well; Shenandoah, I love your Daughter; Young Girls, where are ye bound to* and many other favourites of those days. What a pleasure it would be today to hear those old chanties sung as only the Newfoundland sailors and sealers knew how to sing them.

All started in their turn, the great crowd pulling the East End load to the Cathedral ground, and coming back to give a helping hand to the next in turn. It took two days to complete the great 'haul.' Skipper Din Mealey's big load being left for the next day. On one particular occasion, Skipper Din's big load went through the Brewery Bridge while being hauled down and they had to unload it to get it clear and build it up again. The bridge was broken by the great weight and the fore-part was brought up against the bank. Fortunately, no person was injured except James Fardy and his injury was only somewhat slight.

The decorations were really artistic and beautiful consisting of the drays with the different vessels names on them, young white coats, models of all kinds of ships, particularly the sealing fleet, pictures, etc. There was a large steering stick built into the load with some seven or eight men, specially selected, on hand for guiding the huge mass of wood along the line of the road.

The guy men[5] and steering men held the whole responsibility when once the loads were started. The leading man, such as Captain Din Mealey, Captain Thomas Duff or any other ship master, issued the orders couched in nautical phraseology, as was his custom, even in common conversation. It was always the masters favourite mode of expressing themselves, and they neither knew nor cared for any other.

When all was finished, they retired to the different hotels, or the hospitable residences of the famous sealing masters where they discussed the events of the day – more particularly as to who had the largest load, and I can assure you there were some tough arguments entered into before a decision was arrived at. But it was, in the end, unanimously agreed upon that Skipper Din Mealey carried off the honours of the day.

THE BARKING KETTLE-SPRINGDALE STREET

The corner of George Street and Springdale Street was another landmark in old St. John's associated with brawling and donnybrooks. Sealers often battled each other over the right to retrieve fresh water from the river flowing nearby into St. John's Harbour. The site was known as the 'Barking Kettle'[6] and was one of the many famous locations of old St. John's.

Journalist and historian, H.F. Shortis[7], described this historic location in *The Evening Telegram* November 26, 1921:

> This historic locality was not confined to the barking of sails, twines etc., because all the sealing crews, from Bowring's up to Newman's, filled their puncheons with water from the river which flowed from Mundy Pond, and discharged into the Cove between Newman's and Hounsell's. It was no unusual sight to witness over one hundred sealers there at the one time, waiting their turn to fill their vessels' puncheons, which were brought on catamarans, drays and every other means of conveyance.
>
> The water was dipped up in buckets by the crew of each ship and, when the puncheons were filled, they were conveyed to the respective wharves and placed on board the sealing vessels. Many a good battle was fought on that historic ground of the 'Barking Kettle' by the men endeavoring to get 'first turn' to dip up the water, but, of course, the row was all in the day's work, and was soon forgotten, and friendships renewed over a stiff glass of 'the same again' and it wasn't coca cola either, sucked through a straw.

By 1921, the Barking Kettle had been replaced by Silversmith's Garage. According to Shortis, a Church of England school house was erected near the site and was later torn down and replaced by the Salvation Army Citadel.

TAVERNS AND INNS OF OLD ST. JOHN'S

In 1856, many people from Harbour Grace visited St. John's to purchase their Christmas "cheer." Each person brought along a small keg which he had filled at one of the city's many public houses and inns. *The Harbour Grace Standard* of December 1856 reported, "With spirits selling for one dollar a gallon, there were few homes, except those of the teetotalers, that were without a supply of liquor during the Christmas season."

The taverns and inns of old St. John's were especially popular during the days leading up to Christmas, and they possessed a little of the Dickens' charm as townies and outport men gathered together for refreshments after a hard day's work, or to load up a keg of Christmas cheer to bring home for the season's celebrations. These public houses bore distinctive signs to enable even the illiterate to identify them.

According to the late Michael Murphy, author and city historian, "These Inns of Olde Tyme St. John's carried such colourful names as: The Dove, The Red Cow, The Ship, The Swan, The Rose and Crown, The Britannia, The Nelson, The Tavern for All Weather, The Travelers Joy, The Gamecock, The Flower Pot, The Struggler, The Royal Standard, The Blue Ball, The Shoulder of Mutton, The White Hart, The London Tavern, The Bird in Hand, The Union Flag, The Duke of York, The Calibogus Club, and The Three Crowns."

THE BULL INN – PRESCOTT AND DUCKWORTH STREET

The Bull Inn was located at the western corner of Prescott Street and Duckworth Street, opposite the family home of Catherine Brennan Keating, wife of Captain John Keating, the only man to find the fabulous treasure buried on Cocos Island. It was owned and operated by Abraham Saunders who was a giant of a man. He stood six feet, six inches tall and weighed 250 pounds. Usually a quiet man, but when need be, he could rise to the occasion, and he feared no living creature. The only exception being his wife, a small Irish woman, who weighed 100 pounds, but made up for her disadvantage with her sharp tongue.

THE GAMECOCK INN – LONG'S HILL AND QUEEN'S ROAD

The Gamecock Inn was located at the corner of Long's Hill and Queen's Road where the Theatre Pharmacy operates today. The owner, Peter Sullivan, who lived on Casey's Lane (Barron Street), was a big and belligerent native of County Cork, Ireland, noted for giving unwelcomed customers the 'quick shift' out his front door. He promoted cockfights which took place in the garden behind the tavern. According to author Michael Murphy, "Peter dispensed good rum and ale and also a prime drop of good whiskey that came over on the emigrant ships and had never been contaminated by the rod of the gauger."[8]

When cockfighting became illegal, Peter returned to Ireland and his building was torn down and replaced by the Phoenix Fire Hall, headquarters for the old Phoenix Volunteer Fire Brigade. Outside the fire hall, a bell was installed to warn people when an outbreak of fire occurred. This remained a familiar sight until fire destroyed the fire hall in November of 1876.

THE FISHERMAN TAVERN – QUEEN'S ROAD AND WILLICOTT'S LANE

The Fisherman Tavern is often referred to by writers as The Calibogus House. This tavern was located at the head of Willicott's Lane west of the Congregational Church on Queen's Road. Over its door was a sign depicting a fisherman looking out towards the narrows and wearing oilskins with a sou'wester on his head and a pipe in his mouth.

The owner of this tavern was Andy Brady, a well-educated man who had once served as butler in a Waterford, Ireland mansion famous as the Beresford Mansion. The Fisherman became the home for the 'Calibogus Club' founded by Brady. According to Michael Murphy, "This was a mysterious association that bound its members by solemn promise not to drink any liquor but rum and spruce beer mixed. The mixture was known as 'Calibogus.'

The Fisherman was frequented by, "...a number of jolly seadogs and others who were members of the club." Murphy recalled in his writings, "... many good stories were told there, some of which later found their way into the local press. Dancing, singing and drinking deep of the flowing bowl were kept up until early morning and many were the hangovers that resulted from too much imbibing of the potent Calibogus at Andy's establishment."

For those more literary inclined, Andy Brady kept a supply of newspapers from the Old Country.

THE CROWN TAVERN – PILOT'S HILL

This tavern catered to the military, government officials, merchants and professionals. It was a two story building located near the top of Pilot's Hill where it was built in the 1780s. From the upper windows there was a spectacular view of the harbour, especially the narrows. The Crown Tavern had a gable roof and a large attic with two bay windows at the front. The second flat had four windows facing the harbour. The ground flat, with the main door in the centre, contained two large rooms in front, one on each side of the hall, and a large kitchen at the rear. Wines were stored in one of the front rooms which had a long bar. Kegs of draught beer were plentiful. Several small tables and chairs were also located in this room which had a few cheap paintings on its walls. The other room in front had tables, chairs and benches, and it included a large fireplace which was kept burning throughout the winter. The keeper of the Crown was Henry Fowles, a native of Somerset England, who had retired from the Royal Navy.

THE LONDON TAVERN - DUCKWORTH STREET

One of the elite taverns of early nineteenth century St. John's was the London Tavern located on the north side of Duckworth Street near Cochrane Street and operated by Cornelius Mark. It was here that the Benevolent Irish Society was organized and for a long time held its meetings. This tavern was well-equipped and as the old advertisements said, "...provided accommodation for man and beast."

The London Tavern was equipped with stables, a billiard room and an elaborate barroom which was described as the best bar in early nineteenth century St. John's.

AMPLE SUPPLY OF OUR 'NATIONAL'

In 1807, 220,000 gallons of rum were imported into Newfoundland, which had a population of 20,000. This source alone was enough to supply eleven gallons per head for everyone in Newfoundland. Not included in this figure was the brandy, gin, wine, beer and cider which when combined provided another five or six gallons per head.

H.M. Mosdell described the taverns of old St. John's, "These must have been interesting places. Sailors from warships, soldiers and marines, hobnobbed with merchant seamen, the fisherman, and the wondering Irish youngsters, and each had his tale of marvelous adventure. Some of the navy men had doubtless been with Nelson at Copenhagen or the Nile, or had convoyed ships through thrilling adventures. It is but little wonder then that the taverns were crowded with excited men and that the glass went round and round and round again."

[1] The Barrens was an area stretching from Fort Townshend to Bannerman Park. Some nineteenth century newspapers referred to the Parade Grounds (Parade Street area), as a barrens.

[2] The Parade Grounds, now Parade Street vicinity.

[3] A dray was a cart without sides used to transport barrels and heavy loads.

[4] A hawser is a thick rope or cable used for towing a ship.

[5] The guy men were the workers who steadied the rope or cable on the load.

[6] The place known as "The Barking Kettle" got its name from the Barking Kettle which operated on the site for decades. This iron barking kettle was used to boil the bark and buds of conifers to create a liquid used in the barking of nets, traps and sails. The liquid produced by the barking process helped preserve these items from the corrosive effect of the sea water.

[7] Henry Francis Shortis was described in a Newfoundland Who's Who of the 1930s as a Historiographer of the Newfoundland Museum, journalist and historian. He was born August 19, 1855 at Harbour Grace. In St. John's he lived at 118 Bond Street.

[8] A gauger inserted a rod into each barrel of imported liquor to measure the contents. This was done as a protection against pilferage. Only smuggled liquor escaped the rod of the gauger.

CHAPTER 5

NEWFOUNDLAND SEA ADVENTURES

INCREDIBLE TALE FROM THE SEAL HUNT

One of the most incredible true tales from the Newfoundland seal hunt took place in 1868 off Bird Island Cove, Trinity Bay and involved the barquentine *Eric*.[1]

The *Eric*, owned by Torke & Sons of Carbonear, sailed from that port with sixty-four sealers under Captain Perry on March 5. By the 25th, the vessel and crew had received such a battering and endured so many casualties that Captain Perry decided it was time to return to Carbonear.

However, one man had broken his leg and the others were on the ice hunting seals. It was March 22, and before Captain Perry could call the men back to the ship, the weather suddenly turned strange, and a violent wind with snow struck with a vengeance. The storm hammered the area for thirty-nine hours and by the time it came to an end, two men were lost and fifteen were seriously frostbitten. Hardly a man escaped without some effect of the long exposure to the elements.

Perry organized his men and quickly got all the survivors and injured back on board. He then set out for home. On the return trip the *Eric* encountered another snowstorm, and barely avoided crashing on the breakers en route. Her anchors brought her up just in time.

There was a sea raging and between this and the blizzard, death and destruction faced the *Eric* and her crew. The storm continued until Sunday and the men were giving up all hope of survival. Perry later recalled that every man on board was praying for a miracle. Suddenly, Captain Perry noticed a pale, low-lying narrow strip of something in the water to the north of the ship. Using his binoculars, he took a closer look and recognized that it was a long narrow strip of ice. Strangely, it was moving toward the *Eric*.

It didn't take long before the ice was brushing against the side of the sealing vessel. Gradually, it was pushed and guided between the vessel and the shore. When the Captain and the men realized that this 'ice out of nowhere' had formed a bridge between them and shore, they knew their prayers had been answered. All sixty-three men on the *Eric* made it safely to shore over the mysterious bridge.

Little wonder that for decades afterwards it was described as, "One of the most miraculous events to ever happen at the seal fishery."

INDIAN ISLANDS MEN EARN CARNEGIE AWARD

The Keefe Brothers of Eastern Cove on Indian Islands, Newfoundland, had a very close encounter with death in 1912, and if it had not been for the courage of two fellow Indian Islands men, they would have been swallowed up by the sea.

The following account of the duo's heroism appeared in *The Evening Telegram* on April 1916, at which time they were awarded the Carnegie Award for heroism. The article described the incident which led to the prestigious award. It stated:

> Nathaniel Sheppard, aged sixty, fisherman, helped to save Nicholas and Thomas Keefe, aged sixty and sixty-two respectively, fishermen, from drowning. Tilting, NF, June 28, 1912.

> The Keefe brothers, who were in an open fishing boat, running before a gale on the Atlantic Ocean, struck a submerged block of ice at a point about three miles from land. Their boat began to sink. Sheppard and his son were in their fishing boat about half a mile to windward of the Keefe boat and were also running before the storm in order to reach shelter. They changed their course and sailed toward the Keefes. When they were thirty feet from the Keefes' boat, Sheppard's son let the jib fly in the wind, stood on the bow with his arm around the foremast, and caught the disabled boat with a boathook.

> Nathaniel Sheppard handled the tiller and mainsail. The Keefe boat had sunk so far that the Keefes were in water to their chests. Waves six or eight feet high broke over the boat. Young Sheppard pulled the bow of his boat over the submerged stern of the Keefe boat. A wave

lifted his boat and let it fall violently on the corner of the stern of the other boat, and a piece of plank a foot long and five inches wide was knocked in at a point a foot above the waterline.

Nicholas Keefe scrambled into the Sheppard boat. Thomas fell into the water between the boats while trying to get on board. Sheppard dropped his boat hook and pulled Thomas into the boat, then he used the boathook to work the bow of his boat to the lee of the Keefe boat. He worked feverishly and temporarily mended the hole in the side, and he and the others sailed three miles before the wind to port in safety.

A factor, not referenced in the above article which enhanced this drama at sea, was that seven-year-old Henry Sheppard, son of Mark Sheppard, was on board the rescue boat that day and no doubt was a major concern to the Sheppard men as they risked their lives in their heroic rescue mission.

In recognition of that heroism, Nat and Mark Sheppard were awarded the Carnegie Hero Commission Award for their bravery on June 28, 1912. The award consisted of $500.00 and a medal to each person. The Sheppards are the only Newfoundlanders ever to have won that award.

AMAZING COINCIDENCE AT POUCH COVE

In 1900, John S. Noseworthy of Pouch Cove, east of St. John's, helped save the life of a neighbour named Abram Murray. They were sailing out to the fishing grounds when Murray's boat, a little distance ahead of them, capsized and the two occupants were tossed into the water. Noseworthy's boat rushed to the scene and he succeeded in pulling Murray from the water just in time. Murray couldn't swim and he was near exhaustion when rescued.

Twenty-five years later Noseworthy was out in his boat when a windstorm struck and all the fishing boats moved rapidly to shore, Noseworthy included. However, he noticed that a distance from him there seemed to be a small boat in trouble. It was losing the battle against the wind and appeared to be unable to make any headway towards land. Noseworthy turned his boat around and, at great danger to himself, went to aid the small craft. He reached it and had succeeded in getting the occupant out just before it was swamped. The occupant of the boat was none other than the same Abram Murray he had saved twenty-five years before.

NEWFOUNDLANDER HAD A MOUNTAIN NAMED AFTER HIM
Mount Carroll, a 3000 foot high summit at the South Pole, was named after Captain Tom Carroll, a courageous and daring Newfoundlander, born at King's Cove, Bonavista Bay, in November 1867. His seafaring career took him from the ice fields of Labrador to the winter seas at Greenland and to the South Pole. Carroll began his career in 1885 at the age of eighteen and by the time he retired from the sea in the mid-1940s, he had visited every continent on earth, except Australia.

'Skipper Tom's' first brush with death occurred at age nineteen when he experienced his first shipwreck which was off the coast of Newfoundland. The vessel he was on was ripped open by what he described as 'iron rocks' that cut through the ship like scissors cutting paper. The Skipper recalled that the experience made him a better seaman. Through it, he got his first lesson in survival. The entire crew got off safely then worked as a team in overcoming the ordeal of a precarious journey over heavy ice to Fogo. Carroll was not at all deterred by the dangers, but saw them as part of the training necessary for a career at sea.

After serving on several other vessels, and sailing in rough seas and through ice fields, Skipper Carroll felt he was ready for the tough adventure offered by a whaling expedition to Greenland waters. He joined the crew of the *Eagle II*, and in 1893 was participating in the Greenland whale hunt. During that hunt, the *Eagle II* became trapped in heavy ice and the relentless pressing of the ice against its sides caused some harrowing moments on the ship. The ice pressured the *Eagle II* from all sides until the ship began to break up. It burst through the walls of the engine room and pinned the vessel, according to Carroll, "as though it was nailed to a giant wall."

Carroll's previous experience in shipwrecks prepared him well for what was to follow. To survive, the crew knew they would have to abandon ship and face a dangerous journey to the nearest port. Carroll took a leading role in the escape effort. The lifeboats were put over the side, and the men gathered as many supplies and provisions as space would allow on the escape crafts.

116

They traveled, six men to a lifeboat, sometimes dragging the heavy boats over ice and, at other times, using them to cross small lanes of water.

Fortunately, the good weather prevailed, and they safely reached Cape Fury where they were able to chart their course for Whale Bay. While crossing the sixty-mile stretch to Whale Bay, the crew became separated. Although they were plagued with difficulties, they all made it safely to a point known as 'Yakki Shore.'

The Newfoundlanders were picked up there by Captain Geoffrey Phillips of the S.S. *Esquimalt*, a ship sailing out of Dundee, Scotland, which took them to its home port. From there, they made their way to Liverpool and on December 22, 1893, Tom Carroll arrived in St. John's on the *Serian*, just in time for Christmas.

When Bowring Brothers replaced the lost *Eagle II* with the *Aurora*, Tom Carroll was given the job of bosun and later he held the same position on the *Eagle III*. He soon became a captain and never missed a spring at the ice. He remarked proudly to reporters on one occasion, "I'm glad because that's what kept me in such fine shape."

With the war at its height in 1941, and Nazi submarine periscopes dotting the Atlantic, Tom Carroll joined a British expedition to the South Pole. During the long hours of the expedition, Skipper Tom often entertained the expedition party with hair-raising tales of his lifetime at sea, and, in particular, at the seal hunt.

The high regard held by the British officers on the expedition for Tom Carroll became evident when, after discovering a 3000-foot high rocky mountain at the South Pole, they named it Mount Carroll in his honour.

Skipper Tom's adventure to the South Pole included battles with hurricanes, tornadoes, tropical storms and blizzards. Tom Carroll kept notes and clippings regarding his more than fifty years at sea. He once said that he had enough to fill an encyclopedia.

CAPTAIN ART HOLWELL'S LATE CHRISTMAS

When the cargo vessel *Jessie* set out in December 1902 to deliver a load of lumber to St. John's, the crew had no idea of the danger and adventure that awaited them. They expected to make their delivery and return home to Twillingate Island in time for Christmas. The *Jessie* was under the command of Captain Arthur Holwell and carried a five-man crew, all from the Island.

Soon after departure, the winds increased to storm force and Captain Holwell decided to seek shelter at Seldom-Come-By. By next morning, the winds subsided and the *Jessie* resumed her voyage. However, the vessel was not yet out of danger. By nightfall, another storm struck and, within hours, had developed into a blinding blizzard with hurricane-force winds.

The *Jessie* was tossed around on the raging seas and only the expert seamanship of the captain and crew saved her from being wrecked. All the charts and instruments were washed overboard, making it impossible for Captain Holwell to determine the vessel's position. Hours turned into days and the struggle for survival became more intense. Pumps used to bail out the water became choked with sand from the ship's ballast.

After two weeks lost at sea, and the ship's supplies running out, the captain had to enforce rationing their supply of food and water. Each crewman's daily share was a half pint of water and a piece of hard bread. There was a brief spark of hope among the men when they sighted the lights of a steamer in the distance. They sent up a flare, shouted and waved clothing to attract attention, but their efforts were in vain. It was Christmas Eve and the men were losing hope. Their thoughts turned to their families at home and the feeling was beginning to set in that they would never see their loved ones again. They prayed for deliverance.

Suddenly, out of the distance, their prayers were answered. It was the *Hornsby Castle* out of Galveston, Texas. Captain Holwell set off his last flare and the Texas ship responded. Holwell and his crew were overjoyed to be rescued and they said a prayer of thanksgiving. To their dismay, their dream of being home for Christmas could not be realized. The rescue vessel was on a tight schedule to Antwerp, Belgium and arrived there on New Year's Day. The Newfoundlanders were sent from there to England and from there were given passage on a steamer going to Newfoundland.

Meanwhile, their families had learned of the rescue and delayed Christmas celebrations until the crew's safe-return.

Late in January, the *Jessie's* crew arrived home on Twillingate Island. There was great rejoicing on the island, and a late, but very special Christmas was held. It was one the people of the community never forgot, especially the captain and the crew of the *Jessie*.

FATHER EDWARD MORRIS – MIRACULOUS SURVIVAL

Days before Christmas Eve, 1875, Father Edward Morris, parish priest for an area that stretched from Placentia Bay to Burin, was anxious to complete his tour of the parish so he could spend Christmas at his residence in Oderin. It was not to be. This was to be a Christmas like none other he had celebrated in his life. It started off peacefully enough, but events rapidly changed and with little warning, he found himself on a boat being tossed around on the high seas and wondering if he would survive to celebrate Christmas.

Young Edward Morris had abandoned his family's wealth and comfort for the austerity and hardship of life as a parish priest, serving rugged communities along Newfoundland's coast.

With Christmas approaching in 1875, Father Morris was rushing to finish his visits to the communities in his parish. This was a routine he repeated several times throughout the year. On December 20, he had completed his work and was awaiting the arrival of a boat to take him home. Unexpectedly, he received an urgent message asking that he make a sick-call at Frenchman's Cove on the Fortune Bay side of the Burin Peninsula. The parishioners had looked to Father Morris for medical as well as spiritual support.

Father Morris had no idea when a boat would arrive to take him, so he set out for Frenchman's Cove on foot. He readily accepted the fact that he was not likely to make it home for Christmas. He felt he was blessed when the weather improved and he was able to take a shortcut to the sick parishioner. He tended the sick and made it back to Jean de Bay by Christmas Eve. A boat was ready and waiting to get the priest home for Christmas Day. The weather was unusually calm as the little boat left the harbour. It was therefore surprising to Father Morris when it suddenly went aground on a sandbar.

Skipper Sam Davis and his crew were splitting fish on the nearby shore when they saw the accident. They boarded their fishing boat and rushed to the aid of the stranded priest. When he realized that they couldn't get the boat off the sandbar,

Skipper Davis offered to take the priest to Oderin. Things were moving along fine and Father Morris was content knowing that he would soon be home in the comfort of his own home in time for Christmas dinner. Suddenly, to the complete surprise of the priest and the fishermen, a raging storm erupted and left them wondering if they would survive. Snow, sleet and high winds engulfed the little boat and ripped away its mainsails. The men openly prayed for deliverance as they fought to keep the craft afloat.

The tossing of the sea nearly turned the boat over and she took on water. The captain and crew were attempting to mend the mainsails when a giant wave struck the deck, taking with it the compass and almost dragging Father Morris from the boat. If Davis hadn't seized Father Morris's arm and held tightly, the priest would have been swallowed up by the sea. The Skipper, a man of faith, asked Father Morris to bless the waves and the boat, and the priest did.

It was near 10:00 p.m. on Christmas Eve and miraculously the storm subsided as rapidly as it had appeared. The Skipper dropped anchor off Oderin Harbour, and all on board gave thanks to God for what they felt certain was a miracle. While they prayed, the jib snapped. The Skipper gave each man on board a lit torch in hopes of attracting attention from the beach. There was no response. Now a new danger threatened their safety. The rolling of the sea was pushing the boat closer and closer to the rocky shore. Just when it seemed death and destruction were near, they heard the voices of people in the distance. A skiff, with rescuers on board, was fast approaching. In no time, the priest and crew of the stranded boat were rescued and taken safely to shore. The Christmas ordeal of Father Morris was over and he was home in time to enjoy Christmas dinner with his friends and parishioners. It was said that at mass on that Christmas Day, Father Morris delivered the finest sermon ever heard in the Oderin Church.

Father Edward Morris became the founder of the first boys' orphanage in Newfoundland located at Manuels, and gained a reputation as one of the province's most dedicated and saintly priests. He died in 1888 while tending the needs of sick orphans, victims of a typhoid epidemic at Villa Nova Orphanage, Manuels.

FIFTY HOURS IN ZERO TEMPERATURES

A thirty-five-year-old seaman from Grand Bank, Newfoundland, suffered a broken chest-bone during a winter storm on the Atlantic that ravaged the ship on which he was a seaman, yet he valiantly fought side by side with fellow crewmen in a five-day struggle to keep their ship afloat. When that battle was lost, and the men took to the lifeboat, the same man took his turn rowing in high seas and below freezing temperatures with pelting ice slowly entombing the fifteen-foot long lifeboat in another fight for survival that lasted fifty hours.

The courage and endurance demonstrated by the six man crew of the doomed schooner *D.J. Thornhill* prompted the captain of the Canadian Corvette, *Dundas*, who rescued them, to observe, "A few hours after we picked them up, most of them were A-1 again...new proof, if you need it, that Newfoundlanders are among the world's hardiest seamen. The cold during those two nights when they were adrift in the dory was petrifying."

Captain Gordon Williams of Poole's Island, Newfoundland was in command of the *D.J. Thornhill* which was carrying a cargo of dried cod to an undisclosed seaport on Canada's east coast. They set sail in early April and within days found themselves in the midst of winter's last angry storm. Gale-force winds, blinding snow and below freezing temperatures battered the ship for five days. It was during these storms that a heavy gale tossed seaman James Brown against a barrel, causing his breast-bone to break.

In addition to nature's forces, the Newfoundland six fought hunger and thirst. Their water tanks became salted and their food was washed overboard on the first day of the storm. The men survived on biscuits and a few cans of milk. When they were rescued and taken aboard the *Dundas*, they surprised the Canadian Naval Officers by passing up an offer of rum, for water.

Captain Williams later recalled that the storm and bad icing conditions brought an end to his schooner. He described the first hours of their fight for survival, "The weather began deteriorating and a drop in temperatures started ice forming on the deck. The wind rapidly reached gale-forces and the mounting seas battered the schooner with such violence that she started to leak."

The crew immediately manned the hand pump and laboured non-stop for two days, but the increasing water overtook them and the weight of ice forming on the ship caused her to rapidly settle. The last night on the schooner was their worst night. The crew's quarters had been flooded forcing them to take shelter in the stern. The foresail had torn away leaving the vessel to run without canvas. The battle was wearing the men down. The combination of ice, wind and pounding waves was forcing the schooner under and the men prayed throughout the night that the vessel would stay afloat until morning.

Their prayers were answered. The storm subsided at dawn and the captain decided the time had come to abandon ship. Before leaving, he gave orders to set the schooner on fire and sink it so it wouldn't be a threat to shipping in the area. In addition to Captain Williams, the crew included: James Brown, a seaman; Hugh Branby, a mate; Wilson Price, the engineer; Wilson Taylor, the cook; Berkley Nurse, a seaman.

After setting the ship ablaze, the men pushed off in their dory and watched the spectacular flames and clouds of rising steam and smoke. By then, however, the wind had subsided and the men in their open dory were exposed to extremely cold temperatures. Captain Williams recalled, "The frost was the worst. It got colder every day. The corvette came just in time. We couldn't have stood it another night."

The little dory was covered with ice when the *Dundas* came to its rescue. The oilskins worn by the men were stiffened with frozen spray. James Brown was placed in a hammock to rest and, upon arrival in St. John's, was taken to hospital for treatment of his chest injuries.

Lieutenant-commander R.W. Draney, Captain of the HMCS *Dundas*, was amazed at Captain Williams knowledge of the sea. Draney told reporters that after Captain Williams boarded the corvette, he hazarded a guess at the ship's position. The veteran sailing skipper's estimate, arrived at by dead reckoning and instinct, was within ten miles of the actual point of the expanse of ocean where the *Dundas* had picked them up.

HARDY MEN OF PETTY HARBOUR

Several Petty Harbour landsmen struggled in freezing temperatures with snow pelting in their faces to rescue crewmen of a sinking vessel at Petty Harbour Motion during the winter of 1882.

The *Lizette*, which was not a large vessel and had only a six man crew, was delivering a cargo of pork, flour and other foods from New York to St. John's. On February 6, 1882, with high winds and blowing snow, the little ship ran into Dick French's Rock at Petty Harbour Motion and began to sink. The Captain and two crewmen were drowned during the incident. While the *Lizette* is rarely mentioned in the history of shipwrecks of Newfoundland, the unique battle by the Petty Harbour men to save the crew is worth recording.

The weather in the Petty Harbour/St. John's area had been favourable that year. The people of Maddox Cove were spreading horse manure on their fields on January 18 when the first big snowstorm struck. On January 20, temperatures dropped to freezing and the frost and snow continued until March 8. The change in weather brought hardship to the community. The men and horses were unable to go into the forest to cut wood and the roads to St. John's were completely obstructed by snow.

It was during this bout of severe weather that the Brigantine, *Lizette*, under the command of Captain R. Buttner, met tragedy in Newfoundland waters. Jacob Chafe and several landsmen watched from shore as the tragedy unfolded. Chafe wasted no time in trying to rescue the men stranded on the ship. He made several attempts to get a line to the *Lizette* by tying a fishing line to a ramrod and firing it from an old sealing gun. Due to high winds, it fell short. Chafe repeated this effort until they ran out of powder.

With the Captain and two crewmen already drowned, the remaining three men fought for survival in the freezing Atlantic waters. Chafe was not ready to give up. He tossed a cod jigger line which was attached to a large rope that was caught by the mate. The mate wrapped part of the rope around his body and held the end of the rope in his teeth. The other two men held tightly to him while the Petty Harbour men rapidly dragged them to shore.

Near exhaustion, the group shared a drink of rum and the Petty Harbour men removed their inside shirts and sweaters which they gave to the rescued Americans. In freezing temperatures, and blowing snow, Chafe led the men on a three-mile walk back to Petty Harbour. Given the heavy snowfall over recent days, the walk was a real struggle. One of the Americans passed out and had to be carried on a make-shift slide the rest of the distance.

Once in Petty Harbour, people in the community came together to share what they had and to feed and clothe the rescued men while they waited to get a ship to St. John's and then home. The people of the community managed to retrieve a good portion of the pork and other foods on the sunken *Lizette* by using cod-jiggers, stabbers and bait hooks.

The weather improved and on March 8 the men and horses were able to get into the woods to gather fuel for their stoves. The weather broke on April 20 and fine spring weather prevailed. It was a winter long-remembered in Petty Harbour.

TWICE A HERO

The captain and crew of a wrecked ship wondered if they would survive their ordeal while they sought safety at the peak of a 100-foot high rock at the entrance to a gulch near Trepassey. Strong winds and a rising tide added to the near hopelessness of their situation. While they prayed for divine intervention, unknown to them, John Kennedy from Trepassey had witnessed the shipwreck and went for help. The date was September 1, 1887.

Just twenty-four hours before, Captain Richards of the *Maglona* and his crew had set sail from Little Placentia for Bay Bulls to take on a cargo of salt fish for overseas markets. They ran into problems from the start. Marmaduke Clowe, the ship's super-cargo,[2] cursed the strong headwinds which were significantly slowing the ship's advance.

Near Cape St. Mary's, the *Maglona* ran into a heavy fog. Although Captain Richards altered his course, the ship was moving closer than anticipated to the treacherous rocky shores.

The crew had managed to lower the mainsail by the time someone shouted the warning, "Breakers!" However, it was too late. The *Maglona* struck rocks and broke its rudder at the entrance to the gulch. The ship's only lifeboat was washed away by a crushing wave as the Captain and crew looked on helplessly.

Captain Richards had observed that with each crushing wave that struck the boat, the stern heaved toward a nearby 100-foot high island rock. He viewed this as a chance for all on board to escape the ship before the waves took it to the bottom. The captain observed that in order to escape, they had to leave from the starboard side, but the heavy main boom was swinging back and forth across the quarterdeck. He thought that a blow from it could be fatal. One by one, the crew dodged the swinging boom until all had successfully made the move from the *Maglona* to the rock. The joy over successfully abandoning the vessel was short lived when the men found themselves isolated on a rock that was unscalable and cut off from the shore by a treacherous sea and the gulch.

Just as despair was setting in, they heard muffled voices from shore and felt their prayers were answered. Little did they know, their shouts of "help" were not needed. John Kennedy, the man who had witnessed the shipwreck and gone for help, was now back with one Tom Neil and preparing to put a rescue into action. The two had brought two ropes with them, one, a long heavy rope, and the other, a lighter rope. Kennedy tied the light rope around Neil and the other end to the heavy rope which he had anchored around a large rock. Neil then plunged into the raging sea. Tom Neil was no stranger to courage and heroism. Just ten years earlier, he had risked his life by scaling a three-hundred foot cliff in a storm to recover victims of the wreck of the *George Washington*.

The men watched in amazement at the courage of Neil as he fought through the tossing waves, waves which often tossed him head over heels, causing him to disappear. Just when the stranded men thought he was gone, back he would come to the surface and resume his battle to save them. By the time he reached the rock, he was bruised and bleeding, but not beaten. Neil was determined to get every man safely to shore. After untying the light rope around him, Neil, with the help of the stranded men, managed to pull the heavy rope to them. He, then, secured the rope, and one by one, they made their successful escape to shore. Neil, however, was not yet finished. He volunteered to go with the men over seven miles of open barrens, and fought wind and cold rain all the way to Cape Race.

THE FORTUNE BAY MYSTERY

Imagine walking along a beach and coming upon a vessel that had drifted ashore and rested upside down in the water, then, noticing debris and fish scattered all around it, both in the water and on the shore. Such circumstances would logically suggest a shipwreck. But things may not have been as circumstances suggested. That was the experience of some men from Fortune on March 28, 1873, when they found a wreck on the shore at Dantzic Cove about sixteen miles from Fortune.

From all appearances, the men concluded the vessel was an American fishing schooner. The men made an effort to see if there were any bodies on board. In the foc'scle, they found the decomposed body of a man, and after removing him, buried him nearby. They returned to the vessel, expecting that there would be other bodies inside the vessel, but there was none. Neither could they find anything to identify the dead man they had buried.

However, there was on board an empty firkin marked "coffee" and on the inner side of the cover some writing in pencil. The note offered no explanation for the tragedy, but it sparked a mystery which had never been solved.

The note read:

> Schooner *Thorwaldsen*, Captain G. Phillips, Glousester, Massachusetts. Finished loading the 6th of February with herring. Went into St. Jack's the same evening. Bound home all well. Joseph Fritz, Gloucester, Massachusetts.

That was all. The story of the schooner *Thorwaldeson* would not be anything out of the ordinary, but for this brief note. Why was such a note written, and on the inner side of the cover of a coffee-firkin of all places. It certainly wasn't the sort of place that a person would choose to write a letter.

Based on the note, the vessel was in Fortune Bay and loaded with herring on February 6th and on that same day she went into St. Jacques. She was on her way home and according to the note, all the crew were well. Those who looked into the mystery said it was likely she didn't stay in St. Jacques longer than perhaps a day or two, so that it would be about the 7th or 8th of the month when she put out of Fortune Bay.

Yet, it was not until March 28th, fifty-two days later that the hulk of the "*Thorwaldsen*" drifted ashore in Dantzic Cove sixteen miles from Fortune at the very tip of the toe of the Burin Peninsula. Where was the "*Thorwaldsen*" during all that time?

John Spencer, a Fortune Bay fishermen, observed, "If she was a derelict in Fortune Bay, there's a hundred chances to one she would have been sighted by some craft, or from the coast itself or islands like Sagona or Brunette. To drive ashore in Dantzic Cove, the derelict would have had to pass fairly close to Great Miquelon at Cape Verde. It seemed odd that between February 8th say, and March 28th, no trace of crew, boats, wreckage or anything else from the *Thorwaldsen* was sighted or picked up in or around Fortune Bay."

There were others who tried to explain the mystery. They theorized that when the ship went out of Fortune Bay and into the open sea she could have run into heavy ice which might have shattered her hull allowing sufficient water in to cause her to turn over.

As to the disappearance of the crew, the same people speculated that all the crew, except the man who was likely trapped in the forecastle, had taken to the ice and perished in one of the fierce storms frequently encountered on the south coast in that season of the year.

This theory could explain much of what had happened. The advancing and retreating ice, on and off the land, or up and down the coast, could easily have taken the vessel a great distance over a period of six or seven weeks and finally near the end of March, the tides and winds may have brought her back to the mouth of Fortune Bay where the ice-pack melting in the spring would set her free to drift ashore. There was plenty of time for the captain or any of the crew to have recorded the encountering of a storm and rough seas.

Yet, none of this explains the mysterious note that was found. It reads almost like the entry in a log book. But why would the skipper write it there and not in his log book? If the skipper did not write it, who did?

Could it have been a crewman whose intuition warned him of the danger to come? It is significant that the message states, "Bound home, all well."

It is strange that no one arrived home and the only man who ever made land again was the dead man whose remains are at Dantzic Cove, unknown and unrecognized.

THE SEAL HUNT IN 1840s
During my research for this book, I came across a lengthy letter written by John Pearson Jr. of the merchant family of Pearson's, operating in St. John's during those years. This letter provided an articulate and colourful account of many aspects of life in St. John's in the mid-nineteenth century.

I include here his amazing description of the Seal Hunt. Mr. Pearson wrote:

> The Island has little or no resources within itself, and is entirely dependent upon its fisheries – namely, that of the seal and cod fishery. The first-named is the one that may be considered the mainstay of the Island, and although attended with considerable risk, is much sought after on account of the exceeding lucrative gains, when vessels are fortunate.
>
> It commences early in the month of March, at which time the coast of Newfoundland is usually surrounded by immense quantities of ice on which the seals are found. You will perhaps scarcely credit it, when I inform you that there are upon an average 800,000 of these animals taken every spring, and that in the short space of three or four weeks; in taking of them some 150 vessels are employed, all built purposely for going into the ice, being cased with iron.
>
> A person on your side of the Atlantic can form no idea of the ice what we have upon this coast in the spring. It is not unusual that the ocean is seen as though one solid mass of ice, which extends perhaps for a distance of 300 miles from the land into the main ocean. This is what is termed field ice; but I have seen some pieces that appeared like immense mountains, and unless you knew to the contrary, you would take them for islands in the ocean covered with snow.
>
> These float about, or are rather carried along by the field ice. You can readily fancy what must be the fate of vessels that are not built to withstand it, should they fall into it. There is never a spring but a number of foreign ships are lost in it; indeed if they once become jammed in, they remain so for some months, with the prospect of being at any moment crushed to pieces by the rolling mountains, or on the other hand frozen or starved to death.
>
> I have seen vessels out at sea not more than four miles from the harbour (St. John's), that have been frozen up for weeks and weeks, and have known their

crews to leave them and walk upon the ice to their intended destined haven.

The seals of which I have before spoken are to be seen in endless thousands upon the small ice, and are usually killed by a blow upon the head. They are then skinned, the fat taken from them, and the skin saved. Their value is from 8s to 12s a head. It is not unusual for a man to kill in six weeks as many as will serve him to live for twelve months upon the profits he may derive from the sale of them.

After they are brought home, they are stowed in large vats, where they remain until they become oil, which, I need not tell you, is then shipped to the home country. A merchant here who fits out five or six vessels, should they prove fortunate, will perhaps realize £2,000 upon the cargo of each clear; but then there is a desperate risk of their being lost, etc. which is not of infrequent occurrence, and then they lose quite as much, or more, so that it may be termed a complete lottery.

[1] Bird Island Cove was renamed Elliston after Reverend William Ellis, an early Methodist minister in the community.

[2] The Supercargo was the person representing the ship's owner and responsible for the cargo.

CHAPTER 6

OLD-TIME NEWFOUNDLAND WEATHER

TEMPERATURES GOT WARMER IN OLD-TIME NEWFOUNDLAND BUT NO TALK OF GLOBAL WARMING!
When the Newfoundland climate began warming up in the late 1940s and early 1950s, there was no talk of global warming. Most people enjoyed the milder winters and others cursed it.

The winter of 1948 was an exceptionally mild one. The following item related to the mild conditions appeared in *The Evening Telegram* on January 17, 1948:

> There's no doubt that the winter so far has been outstanding for its mildness, and now comes another true tale to back up the evidence of near summer conditions in January. Mr. John Squires, gardener at the residence of Mr. Herbert Outerbridge, 21 King's Bridge Road, went out in his employer's garden this morning and brought in lettuce, brussels sprouts, parsley and several other vegetables that had lain under the snow until it was melted by the mild weather. The vegetables, Mr. Squires assured *The Telegram*, would be served at lunch Thursday. The lettuce, sprouts, etc. sprung from seeds planted by Mr. Squires.

The warming climate did attract media attention. One newspaper headline in 1953 read "Newfoundland Gets Warmer" and reported:

> Newfoundland is warming up and February this year was more than five degrees warmer than normal – normal in this case being the statistical average at St. John's between 1874 and 1942. The mean air temperature for the month was 27 degrees Fahrenheit. "Normal" used to be 22.4. The warmest day for March 1953 sent the mercury to 49.4 degrees which is not high by old-time standards. On one day back in 1892, the thermometer rose to 56. And residents thought summer had arrived. On

the other hand, we had no extremely cold weather. In 1904, it sank to an Arctic-like 19 degrees below zero.
– *Newfoundlander,* March 1953

MILDEST WINTER

Joseph R. Smallwood reported in one of his Barrelman Broadcasts of December 1939 that the mildest winter ever in Newfoundland was undoubtedly the winter of 1899. He said:

On the 11th of January that winter, William Woodley, a farmer near Quidi Vidi, ploughed an acre of land on his farm, and all the farmers near St. John's were ploughing that day. Some of them top-dressed their fields. Hundreds of sheep were to be seen out in the fields grazing, and up to that time, and even later, not a scrap of their reserves of hay had been touched.

And then, on the twenty-first of February, in Bannerman Park, a game of football was played that some people living in St. John's will remember to this very day, though it was nearly fifty years ago. Amongst the players were the late Hon. F.C. Alderdice, Andrew Thorburn, Joseph Peters, George Langmead and George Tessier. It isn't very often that football is played in the month of February, is it?[1]

THE WEATHER SONG

The changes in weather prompted Mrs. Alfonso Stares of Brooklyn, Bonavista Bay, to write a poem called "Weather Rhyme." The verses explain how to tell the weather.

THE WEATHER RHYME

Quick rise after low
Indicates a stronger blow.
Long foretold, long last,
Short notice, soon past.

When the glass falls low
You must prepare for a blow,
When it slowly rises high
Lofty canvas you may fly.

132

If clouds are gathering thick and fast,
Keep sharp lookout for sail and mast,
But if they slowly onward crawl,
Shoot your lines, nets and trawl.

Mackerel sky, and mares' tails
Make lofty ships carry low sails,
When the wind shifts against the sun,
Trust it not, for back it will run.

With rain before wind,
Your fishing gear mind,
But wind before rain,
Your nets shoot again.

The evening red and morning grey
Are sure signs of a fine day,
But the evening grey and morning red
Makes the fisherman shake his head.

A rainbow in the morning
Is the fisherman's warning.
A rainbow at night
Is the sailor's delight.

In 1954, there was plenty of rain to deal with and that prompted the following song:

UNCLE JERRY'S WEATHER SONG
AUTHOR UNKNOWN

Oh me old bones they squeak and I'm stiff with rheumatic,
I've got pain in me system from cellar to attic.
I'm waste'n away – I'm as light as a feather,
And its all on account of this '54' weather.

I'm goin' to write Joey and I'm goin' to say, "Dear Sir,
The weather this year has been certainly queer, sir,
When your Cabinet next you do get together,
Would you please try to end this calamitous weather.

"Me wife she is mad and she's always complaining,
She can't dry her clothes on account of the raining,
She's gone off her feed, and she's all in a dither,
And it's all brought about by this tarnation weather.

"I've got dew in me whiskers and fog on me brain, sir,
I'm goin' insane with this continuous rain, sir,
We dassn't go yon and we dassn't go thither,
We're tied up in knots with this inclement weather.

I can't tar me punt and I can't do no paintin',
I can't dry me fish– I'm just sizzlin' and rantin',
The fog she shuts in and you can't see a feather,
I'm sure in a fix with his horrible weather.

"I can't see the marks and I don't trust me old compass,
When I'm out in this fog there's one helluva rumpus,
The sunkers they roar and it sure makes me shiver,
Oh, I wish I was rid of this pea soupy weather.

"Now I never did care for this confeddyration,
I was sartin' 'twould be our utter ruination,
I'm savin' me vote for whoever comes hither,
And puts a quick end to this confederit weather.

"Oh, I'm wishin' right now for a tearin' nor'wester,
I'd batten down mitts, rubber boots and sou'wester,
And cackle with glee as this dang-blasted weather,
Took a dive-bombing shoot to the nethermost nether."

CHAFE'S ALMANAC

Chafe's Almanacs were as common in Newfoundland house-
holds as calendars are today. However, some fishermen compiled
their own almanacs, often with great accuracy.

Ambrose Cahill of the Southern Shore recalls the stories of
an old sea captain from Renews who compiled his own almanac
and was consulted by scores of Southern Shore fishermen
regarding predictions about the weather. Mr. Cahill explained

that the captain would compile his book beginning on Christmas Day, using a board which he had divided into four parts. He said, "The captain divided the first day after Christmas into four parts and took notes of the quarter the wind was blowing from, and made his observations on the same. That board was then called January and each quarter of the day represented a full week. He did one for each day up until January 6th. The twelve days represented the twelve months of the year." The almanac predicted how the summer would turn out, when the ice would leave the harbours, and the date of the first snowfall.

According to Mr. Cahill, these almanacs were made for nearly fifty years, and fishermen swore by their accuracy.

WEATHER BELIEFS

Newfoundland fishermen have the reputation of possessing the ability to predict weather. During the nineteenth century the following verses were commonly quoted among fishermen:

When the wind shifts against the sun
Trust it not, for back 'twill run
When the wind is in the east
'Tis neither good for man nor beast
Mackerel sky and horses' tails
Make the sailor furl his sails

Indications of impending rain included: soot falling to the ground, dogs sleeping all day, spiders very active, and elderly people with rheumatic pains.

When gulls were viewed flying hard, fishermen knew stormy weather was near.

A thick coat of fur on wild animals indicated a bad winter to come.

When distant hills seemed near, rainy weather was on the way.

Hoarfrost in autumn meant south wind and rain would follow.

A brilliant display of northern lights meant a fine day that would be followed by stormy weather.

THE WEEKDAY UPON WHICH CHRISTMAS FELL
PREDICTED THE FOLLOWING YEAR'S WEATHER

During the nineteenth century, Newfoundlanders believed the weekday upon which Christmas Day fell determined the weather for the following year. The predictions were based on English tradition and are mentioned in writings which are now stored among the Harleian Collection, in the British Archives. The tradition was brought to Newfoundland by early English settlers and fishermen. A description of the practice appeared in the *Newfoundlander*, December 1948.

If the Christmas Day falls upon a Sunday, there will be a good winter, but a windy one and the summer will be fair and dry. Peace throughout all lands will reign, and thieves will be readily taken.

A Monday Christmas also indicated a good winter but very windy followed by a stormy tempestuous summer. Many battles will occur, and a great mortality among the cattle, but little among men.

However, Tuesday was considered an unlucky day for Christmas:

A dry summer that year shall be
As all are born therein may see:
They shall be strong and covetous,
If thou steal aught, thou loosest thy life,
For thou, shalt die through sword or knife.

Christmas falling on Wednesday brings a stormy and hard winter, but a good summer, with wheat in plenty. It will be a disastrous year for young people; and particularly fatal for ships.

A Thursday Christmas on the whole is a propitious day. A windy tempestuous winter will be followed by a good dry summer, in which crops and cattle will thrive. "Kings and princes, it is said, shall die by skill. The sick shall speedily recover."

In this weather predicting method, Friday loses its unlucky character. A Friday Christmas means the first of the winter will be severe, with frost, snow and flood in abundance; but it will end well and a good summer will follow. Crops cattle and children will thrive and the sick prosper.

A Christmas Saturday meant a dreadful and severe winter will follow; disastrous to man and beast and fatal to old people. The summer will be wet, crops will fail, and sickness will generally result fatally. The practice of predicting a year's weather by the day on which Christmas fell was carried on in the St. John's area into the late 1920s.

1 *The Best of the Barrelman* (1938-1940) Edited by William Connors, Creative Publishers 1998.

CHAPTER 7

BURIAL SITES OF OLDE ST. JOHN'S

ANCIENT BURIAL SITES IN OLDE ST. JOHN'S

The city of St. John's has several long-forgotten cemeteries and burial places, and some of these were even covered over with new developments and road expansions without the removal of the corpses. The cemeteries in the city were closed by law in 1849 due to public concern over epidemics that frequently hit the city and new cemeteries were opened outside St. John's. When closed, each of the existing cemeteries were covered with twelve inches of lime.

Decades later, newspaper records indicate that bodies were removed from both the Church of England Graveyard on Church Hill and the Long's Hill Roman Catholic Cemetery. Researching archival records and comparing information with archival maps, I came up with the following revelations about ancient burial grounds throughout St. John's.

THE LONG'S HILL AND CHURCH HILL CEMETERIES

The Encyclopedia of Newfoundland and Labrador estimates that the old Church of England Cemetery adjacent to the Anglican Cathedral on Church Hill goes back to at least 1583. However, the earliest archival Church burial records for the cemetery start at 1756 with the first person to be buried that year being recorded as "Thomas Lee, old sexton." Based on Anglican Church records, the total number of burials from 1756 to 1849, when all cemeteries in St. John's were ordered closed, is 4985. The official name of the C of E cemetery was the Established Protestant Cemetery.

The Long's Hill Catholic Cemetery dated from 1811 to 1849.[1] It is not possible to obtain the number of burials in that cemetery because burial records were not kept. For the sake of comparison, the number of burials that took place in the Established Protestant Cemetery from 1811 to 1849 was 2796. Statistical records for 1845 show approximately 20,000 people living in St. John's and nearby. The number of Roman Catholics was about 16,000 and there were 3,000 Anglicans. Other faiths numbered 1,000.

After the Great Fire of 1892, major rebuilding and realignment of streets took place in St. John's. During these changes about 800 bodies were exhumed from the Long's Hill Catholic Cemetery and placed in a pile on Livingstone Street. They remained there for several days while preparations were being made to move them to the Belvedere and Mount Carmel cemeteries. During this time, children playing among the dead came down with a contagious fever which rapidly spread and left thirteen dead by the time it ended.

A letter appearing in the October 26, 1906 edition of *The Daily News* indicates that there were still bodies in the old cemetery. The letter stated:

Dear Sir:
   I thank Councillor Carew, and the other members of the Council for the interest they are taking in the Long's Hill neglected, cemetery grounds. Plant the place with some of our Newfoundland juniper and fir trees, and make some mounds for receiving flower trees and seeds which many persons having old friends and relatives buried there, will gladly contribute to beautify the sacred ground.

Sgd. Citizen

Both the Methodists and Presbyterians had property adjoining the RC Cemetery. After the Great Fire of 1892, the RC church leased their property to the Presbyterians to give them a Queen's Road access to their parking lot. The rent was one dollar per year with a request that the remaining graves not be disturbed.

The Catholic Cemetery did not become known as the Long's Hill Cemetery until decades after it closed in 1849. The geography of that total area of the city has undergone widespread changes in the 160 years since that graveyard was closed.

THE LONG'S HILL WESLEYAN CEMETERY

Wesleyanism was introduced into Newfoundland in 1765 by the Reverend Laurence Coughlan, a Church of England minister. At the time, Wesleyanism was a movement within the Anglican Church. Its founder John Wesley lived and died as a member of the Church of England. In time, the Wesleyans formed their own congregation after being forced out of the Anglican community.

While history books make no references to the Wesleyans having their own cemetery, an 1851 map of the city shows that there was, indeed, a small Wesleyan Cemetery which today is the portion of Long's Hill between Queen's Road and Gower Street. Today, that cemetery has been covered over by the portion of Long's Hill connecting Queen's Road to Gower Street. I have yet to see any record showing that the Wesleyan graves had been removed.

QUEEN'S ROAD–CHAPEL STREET BURIAL SITE

During the reconstruction of St. John's after the Great Fire of 1892, workers rebuilding the Congregational Church at the western corner of Queen's Road and Chapel Street made a discovery that brought all work in the area to a standstill. As word of the unusual discovery spread, people from all over the city rushed to the area.

The centre of attention was a coffin unearthed by the workers. Encouraged by spectators, the workers decided to open it. When they did, they found three people in the coffin, a woman and two children. The woman had long blond hair and the hairpins, although rusted, were still in place. While people speculated on the contents of the coffin, another coffin was found, then another and another, until a total of twelve were exhumed from the grounds.

One spectator commented, "There's enough disease in one coffin here to kill the whole city." It was believed the site had been a private burial place used during the cholera epidemic that swept the city in 1846.

MYSTERY BURIAL SITE IDENTIFIED

If the true history of this burial site was known in 1893, it was not reflected in the newspaper reports of the discovery. In tracing the history of the site, I learned that prior to 1849 this land was the site of the Congregationalist Cemetery. That cemetery was closed in 1849 along with all other cemeteries in town. The Congregationalists joined with Methodists and Presbyterians in securing land at Waterford Bridge Road (then Riverhead) for a General Protestant Cemetery.

In 1853 the Congregationalists built a stone chapel on the grounds of their old cemetery. This chapel was destroyed in the Great Fire of 1892 and was replaced with a wooden chapel in 1893.

In 1936, the Congregational Community joined with the Presbyterian Church of Canada and the Queen's Road Church became known as the Queen's Road Presbyterian Church.[2] By the 1950s the Congregation had decreased and they decided to become members of the Presbyterian Kirk at the corner of Queen's Road and Long's Hill. They sold their building to the Seventh Day Adventists in 1956/7 who sold it to developers in 1979 when it was turned into a condominium.

EPIDEMIC

In 1846, extraordinary precautions were enforced throughout town and most people were panic-stricken. Interdict signs denying access to anyone were placed on the entrance doors to homes where the cholera had struck. In one case, a seaman returning from abroad was prevented from entering his home where his wife and children had contracted the disease. Constables arrested the man and detained him in the city jail.

Authorities, fearing the contagious disease, dropped coffins off in front of homes where people had died from the disease. Preparation and burial of the dead were left to individual families. During this epidemic, the Mercy Nuns went from house to house, providing food, caring for the sick and preparing the dead for burial. Amazingly, not one of the nuns contracted the highly contagious disease.

There may have been many such small burial sites around the city resulting from deaths due to a variety of epidemics. J.W. Withers, writing in *The Royal Gazette*, 1907 stated:

> The terrible scourge of the eighteenth century was smallpox – a loathsome disease, which when it did not kill, it most generally disfigured. We can hardly imagine the hopeless dread with which a visitation of this disease was viewed. It passed over the land like a destroying angel against whose sword there was no shield. It was awfully prevalent in St. John's one hundred years ago, especially amongst the Irish emigrants.

JOB STREET GRAVES

Workmen digging up the foundation of the old shoe factory on Job Street made an alarming discovery during the summer of 1922. They unearthed a gravesite containing ten skeletons. Newspaper reports stated that one skeleton had "...a completely black head." People in the neighbourhood, as well as old-timers around the city, could not recall any information relating to the burial site. There was speculation that all ten bodies were men and all displayed signs of having been tortured. It was claimed that each had the right arm and left leg broken and two of them had their hands broken off. This was not the first time graves had been uncovered on Job Street. Newspaper reports over previous decades had reported the findings of two other graves with bodies in the same condition.

The Sunday Herald reported in 1947 that a complete investigation was never carried out into the discovery. News of the finding caused a sensation around St. John's, but, in time, interest dissipated and the ten remains were never identified.

THE OLD SOUTHSIDE ROAD MILITARY CEMETERY

This burial ground is located on the portion of Southside Road directly south of Patrick Street. According to the *Encyclopedia of Newfoundland* by J.R. Smallwood, the British built several military hospitals around St. John's during the eighteenth century while establishing a permanent garrison in the town.

One of these was constructed on Water Street near Patrick Street on the site known later as the gas-house. *The Encyclopedia* recorded:

> Moreover, there was doubtless a military burial-ground in a line directly south from this, at the foot of the Southside Hills, as some years ago, when excavating this spot, workmen found skeletons and the remains of coffins, together with many military buttons. It is quite reasonable to suppose that this building may have been used for infectious cases only, being at this time isolated from the main garrison which was situated at Fort William.

It was the discovery by Andrew Churchill of a skeleton on his property on Southside Road during road excavation in the 1960s that drew attention to the area as a possible burial site. When interviewed recently by this author, Mr. Churchill recalled that when he reported the find all work on the road was temporarily suspended and some people from Memorial University came to the area and carried out a study. Other bodies were unearthed.

FEVER HOSPITAL GRAVES–NEAR PATRICK STREET

Between the years 1814 and 1871, the area of St. John's now known as Victoria Park was the site of a hospital called the Victoria General Hospital. Between 1871 and 1888, it became the Victoria Fever Hospital. Prior to being converted into a fever hospital, the building was used as a public hospital for the people of St. John's. A report on the hospital's condition stated, "It's a wonder that the poor patients did not freeze to death during winters." The land was given to the city of St. John's in 1883, and by order of Council the Fever Hospital was burned to the ground in 1888. Between 1840 and 1860, victims of the cholera epidemic were buried near the old hospital. Today the site of that old hospital is part of the popular Victoria Park. Old records mention that the dead from the hospital were buried on a site near Patrick Street.

THE MAGOTTY COVE CEMETERY–WATER STREET EAST

There was a cemetery at Magotty Cove which was located in the east end of Water Street near Temperance Street. Temperance Street was a river at that time. During the late eighteenth century, fishermen operating from Magotty Cove petitioned the Governor, asking that the cemetery be removed. They complained that a cemetery near the cove was interfering with their work. Considering the extensive developments that have taken place in that area over the past 200 years, one can only speculate that if the bodies had not been moved from there, the remains have since been spread all over.

GROVES ROAD CEMETERY

There is a little-known, private graveyard on Groves Road which contains about a dozen graves, with all but one marked with a tombstone. The famous Newfoundland-born Canadian author Harold Horwood, who passed away in 2006, is buried there. Other members of the Horwood family also buried there include:

Harold's brother Charles Russell Horwood, his father Andrew, also an author, and his grandfather John Horwood, a master mariner. Others buried in the Groves Road Cemetery include members of the Ross and Hodder families.

GALLOWS BURIALS

In the earliest days of executions in Newfoundland, those who were hanged were cut down and buried near the gallows. Gallows burial places around St. John's include: On Water Street near the Royal Trust Building, Gibbet Hill on Signal Hill, Military Road at the eastern entrance to the Basilica grounds, the old prison property which was located in the open area east of the Court House between Duckworth and Water Streets, and at the eastern corner of Queen's Road and Bate's Hill. One man, sentenced to hang for the murder of his family, cheated the executioner by strangling himself with the braces of his pants. His body was unearthed at Rawlins Cross.

[1] During the history of the Catholic Cemetery 1811 to 1849, it was never known as The Long's Hill Catholic Cemetery. Long's Hill did not exist. What is known today as Long's Hill was part of Freshwater Road. It was realigned from Lemarchant Road to Queen's Road and that section was renamed Long's Hill in the late 19th century.

[2] Encyclopedia of Newfoundland, Vol. I, Joseph R. Smallwood, Newfoundland Book Publishers (1967) Limited. 1981.

CHAPTER 8

DAYS OF ELECTRIC STREETCARS

LAST RUN OF CITY STREETCARS
After forty-eight years of providing public transportation to the City of St. John's, the electric trolleys, also referred to as the Trams or Street-railway System, came to an end on Wednesday, September 15, 1948.

BACKGROUND
In a contract between the Newfoundland Government and R.G. Reid, signed in 1898, Mr. Reid undertook to operate the railway system across Newfoundland for fifty years and to provide a streetcar service for the City of St. John's. In addition, he committed to the paving of Water Street.

The old railway terminus was located at Fort William in St. John's in the Cavendish Square area. The tracks came into St. John's by a route which later became known as Empire Avenue. The Reids diverted the line from Donovan's on Topsail Road to make the terminus in the west end of the city on Water Street opposite Job Street. There, they built a modern station which today houses the Railway Museum and the City of St. John's Archives.

The Reid Newfoundland Company, which operated the street-railway and the Petty Harbour Power Development, sold out their interests in 1924 to the Royal Securities Corporation. The properties were then passed to the Newfoundland Light and Power Company, owners at the time of the termination of the streetcars.

Creative Publishers
The first of the new street-cars which replaced the original ones in 1925 is shown in front of the Newfoundland Light and Power Company Barn near the railway station on Water Street.

CITY IN 1900

When a hydroelectric plant was developed at Petty Harbour, only gaslights and a small supply of electric current from the Flavin Street Steam Plant supplied the town with its lighting. Water Street was a sea-of-mud in wet weather and one continuous line of gulches in winter. Wooden planks were used to cover sidewalks in some places, and wooden blocks were used in others. In cases where neither were used, there was gravel.

Commissioners ran the city and there was plenty of work, but salaries were low. For example, coal-heavers were getting fifteen cents per hour with nothing extra for overtime. After they went on strike, their salary was increased to twenty cents per hour for night work. In comparison, Bell Island oar-shovelers were paid twelve and a half cents per hour and general labourers were paid eighty cents per day.

Although pay was low, commodity prices were also low. Coal was sold at six dollars per ton, a barrel of beef could be purchased for nine dollars, ham went at ten cents per pound and seven pounds of tea cost $1.12.

Men's ready-made suits could be bought for prices starting at three dollars and up, and a collar shirt and tie was priced at fifty cents. Tailor-made suits sold for fourteen dollars each and ladies costumes in cloth or felt sold for six dollars.

There were cricket matches and football at Pleasantville. The Regatta was held at Quidi Vidi Lake. Movies, television and radio were things of the future, but there was what newspapers described as:

> A crude sort of movie called the Biograph was shown here for a brief period in 1900, and there was also a phonograph which could only be heard by placing sound tubes resembling a stethoscope in one's ears. The Boer War was still being fought. Water Street businesses were still rebuilding in the aftermath of the Great Fire of 1892.

STREETCARS

The first streetcars (trams) used by the City of St. John's were six used trams which were delivered here by train from mainland Canada. These wooden trams were painted yellow and the seating was installed lengthwise. Each tram had a front basket-like guard made of hickory which automatically dropped to the ground on contact with any obstruction on the tracks in front of the tram. They were the same size as the steel body cars which were imported to replace them in 1926.

Reporting on the initial run of the trams, *The Evening Telegram* on May 2, 1900, stated:

> For the first time, two electric streetcars started from Fort William at 12:45 today, and in the charge of Engineer W. Mckay, came slowly along Ordnance Street and up Duckworth Street as far as Holloway Street where the rails run into Water Street. A large crowd of people were attracted to the novel sight. A few passengers were in the cars, among whom were Messrs. W.D. and R.G. Reid. At 1:00 p.m., the rail was cleared and made ready on Holloway Street and the cars came down into Water Street, where, although it was dinner hour, a large number of spectators waited. After a little delay on Water Street, during which the car behind was filled up with passengers, both cars moved up Water Street with a good degree of speed, the sidewalks being lined with people all the way up town.

Creative Publishers

The introduction of electric streetcars in St. John's was viewed as a sensational event by townspeople. Free rides were given on the first day of operation May 1, 1900. Just about every child in St. John's turned up to participate on opening day. These streetcars are shown on Water Street east of Holloway Street.

It was a day of free rides. The cars ran smoothly throughout the day patronized by crowds who enjoyed the novelty and the free ride.

Conductors were required to announce to passengers the names of car-stops as they were reached. The operator had to sound a gong when within fifty feet of each street crossing. Patrons had little problem in jumping on or off the streetcars even at their top speed of eight miles per hour.

Problems
On that first day of operations, the new transportation system ran into problems. The regular service was initiated with two cars running from Prescott Street to the Long Bridge, but got stuck in mud several times on the trip.

Another problem developed when a switchboard at the central telephone office and some electric poles near Waterford Bridge Road caught on fire. This was caused by a strong surge of electric current in the power lines from Petty Harbour. There was a short interruption in streetcar service.

Hoisted Union Jack
Along the unpaved portions of the west end of Water Street, men were constantly working to keep the rails clear and by May 4th the cars ran as far as Victoria Park. In honour of this event, the park keeper hoisted the Union Jack on the park flagpole. By May 11th, a streetcar was running on the Beltline[1] up Military Road to Rawlin's Cross.

Each car was operated by two workers, a motorman and a conductor.

Mood in Town
Joseph R. Smallwood, in his radio show *The Barrelman* during December 1939, described the mood in the town on the day the streetcar service was introduced.[2] He told listeners:

There were excited arguments all through the day, and the tensest impatience existed for nightfall to arrive so they could actually see whether the car would be lighted up after dark and so be able to continue running just as in the daylight. Hundreds and hundreds of people didn't go home to tea – they just followed the streetcar back and forth along Water Street. And there were dire prophesies to be heard about the streetcar. To some people it just didn't seem natural or proper – it had the appearance of flying in the face of providence to be operating such a strange contraption.

FUNNIEST THING

There was a general concern throughout the town for the affect the new form of transportation moving up and down Water Street would have on horses, which were the source of transportation of individuals and merchandise up to that day. Smallwood reflected upon that concern:

> But the funniest thing of all connected with the inauguration of the first streetcar system that day thirty-eight years ago was the sight of hundreds of men leading horses, or riding bare back, around the town to get them accustomed to the new fangled contraption. Horses drawing long carts, box carts, wagons, victoria cabs, slovens – horses carrying their drivers on their backs – big horses, small horses, all kinds of horses were to be seen that day and night, and there were dozens of upsets, dozens of horses reared and bucked and finally bolted like wild things up the first side street as the streetcar approached them.

COMPLAINTS

By the fifth day of operations, over two thousand people had traveled on the streetcars. There were a few complaints. One traveler wrote:

> The officials who run the cars are courteous and obliging. The fault of hollering for fares in a loud harsh voice might, to a great extent, be remedied. One would think last evening that passengers wanted to beat their way, for from the time the cars started in the east end, till nearly up to Riverhead, passengers' brains were pestered with the din of fares. A voice, a little modulated, will have more effect than hollering.

PAVING OF WATER STREET

Prior to the laying of the railway tracks, the paving of Water Street and the laying of concrete sidewalks was carried out at a cost of $140,000. The stone blocks used for the streets were laid over six inches of concrete and two inches of sand.

The paving work began on August 5, 1899, when a large number of men with picks and shovels gathered near the intersection of Springdale and Water Streets and then began digging and shoveling the gravel surface into box-carts for hauling away. By August 12th, enough progress had been made to lay the first block. The stones were procured and dressed at a quarry on the Southside Hills.

The Evening Telegram reported:

> The first (cobble) stone was laid at 10:45 a.m. in the presence of a large number of spectators who expected a grand ceremony or, at least, a speech on the occasion. The stone was laid by James McLoughlan, who, it appeared, had no remarks to make about the subject. A cheer was called for and a feeble one given. The beginning of the work is being done with blue whinstone from the Southside quarry.[3] The downtown portion will be done with granite.

There had been some debate on whether whinstone or granite would be used. Advocates of granite blocks over whinstone had won out, and only a short section west from the starting point was laid with whinstone. The paving was not completed until sometime after the trams went into operation. By September 27, 1899, the work had been pushed east to just opposite the General Post Office when the supply of granite blocks ran out. A new supply was arranged and paving was finished sometime later.

THE RAILS

Two lines of railway track were laid along Water Street ending a few yards beyond the National War Memorial. These were later removed and replaced by a single line. A small section of the track east of Holloway Street was left and was still there at the time of Confederation in 1949.

RETIRED STREETCAR MAN RECALLED FIRST YEAR

Michael Walsh of Springdale Street, St. John's, was one of only two men still alive in 1948 who had worked with the tram service from its beginning until his retirement. On the occasion of the closing down of the operation, he recalled those first days:

> One of the most difficult tasks in the first days of the streetcars was keeping the tracks clear. There were two sets of tracks with grooved rails on Water Street from Holloway Street to Hutchings Street. Dust and mud would get pounded into the grooves by the flanges on the wheels until it was as hard as concrete. It was an awful job keeping these grooves clear.
>
> Then there was the problem of snow in winter. At first, they had no snow-fighting equipment and after a snowstorm came, on or about Christmas, the cars could not be kept running and had to be put away for the winter. They were not put in operation again until the spring.[4]

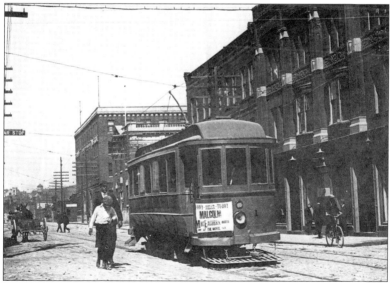

PRL

Streetcar on Water Street east of Prescott Street in 1920. Notice the horse and wagon on the left. In time, cars, trucks and buses were competing for street space with the streetcars.

Several weeks passed after the first ride before the service got into full operation. At first, four of the cars operated on the Beltline, that is: Adelaide St., Queen's Rd., and Water St. to the starting point. Two cars operated on Water Street West. Then it was decided to take two of the cars off the Beltline. One of them was placed on the route along New Gower Street from Adelaide Street to the junction of Alexander Street. The other cars started at Rawlin's Cross and went along Harvey and LeMarchant roads to the head of Barter's Hill where the track ended.

They intended to make a second loop by joining up with the New Gower-Hamilton Street rails. The higher levels service area did not pay because of the thin population and it was discontinued. The gap in the Beltline was never completed and the rails were taken up after it was shutdown. The rails on Hamilton Avenue and New Gower Streets were also removed.

Mr. Walsh recalled that up until the Great Fire of 1892, Springdale Street ended at Gilbert Street and all above that was John Casey's Farm, which took up a big area.

Because of his status as one of the workers on the first run of the streetcar on May 2, 1900, Michael Walsh was given the honour of taking the last tram into the barn, near the Railway Station on Water Street, on September 15, 1948, when the streetcar service came to an end.

TORRENTIAL RAINS

The ending of the streetcar service was not the only memorable event on September 15, 1948. Many people remained indoors due to a torrential rainstorm that struck the city on that day. The storm immobilized trains, closed Torbay Airport and washed out roads. All train traffic to and from St. John's ground to a halt as the result of the washout on the Southside, which buried the tracks under hundreds of tons of silt, and other disturbances along the line from the city to Holyrood.

REACTION

Mixed reaction greeted the passing of the streetcar system. Newfoundland was preparing to join Canada and the trams being lost seemed a trivial affair. The habitual users of the service looked upon it as a sorrowful experience.

Albert Perlin, editor of *The Daily News*, recalled the joys of the service:

> The friendliness of the cars' atmosphere was established by the conductors. Many of them have been more than a quarter of a century in the service. If they saw you running down a hill, they waited patiently and sometimes signalled to you not to risk heart failure from over-exertion since the car would wait.
>
> They got to know the time to expect you and did not leave your stop until they had had a good look up the hill to see if you were on your way. Good humour was their prevailing mood and they were all old friends. When a car was jammed tight until hardly a sardine could have been squeezed in, the good-natured conductor would take on another passenger out of the cold or rain and the late Albert Joy's voice calling to his fares to get to the back of the car was in such circumstances always good for a hearty laugh.

William Bennett, a WWII veteran who lived in the east end of St. John's, remembered some of the casualness associated with the old streetcars. He recalled conductor Albert Joy stopping in front of houses along the west end of Water Street to pick up notes from housewives, asking the conductor to pick up a message along the way. They might have ordered fresh meat from Whitten's Butcher Shop, an item from a hardware store, or something from one of the many stores along the way or may need mail dropped off at the post office. The ladies knew the trams schedule well, and would be watching for its return trip at which time the good-natured Mr. Joy, or one of the other conductors, would hand them their packages.

IRIS POWER'S EXPERIENCE

Iris Power, a columnist with *The Daily News* and a commentator with CBC radio in the 1950s, nostalgically recalled the days of the streetcars and, in particular, how they competed with the horses for the right of way along the course. She wrote:

> Those were the days of the horses – and nobody ever accorded horses the consideration shown them by street-

car conductors. When Dobbin happened to be jogging along the car tracks ahead of the streetcar, no conductor was impolite enough to hurry him. The car just tagged along behind and only picked up speed when the horse had safely turned off into a side street. Nobody complained about the delay in getting to a destination, taking it for granted that the horse had just as much right to the tracks as the streetcar had. Besides, it was very restful looking at the horse ambling along in front with its driver, giving the impression that he was going no place and was in no particular hurry to get there.

Once, while taking the streetcar to work, Iris found herself in a standing-room only situation. Men were chivalrous in those days and no lady would be left standing very long. In this case, the first gentleman to offer her a seat was the town character, Frank Milley. Iris declined the offer at first because Mr. Milley had one leg and, at the time, was living in the Infirmary for the Aged and Infirm better known as 'The Poor House' on Sudbury Street. But Frank insisted that she take his seat. So as not to disappoint him, she graciously accepted his offer and thanked him. Iris recalled witnessing another act of chivalry:

> One day, a lady richly dressed in a Persian lamb coat, got in and was standing a few moments until a longshoreman noticed her. In a voice typical of a Newfoundlander who seems to think everyone else is deaf, he said, 'Here's a seat, ma'm, you're older than I am.' The lady wasn't affronted. It was his way of being courteous – and that was all.

On stormy days, the conductors made it their business to load everyone into their cars, even if it meant getting up from their seats and pushing the customers down the aisles themselves. By cajoling and good-natured threats, they got them all in, and the car would then creak along the street with its springs sagging against its axles.

A Traffic Jam!

The following extract from *The Evening Telegram* of February 25, 1943, describes an unusual traffic confrontation involving a streetcar:

Claims Bus Obstructed Streetcar

At 6:55 last night, when a streetcar left the side switch at the head of Cochrane Street to continue up Military Road, one of the Golden Arrow buses, en route to Fort Pepperrell, stopped on the track in front of the tram. The conductor in charge of the streetcar asked the driver of the bus to back up in order to give sufficient room to pass, but the latter claimed right-of-way and held his vehicle to the track. It was about thirty-five minutes later when a policeman arrived on the scene and ordered the bus to give right-of-way for the streetcar and other vehicles to proceed on their way. As a result of the tie-up, the entire streetcar system was interrupted, and passengers were naturally displeased.

Section 28 of the Street Railway Act stated that a streetcar cannot be obstructed or hindered by other vehicles.

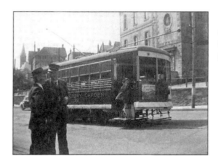

City of St. John's Archives
A 1940s picture of a streetcar stopped in front of the BIS on Queen's Road.

REASON FOR ITS DEMISE

Among the reasons for the demise of the streetcars was the growing population of the city and its geographical expansion. The trams couldn't handle the growing numbers needing the service, and the streetcars were limited to the downtown area. The owners of the system wanted to add new trams and extend the route but also requested that council increase the fare from five to seven cents. Council turned down the request, and the franchise for a bus service was given to the Golden Arrow Bus Company which was permitted to charge ten cents per passenger. The streetcars were bought by Geoff Stirling who sold them off to people who carted them to country sites for use as summer cabins or work sheds.

There was some public support for a proposal to combine the bus and tram with the Water Street route still handled by the trams, but, in the end, the bus system won out and the Golden Arrow Bus Company took over public transportation in St. John's.

WHAT HAPPENED TO THE STREETCAR RAILS?

The last link with the streetcar system in St. John's was severed on August 2, 1949, two days before Regatta Day.

During the spring of 2008, exposed streetcar railings discovered on Water Street just west of Patrick Street caused much public speculation that the streetcar rails had not been removed but were simply paved over. If anyone was left with that impression, they were certainly mistaken.

In seeking out the background to the removal of the tracks, I was able to verify what actually took place when the streetcars were removed in St. John's.

When the streetcar system was abandoned in 1948, the Newfoundland Light & Power Company made a deal to pay Council fifty-thousand dollars for the removal of the rails. That amount was paid to Council before the project started.

On Tuesday morning, August 2, 1949, machines and men began working on the rail removal project. The contract for the work was awarded to Concrete Products Ltd.

The truth concerning the track removal is that most of the tracks of the streetcar system were removed, sent to the City Council yard and likely sold as scrap. The procedure used by the workers involved removing the tracks from sections of the rail channel badly in need of repair. The remaining sections were concealed by paving them over with asphalt.

The work started along what was known as the Beltline near the intersection of Adelaide Street and Water Street. On Adelaide Street, the strip between the rails was excavated and repaved with asphalt. *The Telegram* reported:

> On the short section of New Gower Street between Adelaide and Queen's Road, only that part of the rail channel which is badly in need of repair will be excavated, while on the remaining section the rails will be covered in by asphalt.

The whole of Queen's Road, including the rail bed, is to be resurfaced. On Military Road and Duckworth Street the procedure will be to remove the rails and resurface the excavation where the street is in poor condition, and to resurface over the rails where the pavement is in good shape.

On Water Street West, also a paved street, this will be the order of things. The alternate methods of removal of the rails and repairing of the street will depend on the condition of the pavement.

[1] The Beltline referred to one of the routes taken by the trams.

[2] *The Best of the Barrelman* (1938-1940). Edited by William Connors, Creative Publishers, 1998.

[3] Whinstone was imported from Scotland and was considered too expensive for the project. The granite stone was quarried at Southside Hills.

[4] This applied only to the first couple of decades of streetcar operations. In the 1930s, a special snow clearing tram was used to remove snow from the line.

CHAPTER 9

CHRISTMASES PAST

TWO VERSIONS OF THE MUMMER'S PLAY

The tradition of mummering in Newfoundland was brought here by the first English settlers. The practice was declared illegal in 1860 after one Isaac Mercer was killed by mummers in that same year. Although it had been outlawed, the going door-to-door continued. In the first part of the twentieth century, this led to multiple arrests after criminals in the guise of mummers robbed homes in the Gower Street area of the city. However, there was also the *Mummer's Play* which was performed on stage and continued up until around 1900 and was revived again a decade or so later.

In December 1949, *The Newfoundlander* presented to readers what it described as:

> An historic document relating to old-time Christmas folklore in Newfoundland. The original Mummer's Play, which has been revived in some areas of the province over recent years, was adapted over a period of time and led to a Newfoundland version of the popular Christmas tradition.

The Newfoundlander drew upon the knowledge of two contributors to the newspaper, a Mr. Barney Moss of Salvage, Bonavista Bay, and a Mr. J.J. Peckford of Gander Bay, to present to readers both versions. The Newfoundland version is slightly shorter than the English play.

Writing in 1949, Mr. Peckford recalled that the Newfoundland version, "...was performed at Change Islands, Fogo District, when he was a boy of ten or twelve, about fifty years ago."

Remarkably, Mr. Peckford, who had never seen either of the plays in print, committed the Newfoundland version to memory after repetitively seeing and hearing the play performed.

Mr. Peckford recalled:

> The play was introduced to our young people by an English schoolmaster, Mr. Justinia Dowell by name. The

'soldiers' as we called them – actors in the play – would start on St. Stephen's Day and visit all the houses in the town and would keep it up for several days. They would have quite a jolly time, and they looked very smart in their trimmed pants(blue with red side stripes), white shirts and high hat with ribbons and tassels. They also carried swords made from birchwood, and they made other items to use in the play, too.

Mr. Moss wrote that the original version was performed on stage as well as house-to-house in villages and communities around Newfoundland. He felt that the tradition had died out in most of the colony by about 1900. He remembered, "They used to start out St. Stephen's Day and visit from house to house. They would keep it up for twelve days, everyone clad in war equipment that was required to do battle in those days. It's a great play, well-worth resurrecting for the benefit of future generations. I have seen the old fellows acting it, all dressed in uniform. There's no play today can come up to the old-fashioned mummering play."

St. Stephen's Day was notable in the theatre as the beginning of the pantomime season. In England and Newfoundland, as well as other parts of the world, it was also the day the mummers began their rounds of the community.

The first version presented here is the Newfoundland version.

SOLDIERS ACTING AT CHRISTMAS

1. Roomer (Introduction Officer)
Room, room, gallant room, room required here tonight,
For some of my bold champions are coming forth to fight.
Old act, new act, acts you never saw before,
For I am the very champion that brings old Father Christmas to your door.
And if you don't believe these words I say, step in Father Christmas and boldly declare thy way.

2. Father Christmas
Here comes I old Father Christmas, welcome or welcome not,
I hope old Father Christmas will never be forgot.
Here comes I old Johnny Jack, my wife and family on my back,

My wife so big and my children so small,
Takes more than a crumb of bread to feed them all,
And if you don't believe these words I say, step in King George
and boldly declare thy way.

3. King George
Here comes I, King George,
from old England I did spring,
Some of my victorious works I am going to bring.
I fought the fiery dragon,
I brought him to the slaughter,
And by those very means I'll win fair Zebra, King of Egypt's
daughter.
And if you don't believe these words, I say,
Step in King of Egypt and boldly declare thy way.

4. King of Egypt
Here comes I, the King of Egypt, in uniform do appear.
King George, King George, thy comrade is here.
He is a man of courage bold,
I am his armour-bearer
To cut down his enemies if there are any of them here.
And if you don't believe these words I say, step in Valiant
Soldier and boldly declare thy way.

5. Valiant Soldier
Here comes I, the Valiant Soldier,
Slasher is my name,
Sword and pistol by my side I hopes to win the game;
One of my brothers I saw wounded the other I saw slain.
And by those very means I'll fight King George all on the
plain
(Takes a step).

6. Next scene, King George
Whist, whist, bold man, what thou art telling
Apple dumplings thou are selling
Stand where thou are and call in
Brother Turk to act thy part.

7. Valiant Soldier
Turk, Turk, come with speed,
help in my time of need,
Thy time of need I do implore
I was never in such need before.

8. Turkish Knight
Here comes I, the Turkish Knight,
come from the Turkish land to fight.
I'll fight King George with courage bold,
if his blood is hot, I'll make it cold.

9. (King George Again)
Who art thou that speak so bold?

10. (Turkish Knight)
Haul out thy purse and pay for satisfaction I will have before
I go away.

11. (King George)
No satisfaction thou shan't get,
while I have strength to stand,
For I don't care for no Turk
stands on this English land.

12. (They cross swords and both say)
You and I the battle try, if you conquer I will die.

13. (Turkish Knight)
I am cut down, but not quite dead,
It is only the pain lies in my head,
If I once on my two legs stood,
I'd fight King George to my knees in blood.

14. (King George)
On the ground, thous dost lie, and the truth I'll tell to thee,
That if thou dost but rise again thy butcher I will be.

15. (Turkish Knight)
Come Valiant Soldier, be quick and smart,

And with my sword I will pierce
King George's heart.

16. (Turkish Knight on his feet again, and continues)
I do not care for thee, King
George, although thou art a champion bold,
I never saw that Englishman yet could make my blood run
cold.

17. (King George)
You Turkish dog, King George is here, happy for another
hour to come,
I'll cut thee and I'll hew thee, I am bound to let thee know,
I am bold King George from England before I let thee go.

18. (Turkish Knight)
Now the battle I have won, thank
God, I am free,
And if that man do rise again his butcher I will be.

19. (King George)
(King George rises from the floor and strikes the Turk)
I suppose you thought that I was dead, but yet alive remain,
And go and tell the doctor the Turkish man is slain

20. (Father Christmas and the Doctor)
Doctor, doctor, come with speed,
Help me in my time of need.
My time of need I do implore,
I was never in such need before.

21. (Father Christmas then tries to revive the Turk himself, but with no success, He says)
Is there a doctor to be found
Can heal my son of his deadly wound?

22. (Doctor)
Yes, there is a doctor to be found
Can heal thy son of his deadly wound.

23. (Father Christmas)
What is thy fee?

24. (Doctor)
Fifty guineas is my fee, but if the money is paid down,
I will do it for ten pound.

25. (Father Christmas)
What can you cure?

26. (Doctor)
I can cure the hits, fits, palsy and the gout,
If there is any evil spirit in this man I can sure drive it out.
.
27. (Father Christmas)
What kind of medicine have you got?

28. (Doctor)
I have a little bit of hare's grease and mare's grease,
The wig of a weasel and the wool of a frog,
And twenty-four ounces of September fog.

29. (Father Christmas)
Where do you rub all this stuff?

30. (Doctor)
I rub a little to his temple, and a little to the crack-bone of
his heart.
Arise, arise, hold champion, and boldly act thy part.
Arise, arise, my lofty man, I long to see you stand.
Open your eyes and look about,
I will take you by the hand.
(The man gets up and comes to his feet)

31. (Pickedy Wick)
Here comes I, Pickedy Wick, put my hand in my pocket
and pay what I thinks fit.
Ladies and gentlemen, sit down to their ease.
Put their hands in their pockets and pay what they please,

And if you don't believe those words I say, step in
Beelzebub and boldly clear the way.

32. (Beelzebub)
Here comes I Beelzebub,
under my arm I carries my club.
In my hand I keeps my pan,
I thinks myself a jolly fine man.
Money I wants, money I crave,
and money I'll have to carry me to my grave.
And if you don't believe those words I say,
step in bold Hercules and boldly clear thy way.

33. (Bold Hercules)
Here comes I, bold Hercules,
I boldly stem the weather,
I took the rainbow from the skies and spliced both ends
together,
And if you don't believe those words I say, step in Jack Tar
and boldly clear the way.

34. (Jack Tar)
Here comes I, Jack Tar, just returned from sea, sir.
With the shiners on my breast, and what do you think of me,
sir?
I am a brisk young sailor and always on the sea,
And now I am home, my heroes,
I am full of life and glee.
The battle will soon be over and now we will sing one song,
And we will cheer our hardy comrades as we gladly march
along.

**All the company then form into a ring, with Father Christmas
in the centre, they sing the following ditty.**

The pig and the bug and the bumblebee,
There is one more river to cross.
The pig and the bug and the bumblebee
There is one more river to cross.

One more river and that's the river of Jordan.
One more river, there is one more river to cross.

THE ORIGINAL MUMMER'S SONG
1. Beelzebub
Here comes I, Beelzebub, and on my shoulder carries my club,
And in my hand a three penny pan;
Ain't I a smart jolly old man.
If you don't believe what I do say,
step in Father Christmas and clear the way.

2. Father Christmas
Here comes I, old Father Christmas, all in my merry bloom,
Come, gentlemen and ladies, come, give me little room;
Room, room brave gallant, room; give me room to rhyme
And I will give you some revels to pass away old Christmas time.
Old activity, new activity, the like was never seen,
I pray you now Dim Dorthy step in.

3. Dim Dorthy
Here comes I, Dim Dorthy, with a fair face and a flat commarity
Although my commarity is but small, I'm the biggest bully of them all.
If you don't believe what I do say, step in Sir Guy and clear the way.

4. Sir Guy
Here comes I, Sir Guy, a man of mighty strength,
Who slew down Duncow, eighty feet in length;
Is there anyone here holds King George a spleen,
I'm resolved to conquer, it's for King George I'll die
If you do don't believe what I say, step in King George and clear the way.

5. King George
Here comes I, King George, a man of courage bold,
And with my glittering sword I won ten crowns of gold,

I fought the fiery dragon till I brought him to great slaughter,
And by those bloody means I won the Queen of Egypt's
daughter.
Close in a closet I was kept, then upon a table rack,
And after that upon a rock of stone,
'Twas there I sat and made my grievous moan.
Then the Turkish Knight put his foot on land to fight;
To fight I would even, if I was slain, till every drop of blood
would quiver in his veins.
If you don't believe what I do say, step in, Valiant Soldier,
and clear the way.

6. Valiant Soldier
Here comes I, the Valiant Soldier bold, Slasher is my name,
Sword and buckle by my side in hopes to win the game;
My head is made of iron, my ribs are made of steel
I means to fight the Turkish Knight and slay him in the
field.

7. King George
 Hark, I hear a footstep.

8. Valiant Soldier
 That may be the Grand Turk.

9. King George
If that be the Grand Turk, let him appear.

10. Grand Turk Enters
Here comes I, the Grand Turk, out of prison for to fight,
To fight King George, that man by name, if I had him what
dreadful work I make;
I would cut him and slay him as small as dust,
And send his body to the devil for a Christmas pie crust.

11. King George
Stop! Stop! Don't speak so hot,
There's a man in this room thou knowest not,
I'll cut thee and slay thee and when that is done,
I will fight the bravest champion that's under the sun.

12. Grand Turk
Why, King George, did I ever do you any harm?

13. King George
Yes! Therefore you deserve to be stabbed.

14. Grand Turk
Stab for stab, I will punch you to the ground,
Where I mean to lay your body down.

**15. (The battle is set in array between King George and
the Grand Turk, King George slays the Grand Turk,
his body lying dead on the ground. King George,
sorry for his brother champion calls for a doctor.)**

16. Doctor, doctor, come with speed,
And help me in my time of need;
The time of need I never saw before
Till I saw my brother champion lying dead upon the floor.
Is there a doctor here to be found?

17. Doctor
Yes, there's a doctor here at hand
Who can cure your brother champion
Of his deadly wound and make him stand.

18. King George
What can your cure, noble doctor?

19. Doctor
I can cure all things: itch, stitch,
the pox, the palsy and the gout,
And if the divil is in him I can root him out.

20. King George
How far have you traveled noble sir?

21. Doctor
I've traveled from England through France and Spain,
And always back to old England again.

I have a little bottle in the waist band of my breeches pocket
Called ice, some tice; some gold for lice; some, the wig of a
weasel:
The wool of a frog and eighteen inches last September's fog.
Hold it over a slow turf-fire in a wooden saucepan,
Mixed with a hen's tooth and a cat's feather;
Three drops to his temple and one to his heart,
Rise up, brother, and play your part.

**22. (The dead Turk is brought to life by the doctor's
medicine. The Grand Turk cries out):**
Terrible! Terrible! The like was never seen,
A man knocked out of seven senses, into a hundred and
nineteen;
Not be bucks nor it by bears, one of the divil's whirligigs
blowed me up in the air.
If you don't believe what I do say, step in Turkish Knight
and clear the way.

23. Turkish Knight
Here comes I, the Turkish Knight,
All from the Turkish land to fight
To fight King George or the valiant Soldier bold,
Slasher is his name;
Show me the man before me will stand
I'll cut him down with my
Courageous hand.

24. Valiant Soldier
I'm the man before you will stand
And that you soon shall know,
And if you do your worst or best
I'll give you blow for blow

25. Turkish Knight
I don't mind your words as figs.
Neither your blows or bumps,
If you cut me off my legs,
I'll fight you on my stumps.

171

(The battle is on between the Turkish Knight and the Valiant Soldier. The Turk, wounded, falls to the ground).

26. Valiant Soldier
O see, O see, what I have done,
I have cut him down like the fallen sun;
Ten thousand more such men I'll fight,
For to maintain King George's rights.

27. Turkish Knight
O stop, O stop your hand, there's one thing more I crave,
If you spare me my sweet life
I'll be your English slave.

28. Valiant Soldier
Arise, arise, you Turkish dog, and to your country make your way,
And tell unto your Turkish fleet what a champion old England bears today.
Step in Oliver Cromwell and clear the way.

29. Oliver Cromwell
Here comes I, Oliver Cromwell, as you may suppose
I conquered many nations with my copper nose;
I made the French to tremble, the Spanish to shake,
I fought the jolly Dutchmen until I made their hearts ache.
If you don't believe what I do say, step in the captain of the play.

30. The Captain and his wife appear
Here comes I, the captain of the play,
And to my men I lead the way,
As I stood on the pewter rock of fame
And on the champion bear the blame.
I'm not like some of those Turkish dogs
That go out after night and disturb the people and make a noise
Step in the wren and clear the way.

31. The Wren
The wren, the wren, the king of all birds,
St. Stephen's Day I was caught in the fire;
Although I am little my honour is great,
Rise up, Skipper, and give us a Trate (treat);
If you got no rum, give us some cake.
If you fills the plate of the small,
It will not agree with those boys at all,
But if you fills it of the best,
We hope in Heaven your soul will rest.

(Song follows, sung by the crowd)
Ye midwives and widows, come now pay attention
To those few lines I'm now going to mention,
Of a maid in distraction who is now going to wander,
She relied upon George for the loss of her lover.

(Chorus after each verse)
Broken-hearted I'll wander,
For the loss of my lover,
My bonnie light-horseman
Was slain in the war

Three years and six months since I left England's shore,
My bonnie light-horseman will
I ever see more.
She mounted on horseback,
So gallant and brave,
Amongst the whole regiment respected he was.

If I had the wings of an eagle as
Swift as the dove I would fly
I would cross the salt sea where
my true love do lie,
And with my fond lips I would
bear on his grave,
And kiss his pale cheeks so colder
than clay.

END OF THE PLAY

SPAWNED WREN TRADITION

On the Southern Shore, near St. John's, mummers used the wren portion of the Mummering Play to solicit treats on their door-to-door visits. This is fondly remembered as "Hunting the Wren." It involved a group of neighbours, led by a young raggedly dressed boy, going door-to-door. The boy carried a fir bough decorated with coloured ribbons and in the centre a dead bird, representing the wren, was laid on a piece of red cloth. When someone answered the door, the group would say:

The wren, the wren, the King of all birds,
On St. Stephen's Day was caught in the firs,
Although I am little my honour is great,
Rise up landlady and give us a trate (Treat).
If you got no rum, give us some cake.
If you fills the plate of the small,
It will not agree with those boys at all,
But if you fill it of the best,
We hope in Heaven your soul will rest.

St. Stephen's Day became known as Boxing Day because of the tradition in the early Christian church of opening the alms box on that day and distributing it to the poor. In some parts of England, there was a habit of giving a 'Christmas Box' on St. Stephen's Day rather than Christmas Day which they devoted exclusively to celebrating the birth of the Christ child.

Another explanation was that on Boxing Day the parson would give bread, cheese and beer to paupers. The farmer's wife would set apart a very large pie to be cut up on Boxing Day and distributed to the labourers' families. A gentleman, compelled to travel on Boxing Day, would find that the innkeeper charged him less for his dinner. On Christmas Day, citizens showed good will to members of their own household, but, on Boxing Day, to a wider circle.

SKATING STARTED AT CHRISTMAS

Kevin Jardine, for years a columnist with *The Evening Telegram*, delighted readers with his memories of life in old St. John's. He once recalled:

Going back, it would seem that our weather changed a lot after the Burin Tidal Wave. There is no doubt that the winters are shorter. I remember quite well that in the month of November, the Catholic Church bells would toll during that month of the holy souls. The bell tolled to remind us to offer our prayers for those who had departed. We were allowed out until nine o'clock Friday nights, but had to hurry home for that prayer. We usually brought out our sleds in late October. The streets would be well-coated with snow and frost at that time. Skating officially started at Christmas, and it was a great disappointment if the ponds and lakes were not frozen over for Christmas Day.

TIPS EVE

Tips Eve was the day before Christmas Eve. In olden times, parents were busy on Christmas Eve putting up and decorating the tree, and getting the children off to bed. The evening before, neighbours would get together for a few drinks, usually of home-brew, to relax before the start of Christmas. This became known as Tips Eve and is still observed in many places around Newfoundland today.

SPOOKS AND SPECTRES OF CHRISTMAS SEASON

Christmas is a fitting time to tell tales of wandering spooks and spectres. Yuletide family gatherings in the glow of a fireplace or Christmas tree lights make the ideal setting for telling such stories. When the window pane rattles in the night, are you sure it's just the wind? Maybe it's a long lost soul attempting to manifest its presence. While walking along one of the old St. John's streets alone and late at night, did you ever have the eerie feeling of being watched or hear the sound of crunching snow behind you as though someone is following you? Just your imagination! Or could it be a ghost haunting the area it once inhabited as a mortal being? Who really knows?

CARTER'S HILL AREA GHOST

A hundred years ago, everyone in town knew the story of Nancy Coyle, the Queen of the Dead. Nancy lived in a three-story house at the corner of Queen's Road and Carter's Hill and some whispered she was in league with the devil. It's not surprising then that after her death ghostly stories of Nancy Coyle circulated and spread fear among the residents of the City. Nancy had the unique job of preparing the dead for burial in the 1850s. She worked from her home. On more than one occasion, a corpse brought to her was seen walking around St. John's the next day. The truth was that they were not dead in the first place but merely in a coma. Yet superstition prevailed and after her death many swore to have seen her ghost haunting the quaint, old charming streets in the Carter's Hill area.

PHANTOM FUNERAL PROCESSION

The city abounded with tales of the supernatural which sometimes included the spectre of a phantom scene from the life of a person or persons long departed from this earth as in the case of the Duckworth Street funeral procession. Around the same time stories of the Queen of the Dead were sending chills up the spine of townspeople, there were stories of an apparition of a funeral procession along Duckworth Street near the Court House.

A couple out for a quiet walk in the crisp night air during Christmas of 1898 heard the sound of crunching snow behind them. Thinking it was a horse-drawn sleigh approaching, they moved in off the street and turned to have a look. To their astonishment, it was a hearse followed by a lady with her head bowed as they looked, the vision disappeared into thin air.

When the story was told, older folks remembered hearing tales of the same phantom-like apparition. It is believed it was an apparition of the funeral of Lt. Richard Lawry who was murdered in 1794 by a bunch of Irish thugs in the vicinity of Steers Cove. He was laid to rest in the old cemetery adjacent to the Anglican Cathedral on Church Hill. The lady behind the hearse was the spirit of a girl named Molly who met and fell in love with the young lieutenant. She was so distressed over his death that she drowned herself in the harbour.

ETERNITY PLAYING CARDS

A house near Signal Hill was believed to be haunted by a mean, old man named Earl Cahill. Earl was known around town for his gambling and disrespect for the Sabbath. He is said to have lost his soul while gambling with the Devil, and was condemned to play cards with his diabolic adversary until Judgement Day.

176

HAUNTING ON SOUTHSIDE ROAD

A family occupying a two-story house at the lower end of Southside Road in the 1840s was forced out of their home by the ghost of a woman hanged in St. John's in 1804. The haunting started with the sound of windows rattling in the house. Nothing unusual in that, after all the house overlooked the harbour and winds would cause windows to rattle. But the windows rattled on nights when the sky was clear and there were no winds. While in the downstairs kitchen, the family would hear someone walking around upstairs and opening and closing the doors. Always, they would search each room and find no one and no explanation.

Then a night came when the winds swept through the narrows and a blinding snowstorm raged. But the windows did not rattle. The house was strangely quiet. The family had gathered around the kitchen stove when the sound of someone walking down the stairs was heard. A chilling feeling gripped everyone in the room as the sound came closer and closer. Then the door opened and there, standing in the doorway, was the spirit of a woman with a hangman's rope around her neck. The family fled the house screaming and refused to return, not even to get their belongings. Because of the known haunting, nobody would ever live in the house and it fell into disrepair and was torn down. The house was once owned by Catherine Brown who was hanged in public in St. John's in 1804 for murdering her husband in the same house.

COURT HOUSE GHOST

As late as the 1950s, there were claims that the courthouse in St. John's was haunted by an apparition of a lady in white. Those who claimed to have seen the apparition said it never made a sound. The lady would be seen walking down a hallway and then disappearing. It is believed it was the ghost of Catherine Snow who was hanged near the Courthouse in 1834 after being found guilty, along with two others, of murdering her husband. Stories of ghostly appearances of Catherine Snow spanned more than a hundred years. There were newspaper reports that her spirit was seen in a laneway near the courthouse and in the buildings that occupy the site of the old courthouse between Duckworth Street and Water Street.

SWISH BARRELS FOR CHRISTMAS

For many people, getting a swish barrel in preparation for Christmas Season was as important as getting a turkey or a Christmas tree. People lined up to purchase these because they were a cheap source of a good supply of Christmas liquor.

Swish was sold by the Board of Liquor Control. The Board used to import barrels of rum; in the 1930s and 1940s they stored them at the Newman Wine Vault at the corner of Water and Springdale streets. Owen Moore, a truck driver with Barrett's Wholesale at that time, in an interview with the author, recalled the popularity of 'swish' in old St. John's. Mr. Moore said he would pick up the barrels of rum and brandy from the waterfront and unload them at Newman's.

The vault was used at the time to store imported alcohol until it was taken to the Board of Liquor Control Store on Duckworth Street in the old Avalon Telephone Company building. There it was bottled as Newfoundland Screech and then distributed to the BLC outlets in the colony. Delivering the liquor involved a regular practice whereby the custodian would pry open the small circular covering at the top of the barrel and dip a stick into it to measure the contents. However, before beginning the bottling process, an amount would be extracted to fill a bottle that was shared among the workmen. The custodian would then record the remaining measurements in the record books. After the barrels were emptied for bottling, they would be placed on public sale and advertised as 'Swish Barrels For Sale'.

In the 1930s and 40s these sold for three to five dollars a barrel. People lined up to buy them and were able, by the following process, to retrieve ten to twelve bottles of liquor. An advertisement in *The Daily News* explained the swish process.

Into the barrels from the store
So much hot water you would pour,
A three buck deal,
But now it's more,
Swish will cost ten dollars.

Liquor soaked into the wood
Drawn out by water as it should

A swishy product makes that good
Swish will cost ten dollars.

Mr. Moore explained that by pouring hot water into the barrel and leaving it for a day or more, the alcohol would come out of the wooden sides of the barrel and form what was known as swish. He said many people purchased these barrels in the fall to get their Christmas liquor supplies. The annual St. John's Regatta season was also a busy time for the sellers of swish-barrels.

AN OLD TRADITIONAL HOMEMADE PUNCH

In modern times, Christmas revelors pick up a supply of liquor from the liquor store to make their Christmas Punch. In the old days, in pre-Confederation times, people were more resourceful and made do with what could be found around the house to make a good brew. They would:

Take a cup of strong tea, ¾ cup of orange juice, 1 cup pineapple juice; ½ cup lemon juice. Mix juices and tea. Chill. Just before serving, add one pint of ginger ale and sweeten to taste with the sugar syrup. Top each serving glass with sliced oranges and lemons and add ice. It's truly delicious!

The sugar syrup is made by boiling one cup of sugar with one cup of water. Put together into a saucepan and stir until dissolved. Then boil without stirring for about five minutes. Pour into covered jar and keep cold until needed. Even the kids can drink this Christmas Punch.

PRISONERS SET FREE CHRISTMAS EVE

The following story, anonymously written and published in the Christmas Messenger of 1928, tells a humorous but true story of how one police sergeant got carried away with the Christmas spirit one Christmas Eve. The article reads:

It happened on a Christmas Eve when the late Mr. Sullivan was Inspector-General Sullivan and the guard at the lockup was a most jovial police sergeant. It happened when the public houses did not close till 10 p.m.. Quite a number of otherwise well-meaning citizens indulged a little too heavily on that particular Christmas Eve, and accordingly, one by one, were brought into the custody of the sergeant.

The visitors who happened to have reserve flasks in their pockets were accordingly stripped of them, and so the jovial sergeant became irresistibly attracted to imbibe some of their contents, with the result that by 10 p.m., when the last of the delinquents were brought in, he felt himself in a merrier mood than usual. Realizing what the occasion was, his heart expanded in sympathy with his fellow men who were destined to spend the night behind the bars away from their families, and so with a prompt and generous impulse, he opened up all the prison cells, and then giving fatherly advice, urged the inmates to, 'Depart in peace and go straight to your home and families and have a merry, merry Christmas.'

After they left, the Inspector-General turned up and at once asked the following question, 'Sergeant, how many prisoners have you here?'

'Oi begor, sir,' replied the happy guard, 'neither one at all now, sir. There was about twenty brought in, but on account of it being Christmas times, I let them all out again.'

The shock of that answer nearly caused the Inspector General to collapse. He was amazed beyond description at such a reply. But when he fully realized and verified what had happened his indignation knew no bounds, and accordingly, after giving a severe lecture to his subordinate, he promptly suspended him from duty. However, thanks to the good offices of Sir Edward Morris, then Minister of Justice, the good natured guard was restored to his position again but on condition that never more would he be permitted to stand guard at the lockup on a Christmas Eve.

NEW RESEARCH ON COCOS ISLAND TREASURE

Following the publication of my book *Treasure Island Revisited*, which is a true Newfoundland story about two Newfoundlanders who found treasure caves on Cocos Island in the Central Pacific, some fascinating information began to surface revealing that portions of the Cocos Island Treasure can still be found in Newfoundland.

Captain John Keating, who lived on Water Street in the early nineteenth century, and Captain William Boig, who lived on George Street, found the treasure which sparked more than four hundred expeditions over the next hundred years in search of the fabulous Lost Treasure of Lima.[1] Boig died under mysterious circumstances on the first expedition to the Island, and it is believed he may have been murdered by Keating.

EXTRAVAGANT WIDOW

An intriguing piece of information not available at the time of publishing *Treasure Island Revisited* is that following the death of Captain Keating, who had used his treasure from Cocos Island to start a business at Codroy Valley, his wife had sufficient money to mount an expedition of her own in search of the remaining treasure. She traveled alone to Oakland, California, where she chartered the schooner *Meridian* for three months to bring her to Cocos Island. The wealthy widow even supervised the fitting out of the schooner for the expedition.

Jack Fitzgerald Collection
Mrs. Catherine Brennan, wife of Captain John Keating.

Her adventure attracted international attention and was reported in *The New York Journal* of July 29, 1896. *The Journal* stated, "If there are blood stains on the bags which hold the coins or skulls of murdered men lying hidden with the brass-bound chests,

Mrs. Catherine Brennan has nothing to do with the lawless past of which no witnesses remain."

The *Meridian* Expedition failed. Although Mrs. Brennan made two other expeditions to the Island, the *Meridian* Expedition escaped the attention of the many authors around the world who have produced books on the treasures of Cocos Island.

RICHARD SPENCE

Descendants of a Richard Spence of Trinity believe he may have been part of one of Captain John Keating's expeditions to Cocos Island. Soon after *Treasure Island Revisited* was published, I received a call from a man from Trinity Bay, living in St. John's, who said my book may have cleared up the mystery of a Richard Spence of Trinity who died in 1846. Near the mid-nineteenth century, Richard Spence had gone to South America and brought back treasure, some of which he used and much of which he buried somewhere on his property.

The anonymous caller said that a friend of his, living in Trinity today, brought him to a bank in St. John's and showed him the contents of a safety deposit box. The box contained an assortment of diamonds, rubies, and gold coins that the owner said was part of the treasure brought back to Trinity by Richard Spence from one of his trips to South America.

I recently received information from a direct descendant of Richard Spence who said that around 1900 a valuable piece of the jewelry was used to make a purchase in Trinity. It was a gold and jewel-encrusted necklace. That piece of treasure is today stored in a safety deposit box in a St. John's bank.

AMAZING FACT DISCOVERED

Acting on this information, I did some checking on Spence and found a piece of information that may connect him to Captain Keating, and the Cocos Island treasure. Keating is known to have led at least two expeditions to Cocos Island and brought back treasure to Newfoundland from both ventures. His first was the Edgecombe Expedition which set sail from St. John's Harbour on January 25, 1841, and the second set out from Nova Scotia in late May, or early June 1845.

Keating ran into many problems on his 1845 expedition and was forced to set into Puntas Arenas to recruit some new crew-

men. It was in connection with Puntas
Arenas that I found a piece of evidence
which not only shows Spence had been
there, but that he was there during the same
period of the Captain Keating treasure
hunting expedition.

In researching old records I came across
a newspaper report of Spence's death which
indicated that his relatives in Trinity had
received a notice from "Her Majesty's Consul
in Panama," reporting that Richard had contracted the dreaded disease "Typhoid Fever,"
and had died at Puntas Arenas. The time of
death was Thursday, April 30, 1846. Keating
had stopped at Puntas Arenas to hire new
crew members.

Jack Fitzgerald Collection
Captain John Keating

Keating left his crew in South America and made it back to
Newfoundland with treasure from Cocos Island by late September.

If Spence was part of Keating's crew in 1845, he might have
also been on the Edgecombe Expedition in 1841 when the treasure was first discovered. This would explain where the treasure
in the safety deposit box originated.

THE DOS MUNDOS

Recently, Kay Coady of St. John's, whose late husband is
believed to have been a descendant of Mike Coady who sailed
with Captain Keating on one of his expeditions to South America,
showed me a collection of gold and silver coins handed down in
the Coady family. Mike Coady passed away in 1858.

Carter-Fitzgerald Photography
**Left: The Dos Mundos coin. Right: Gems from the Lima Treasure brought back to St.
John's, Newfoundland by William Boig, Jr. and owned today by his descendants.**

Most prominent among these was a "Dos Mundos" coin minted in Mexico in 1732. A fortune in Mexican gold and silver had been stolen by the same pirates who looted the treasure of Lima. They buried it in the same treasure caves on Cocos Island. Could Mrs. Coady's Dos Mundos coin be from those treasures?

TREASURE COINS SPENT IN ST. JOHN'S

Keating paid his rent in St. John's to his landlord Jonas Barter in Spanish gold coins and purchased items from Bowring's Hardware Store using Spanish silver coins. Some of these coins may still be in the possession of family descendants of Barter and a clerk named McKenzie who served Keating at the Bowring Store.

BOIG'S DESCENDANTS

PANL

Inspector Charles Hutchings, Inspector General of the Newfoundland Constabulary and the grandson of Captain William Boig.

On the first expedition of Keating and Boig, Captain Boig had taken along his son, William Jr. Although Keating fled Costa Rica with several bags of treasure and left young Boig in Central America to get by as best he could, Boig Jr. made his way back to St. John's and brought his mother a leather satchel of gems. In later years, Boig Jr. is believed to have returned to Cocos Island and recovered more of the loot.

Captain Boig's daughter Euphrenia Boig married Charles Hutchings in St. John's on December 19, 1854, and they had a son whom they named Charles. He became Inspector General of Police in St. John's and later Attorney General of Newfoundland.

In the early twentieth century, when Robert Louis Stevenson's *Treasure Island* had become a world-wide classic, and Herve de

Montmorency's *In Search of Buried Treasure*, which directly connected the finding of the Lima treasure with Newfoundlanders, Inspector General Hutchings made a rather startling declaration. He said he knew the story of Captains Keating and Boig was true because he was the grandson of Captain Boig. Even more amazing, at the time, was that he declared he still had some gems which his uncle had brought back from Cocos Island.

TREASURE GEMS STILL IN FAMILY

Steward Fraser, a retired school teacher living near St. John's today, is Charles Hutching's great-grandson and a direct descendant of Captain Billy Boig. He has in his possession several gems which were among the bag of twenty-seven Billy Boig Jr. brought back from Cocos Island. One of these is in a gold attachment connected to the fob of a pocket watch which had been owned by Fraser's great-grandfather. Two other gems, sapphires, were converted into very attractive earrings.

BLOOD-STAINED HISTORY

These gems have a blood-stained history that can be traced from the city of Lima in 1821 during the Spanish American Revolution to 2009 in Newfoundland. They were in the Roman Catholic Cathedral of Lima when rebels threatened to invade Lima. They were on the pirate ship when Captain Marion (William) Thompson and his cut-throat pirates murdered the priests and guards, who were sent to protect the Lima Treasure, and dumped their bodies into the Pacific.

These gems were buried by the pirates as part of a fortune in treasures which they hid in three different caves on Cocos Island. When Captains Keating and Boig removed the large rock hiding the entrance to one of these caves, the gems were among the gold, silver and gems that they removed. They were in the trunk of Captain Boig when Keating, by his own admission, pushed Boig into the Pacific where he was devoured by sharks.

When young Billy Boig Jr. was abandoned in Central America by Keating, he had these gems in a small leather bag containing twenty-seven gems from the lost treasure of Lima. Young Boig made his way back to his family in St. John's, and the gems have been in the possession of descendants of the Boig's since that time.

Lima Cathedral which housed the famous Cocos Island Treasure.

Mr. Fraser vividly described a package being delivered to his aunt's home on Glenridge Crescent in St. John's when he was a child, and all his relatives being summoned there for its opening. The package came from England, possibly the remaining estate of William Boig Jr., and contained a collection of gems. These were divided among his uncles and aunts, and most of them were converted into jewelry and survive to this day.

Another interesting piece of information, which I discovered, is that Captain Keating may have made a third visit to retrieve treasure from Cocos Island. According to that claim, made by St. John's neighbours of Keating in a letter to the press, Stephen Johnston, one of the founders of Baine Johnston & Co. Ltd. of Newfoundland, financed a third expedition to the Island and brought back more of the pirates' loot. Johnston had Michael Kearney build him a four-yarder[2] one hundred ton vessel for the expedition. He named it the *Gauntlet* and he sailed with Keating and a twenty-six man crew to Cocos Island.

The last person in Newfoundland to possess the maps and directions to the treasure was Captain Nicholas Fitzgerald of

Harbour Grace. Nick Fitzgerald died on June 1, 1906, at the residence of his son Patrick on Water Street in Harbour Grace. Fitzgerald, or someone representing him, visited a bank in Lima while checking the veracity of Keating's story, and removed some documentation that verified the existence of the treasure. It's possible that these papers may today be gathering dust in some basement or attic of a Newfoundland home. These papers, if found, might be quite valuable to modern day researchers.

Cocos Island today is a world heritage site and treasure hunting is no longer permitted.

Carter-Fitzgerald Photography

Steward Fraser, descendant of Captain William Boig of lost treasure of Lima fame and Jack Fitzgerald, author of *Treasure Island Revisited* which tells the story of Captains John Keating and William Boig and their findings of the world famous treasure in 1841.

The major portion of the famous pirate treasures remains hidden on the Island and in recent years has caught the interest of filmmakers and writers on several continents. More than twenty-four books on famous pirate treasures of the world have included chapters on the Cocos Island Treasure and Captains Keating and Boig. In addition, documentaries and feature movies have been made about the story. Writers in several countries claim that this story of the lost Lima treasure with its Newfoundland connections inspired Robert Louis Stevenson to write his classic *Treasure Island*. Only *Treasure Island Revisited* has brought together the whole story with its Newfoundland connections.

[1] Although books and films refer to the treasures on Cocos Island as the Lost Treasure of Lima, that is a mistake. The Lima Treasure was recovered days after it was stolen. The treasure that was stolen and which ended up buried on Cocos Island was the Ecclesiastical Treasure stolen from the Lima Cathedral.

[2] A 'yard' on a ship is a large wooden or metal spar crossing the mast of a ship horizontal or diagonal from which the sails are set.

COCOS ISLAND STORY IN PHOTOGRAPHS

Jack Fitzgerald Collection
Breakfast Island just off the shore of Cocos Island has been referred to in treasure maps and described as having the appearances of a sleeping lion. This photograph was taken in 1898.

Montmorency Expedition arriving on the Island in 1898.

Jack Fitzgerald Collection
In Robert Louis Stevenson's *Treasure Island* there is a character named Ben Gun, the hermit of the island who spent years alone seeking the treasure. Stevenson's character Ben Gun is believed to have been inspired by the German-born hermit of Cocos Island, Augustus Gissler shown on Cocos Island next to his homemade shelter.

189

CHAPTER 11

SHANANDITHIT NOT LAST BEOTHUCK

BEOTHUCK RACE WIPED OUT?

Although historians and writers point out that the Beothuck Race was wiped out by white settlers and that Shanandithit, who died in 1829, was the last of the Beothucks, a letter showing that the Beothucks were still around fifteen years later went unnoticed by historians for almost two centuries.

The letter, published in 1845, included some important historical information about the Beothucks in Newfoundland but was overshadowed by other topics in the letter which reflected upon the character of city merchants. Apart from the very brief notoriety the letter attracted during the controversy, it was quickly forgotten.

MERCHANT'S LETTER FOCUSED ON MANY TOPICS

I came across the letter published in *The Newfoundlander* in 1845, while researching an off-beat story of old St. John's regarding the popularity of cigar smoking among the population of the city in the 1840s. The 2000 word letter covered a variety of topics about Newfoundland including a short, but revealing section on the Beothucks which showed that the race was not extinct. However, that information attracted no public reaction.

Comments regarding a cigar smuggling operation in St. John's Harbour caused quite a stir. Remarkably, if it had not been for that controversial information about cigar smuggling, the letter would still be lost to history.

The Pearson family was well-known in town in the 1840s. John Pearson Jr. the son of a St. John's merchant who had offices in England, sent the letter to a clerk in his father's office at Manchester. Pearson had no intention of having his letter published. The clerk who received it submitted the letter to an English publication named *Simmond's Colonial* which found it interesting enough to publish.

The Newfoundlander was on that newspaper's mailing list and received a copy in the mail. After reading Pearson's letter, the editor decided to publish it. The part of the lengthy letter which attracted public attention accused Spanish ships of smuggling large quantities of cigars into St. John's and selling them to local merchants. This allegation reflected badly on city merchants and angered Pearson Sr., a prominent merchant himself, who wrote a letter to the newspaper disavowing any association with the letter written by his son.

The Newfoundlander responded to the newspaper story by denouncing the statements as, "...so absurd and inaccurate that we felt it to be our duty to comment somewhat sharply on the whole proceeding. The fact of its not having been intended for publication is no justification."

John Pearson Jr. defended his letter saying:

I gave a good deal of information respecting the climate, customs etc. and when I named the cigars and the quantity which I had been told were got on shore by one vessel, I did so, merely to give an idea as to the vast extent which I believe that sort of thing is carried on.

The historic portion of the letter, which was not questioned at all, was the description of the Beothucks being still around in 1845, and even visiting St. John's. This was sixteen years after history recorded the race as being extinct. The letter stated:

I must also tell you that we have occasional visits paid us by some of the Indians, who come from many miles into the interior — some as far as 200 to 300 miles. They usually come in the winter, when they can travel across mountain, river, and plain with greater ease than at any other period of the year.

They come across the country with no other guide than the sun and that natural instinct with which the Indian is known to be gifted. The race of North American Indians is now nearly extinct, having been driven from these shores by the English, French and other traders, who, sad to say, in years that are past, have killed, robbed and deceived them for the sake of their furs.[1]

I have seen three since my residence in St. John's; one was a fine fellow and just what you would imagine from the accounts you read of them. He came to trade in furs and then bought what he needed, such as powder, shot and articles of clothing. He came here also with a party of shipwreck sailors, who had been cast ashore a long way up the country from which they had no means of rescuing themselves had they not been fortunate in meeting with this Indian who undertook to convey them to St. John's. Although he had never been here in his life, he succeeded in bringing them through in seventeen days, with no other guide, save their Indian friend with no place of rest but the ground, at that time covered with snow, dependant also upon the Indian's rifle for procuring them food.

In fact, I never heard of so wonderful a performance. You may imagine what a forlorn looking set of beings they were when they arrived at their desired haven; the poor fellows were nearly dead, but the Indian appeared no more fatigued than if he had only come off one day's journey, although he had carried his gun and a quantity of furs. They were three days at a time without tasting food, but then had the good fortune to kill a deer, which served them some time, or else they would have perished in the snow. How would you or I fancy traveling across a country of that kind under similar circumstances? But what suffering will not man endure to save life?

I fear I am wearying your patience, but as I have no other information to give you, you must take the will for the deed. I find I have already extended this letter to a much greater length than I had anticipated when I took up my pen and think it is now about time that my yarn should be spun out; so as the sailors say I must come to and drop anchor.

Yours ever truly,
John A. Pearson

Not the last Beothuck

Not everyone believed the Red Indian race ended with the death of Shanandithit. Joseph Noad, Surveyor General of Newfoundland, in a lecture he delivered in 1852, said, "The Micmacs still believe in the existence of the Beothucks and say some twenty-five years ago (1827) the whole tribe passed over to Labrador, and that the place of their final embarkation, as they allege, is yet discernible."

BURIAL RECORD

In researching this story, I found the following item recorded in the Church of England burial records for that decade. Her burial record was entered in church records two days after she had passed away. It stated:

June 8, 1829. Interred Nancy, Shanawdithe [sic] at 23, South Side. (Very probably the last of the aborigines). (Signed) Frederick H. Carrington A.B. Rector. St. John's.

Her obituary was published in *The Conception Bay Mercury* on Friday, June 19, 1829, and reads as follows:

On Saturday night, the 6th instant, at the Hospital[2], Shanandithit, the female Indian, one of the Aborigines of this Island. She died of consumption, a disease which seems to have been remarkably prevalent among her tribe, and which has unfortunately been fatal to all who have fallen into the hands of the settlers.

Since the departure of Mr. Cormack from the island, this poor woman has had an asylum afforded her in the house of James Simms, Esq. Attorney General, where every attention has been paid to her wants and comfort; under the table professional advice of Dr. Carson, who has most kindly and liberally attended her for many months past. It was hoped that her health might have been re-established. Lately, however, her disease had become daily more formidable, and her strength had rapidly declined, and a short time since, it was deemed advisable to send her to the Hospital, where her sudden decease has but too soon fulfilled the fears that were entertained for her.

With Shanandithit, has probably expired nearly the last of the Native Indians of the Island; indeed it is considered doubtful whether any of them now survive. It is certainly a matter of regret that those individuals who have interested themselves most to support the causes of science and humanity by the civilization of these Indians, should have so unfortunately failed by this sudden termination to their hopes.

They have, however, notwithstanding the calculating apathy with which their views have been met by some, the satisfaction of knowing that their object has been to mitigate sufferings of humanity, and that at least they have endeavoured to pay a portion of that immense debt which is due from the European settlers of Newfoundland to these unfortunate Indians, who have been so long opprest [sic] and persecuted, and are finally almost exterminated.

The account of her death which appeared in London newspapers was more certain about the fate of the Native Newfoundland Indian Race. It described Shanandithit as the last of the Beothuck Race. A half century later writers were claiming that the Beothuck Race had been wiped out and that Shanandithit was the last of the Beothucks.

HEAD SEVERED

Before her burial, Dr. William Carson removed her head and sent it to London for medical study. The head ended up in a British Museum and was destroyed when the building was bombed during World War II. St. Mary's Church was later built near Shanandithit's burial site.

BEOTHUCKS IN NOVA SCOTIA

Newfoundland author and historian, the late Harold Horwood believed there is still Beothuck blood among the Micmacs of Nova Scotia. In his book *Newfoundland,* Horwood stated:

At least one Beothuck boy was adopted into the Micmac tribe as a few had been adopted earlier, and grew up speaking his native, as well as adopted, language. This boy, named Hop, has descendants living today among the Micmacs of Nova Scotia, and though a few other Micmacs also claim Beothuck descent, these are the only people for whom there is clear evidence of descent from even

195

one of the original Red Men, who, because of their attachment to red ochre, gave their nickname to all the other native tribes of North America.

SEEKS BEOTHUCK GRAVES

Over recent years, a man who is a descendant of a man who captured Beothucks has taken up studying their history and has traveled the places where they lived in search of grave sites. He is certain he has located a Beothuck burial site and has in his possession what he believes to be Beothuck bones. He feels that DNA testing using these bones could determine whether or not there are still people living in Newfoundland with Beothuck blood.

[1] In the period this letter was written, it was not accepted as fact that Shanandithit was the last of her race as noted in the church death records. Only decades later did writers become more certain that Nancy Shanandithit was the last of the Beothucks.

[2] The Hospital, likely referred to the hospital at Victoria Park which was the only non-military hospital in the St. John's area in that period.

CHAPTER 12

VAUDEVILLE OF OLD ST. JOHN'S

FIRST IN ST. JOHN'S

The first vaudeville company to show an interest in establishing in St. John's was the Acker Vaudeville Company of Halifax. In March 1910, Mr. A. West, business representative and part owner of the company, leased the Star Hall on Henry Street to present vaudeville shows. West and his wife were known in vaudeville circles in Canada and the United States for their comic and acting abilities. They starred in the first Acker Vaudeville Show produced at the Star Theatre on March 30, 1910. The show went on for nine nights and drew capacity crowds each night. The program included:

The Irish Champion Dancers, Riley and Fleming
The comedy play, 'Taming a Husband' with the Wests
The pretty breezy comedienne Greta Byron in 'Some Class'
The funny jugglers, Owley and Randall in 'Tumble Tom'
The Roberts Indoor Circus that included 'A marvelous troupe of trained bears, monkeys and dogs.'

Supplying music was the famous local Star Orchestra. Two shows were held each evening at 7:15 and 9:00 p.m. Prices were ten cents for general admission and twenty-five cents for choice seating.

Mr. West told reporters, "St. John's is indeed the liveliest and prettiest little city I have visited in years." He said his company had plans to establish a full-time theatre in St. John's. These plans did not materialize, and this was the last we heard of the Acker Vaudeville's intention of permanently setting up in St. John's.

THE ROSSLEYS STORM THE TOWN

Vaudeville was immensely popular in old-time St. John's. Its shows in the city attracted crowds at church halls and public theatres. Initially, the main vaudeville theatres were the Nickel on Military Road and the Casino in the Total Abstinence Building on Duckworth Street. The British Hall later turned to vaudeville. In 1911, the Casino Theatre brought in the Rossleys, a Scottish family famous on both sides of the Atlantic. They came to St. John's for a six-week booking, but their instant popularity with theatre goers in St. John's extended their stay at the Casino to nine months.

RAZOR JIM

Crowds lined up at the Casino in the summer of 1911 for the Rossleys' performance of 'Razor Jim.' Jack Rossley played Razor Jim; J.J. O'Grady, Manager Sokum; Marie Rossley, Adlina Patti; Vivian Densmore, Anna Held and Bonnie Rossley played Chrattea. Two stage backgrounds were used: one, a street in Chicago and the second, Sokum's Office. The show was billed as "A laugh from start to finish," and lived up to its expectations.

Other summer shows that had crowds lining up to get a seat included 'Via Wireless' and 'Before the Vacation.' A review of 'Via Wireless' in *The Evening Telegram* on August 19, 1911, described the play as, "A great success. It was a merry melange of fun from start to finish. As usual, Mr. and Mrs. Rossley were the leading figures and their comedy was of a most mirth provoking quality."

The newspaper advertisements for 'Before the Vacation' described it as, "A screaming adaptation of Gus Edward's great musical comedy success."

Another great hit for the Rossleys at the Casino was the comedy "Tony the Tailor." It was described as, "The greatest of all farcical comedies." It is interesting to note that while the Rossleys were attracting capacity crowds at the Casino during August 1911, the Nickel Theatre was featuring the silent film, Charles Dicken's *A Christmas Carol* which newspaper ads described as, "Depicting cheerfulness of the festive season."

THE ROSSLEYS OPEN THEIR OWN THEATRE

The people of St. John's lamented the conclusion of the Rossleys at the Casino in September 1911. The vaudeville family was more popular than ever in St. John's, a sentiment which prompted the following commentary in *The Evening Telegram* of September 30, 1911:

Now that the end of the season for the Casino theatrical performances is approaching, the hall is filled nightly

198

by people who recognize in the Rossley trio the most versatile entertainment seen here for a long time. Last night, the house was packed and Jack Rossley especially was greeted with the applause his mirth provoking delineations well deserve. The public will be sorry to lose the Rossleys, who have entertained them now for nine months, and we hope to see Jack, Maria and Bonnie prolonging their stay here.

If anyone in St. John's thought they had seen the last of Jack Rossley, they were mistaken. The Rossleys had fallen in love with the city and decided to stay here and open their own vaudeville theatre. They took up residence at 284 Duckworth Street and negotiated with the Star of the Sea Association to lease its theatre on Henry Street. A little more than a month later on Monday, October 24, 1911, the new Rossley Star Theatre opened. The following item appeared in *The Evening Telegram* on October 25, 1911:

PANL

Star Theatre on Henry Street which was used as the Rossley Star Theatre during the Vaudeville Era.

Rossley's New Star Theatre

Last night saw the opening of the Star Theatre and Jack Rossley was well repaid for his expense and trouble, many being unable to gain admission. Everyone was surprised and delighted at the transformation. The Rossleys on their appearance received hearty applause, and on the second show, Jack, tired as he was, had to give the wooden leg dance before he was allowed to leave the stage. As children are not admitted at night without their parents, a funny farce suitable for children will be given on Saturday afternoon.

In his advertisements announcing the opening, Rossley noted that the theatre was cleaned from floor to ceiling and there was a new stage, new electric light service, new box office, new costumes and new songs and dances.

The general admission at the Rossley was ten cents and reserved seats were twenty cents each. Just a short distance away at the T. A. Hall (Casino Theatre), six vaudeville acts were being staged, but the prices more expensive than the Rossley. The T. A. charged twenty, thirty, forty and fifty cents for night performances. The matinee cost; ten, twenty and thirty cents.

By December, the Rossleys were featuring 'A Big Double Show' on Monday, Tuesday and Wednesday. These included the Brayleys in a comedy act, Buster Brown and the Clown. Dainty Lillie Brayley, a child performer, was featured in songs and dances. Bonnie Rossley, also a child, and, who had become an instant hit at the Casino when she was brought on stage in a small airplane singing, 'Come Josephine in My Flying Machine,' brought the house down with her new song, 'Skinny.' Two shows were held nightly at 7:30 and 9:30 p.m. and included three reels of moving pictures. These were silent films, and the Star Orchestra supplied background music for them.

PRIDE AND JOY OF ST. JOHN'S

In a very short time, the Rossleys became the pride and joy of St. John's. Advertisements for 'The Rossley Star Theatre' billed it as, "The Best Vaudeville Theatre in St. John's." This was a reputation 'The Rossley' lived up to, and in a few years, they were operating three theatres: 'Rossley's East End Star Theatre' was at the Star Hall on Henry Street, 'Ours,' also known as 'Rossley West,' was located at the corner of Hutching Street and Water Street, and 'The Rossley Wabana Theatre' was operated on Bell Island.

200

All the Rossley theatres featured entertainment for the entire family and brought in top vaudeville acts from England, Scotland and the United States. They also brought in circus acts from Barnum and Bailey. The main Rossley Theatre was the one at the Star Hall on Henry Street.

The Rossley family of entertainers included Jack and Marie and their two children, Bonnie and Victor. Jack and Marie were world famous dancers, their daughter Bonnie was a talented singer, 'danseuse' and comedienne. Victor joined the family on stage several years after they opened their theatre in St. John's. Both Jack and Marie were talented writers as well.

Rossley did a hilarious act called *Peg Leg Jack* in which he feigned a wooden leg and went through a routine of dance and song to the delight of audiences. In recent years, Greg Donnehey of Carlton Showband fame also thrilled audiences across Newfoundland, Canada and Ireland with a similar dance in addition to his ever popular Laughing Policeman.

LOCALS INCLUDED
Rossley included local actors in his vaudeville shows. City residents J.J. O'Grady who played Percival Archie Lighthead, and Vivian Densmore who played Dolly Dimple in *Before the Vacation* were regulars with the Rossleys at the Casino and at the new Rossley Star Theatre. The famous character of old St. John's Mickey Quinn performed on stage at the Rossley Theatre, The Star, and the Casino under the name 'Dan McQuinton.'[1]

INSTALLED 'OPERA BALCONIES' AT STAR HALL
While leasing the Star Hall, the Rossleys closed down in the summer of 1915 to have 'opera seats' constructed on the western walls of the theatre so that those who could pay the extra costs could watch the stage shows from the privacy of these seats.[2] They were successful and the seats are still there today.

DAINTY BONNIE ROSSLEY RECITES VETERAN'S POEM
Corporal Jack Turner of St. John's, while in a foxhole at the battlefront in Europe during WWI, wrote a poem describing the soldier's craving for cigarettes. It quickly became popular, first, among fellow soldiers, then, among the people back home in Newfoundland. The poem was simply called 'Fags' and was pub-

lished in local newspapers. In fact, 'Fags' became so popular that the Rossley Vaudeville family included it in their show.

On Tuesday nights, the Rossleys included an act called 'Country Store,' which featured a folksy type entertainment. On one occasion the Imperial Tobacco Company donated five hundred cigarettes which the Rossleys presented as one prize.[3] So on Tuesday April 30, 1917, Miss Bonnie Rossley recited 'Fags' on stage at the Rossley Theatre.

The following is part of that poem:

'FAGS' (CIGARETTES)

When the cold is making ice cream of the marrow of your bones,
When you're shaking like a jelly and your feet are dead as stones,
When your clothes and boots and blankets, and your rifle and your kit,
Are soaked from Hell to Breakfast, and the dug out where you sit
Is leaking like a basket, and upon the muddy floor
The water lies in filthy pools, six inches deep or more;
Tho' life seems cold and mis'rable, and all the world is wet,
You'll always get thro' somehow if you've got a cigarette.

When you're lying in a listening post, way out beyond the wire,
While a blasted Hun, behind a gun, is doing rapid fire;
When the bullets whine above your head and sputter on the ground,
When your eyes are strained for every move, your ears for every sound–
You'd bet your life a Hun patrol is prowling somewhere near–
A shiver runs along your spine that's very much like fear;
You'll stick it to the finish – but I'll make a little bet,
You'd feel a whole lot better if you had a cigarette.

– Corporal Jack Turner[4]

Controversy

The Rossleys caused some controversy when, contrary to the custom of the time, they opened their theatre during Lent. Other theatre owners complained, and a rumour was circulated that the Roman Catholic Church had condemned the theatre. The Rossleys quickly denied the claim and said that all profits collected during Lent would be donated to a charity. Jack Rossley also pointed out that they had hired eighty young children from the neighbourhood and trained them to participate in theatre performances. He explained that this was done to put money in the pockets of poor families. On the last night of Lent the Rossleys held a bread night. Admission to the theatre was a loaf of bread, and all bread collected was distributed to poor families in St. John's. In addition, the Rossleys raised money to help the CLB and to send cigarettes to the troops overseas. They also raised funds for other charitable causes.

Rossleys Leave Newfoundland

When the Rossley lease ended, they moved to British Hall for a year and then in 1917 took their show on the road across Canada and the United States. Before departing, they bid farewell to the people of St. John's through a paid advertisement in *The Evening Telegram* on July 1917.

MICKEY MICHAEL

Vaudeville did not end with the departure of the Rossleys. The remaining theatres in the city continued to mix vaudeville with live films. On May 14, 1924, the Crescent Theatre, which was located on the site later occupied by the Arcade Stores on Water Street, introduced a young male soprano who is still remembered as one of Newfoundland's finest entertainers. Describing his performance the next day, *The Evening Telegram* reported, "Master Mickey Michael, the clever boy soprano, was obliged to respond to several curtain calls. This youthful vocalist seems to get more popular at each appearance."[5]

In addition to the vaudeville shows, the Crescent featured a Friday night Amateur Contest which was open to the public. The introduction of talking movies put an end to the Vaudeville Era in Newfoundland.

REMEMBERING OLD THEATRES

The Nickel Theatre, which became a movie theatre in 1907, was also known as The Irish. On Saturday, June 25, 1960, the Nickel showed its last movie. It was called *Damn Yankees* starring Tab Hunter. The Nickel Theatre was located in the old Benevolent Irish Society Building opposite the Roman Catholic Basilica on Military Road.

THE MAJESTIC

The Majestic Theatre opened to the public on March 3, 1919. Its original owners were Tom Coady and Tom O'Neill. It was later taken over by Stan Condon of Real Estate fame in St. John's. The Majestic closed in early 1953 and was sold on May 15, 1953, to the firm Majestic Sales which converted it into a retail shop and warehouse. The Majestic Theatre was located at the corner of Queen's Road and Duckworth Street.

THE FIRST TALKING FILMS

Although St. John's history books credit the Nickel and Majestic Theatres with being the first theatres in Newfoundland to introduce talking pictures, that distinction was actually earned fifteen years earlier by the Casino Theatre.

Honorable Joseph R. Smallwood in one of his famous *Barrelman* radio shows aired in November 1938 told his listeners:

> If I were to ask you when the first talking pictures were shown in St. John's, you would probably answer: The Desert Song, at the Nickel Theatre, about five or six years ago. But you'd be quite wrong, for it's no less than twenty-three years ago that the first talkies came to this city.
>
> They were shown in the Casino Theatre in the month of May, 1914, and consisted of the Edison Talking Pictures.
>
> John J. McGraw, the famous baseball manager of those days, was shown in a picture on the screen, and you could hear him talking quite plainly as he gave a chat on the game of baseball. Then there was a picture showing a group of grand opera singers doing the famous sextet from the opera "Lucia." You could hear them singing as you watched the picture. There was also a picture of the

vaudeville team of Seymour, Dempsey and Seymour, Kings of Mirth, as they cracked their gags and jokes. The talking pictures ran in the old Casino for a period of two or three weeks.[6]

THE CASINO BECOMES THE CAPITOL

The Casino Theatre became The Capitol Theatre in June 1935. It was located on the top floor of the Total Abstinence Building on Duckworth Street with its entrance from Henry Street. The theatre was destroyed by fire on October 26, 1946, and was rebuilt and reopened on November 20, 1950. It changed hands several times and went out of business permanently because it couldn't compete with the new theatres at the Avalon Mall which opened in 1967.

TALKING MOVIES ON PERMANENT BASIS

The Nickel and Majestic Theatres converted to talking motion pictures in 1929 and jointly became the first theatres in Newfoundland and Labrador to feature talking movies on a permanent basis. These first showings took place on August 26, 1929. The Nickel featured *The Desert Song* which starred John Bola and Myrna Loy while the Majestic featured *The Fall of Eve* which was a narrative delivered by Patsy Ruth Miller.

CRESCENT

The Crescent Theatre was advertising in newspapers in 1910, and may have opened before that year. It was originally owned by Patrick Laracy who drowned on the *Florizel* in 1918. J.P. Kieley, owner of the Nickel Theatre, was also a victim of the *Florizel* disaster. Edward Boulos succeeded Laracy as owner and operated the Crescent until it closed down the late spring of 1947.

THE STAR

The Star Theatre was operated by Stan Condon who leased the top floor of the Star Hall on Henry Street in 1932, after the original Star had been destroyed by fire and was rebuilt soon after. The old Star Theatre had been showing movies since 1911 when Jack Rossley operated it and sometimes included films with live vaudeville shows. On its last day as a theatre on May 25, 1953, a double feature was shown: *Walking My Baby Back Home* with

Donald O'Connor, Janet Leigh and Buddy Hackett followed by *Tumbleweed* starring Audi Murphy. For a short while after it was leased by the Federal Government and used as a post office.

In 1997, the old theatre was cleaned up and used for the Flower Hill Reunion that year. The old theatre accommodated five hundred people for a banquet and was used over the three day reunion for live entertainment, a stage show and several dances. The opera boxes put there in 1915 by the Rossley family were still accessible in 1997.

THE REGAL THEATRE

On the north side of New Gower Street, west of Casey Street, was the Regal Theatre which was also known as the Little Star. The exact date of its closure is not known, but Owen Moore of Hamilton Avenue says it was in the early 1940s. He recalled escaping from the Regal on the day it was destroyed by fire. It later became the Belmont Tavern owned by the Byrne brothers, Jack and Jim.

THE QUEEN THEATRE BECAME THE YORK THEATRE

The Queen Theatre, originally called The Wonderland Theatre, changed its name to the New Queen Theatre and then the York Theatre. Talking movies came to the New Queen Theatre on May 13, 1931. The theatre had been closed for several weeks preparing for the event. The Queen's owner Johnny Duff had the latest RCA Photophone Senior Equipment installed in his theatre which enabled people to hear as well as see "...everything in Paramount Pictures." The first talking features shown at the opening were:

Paramount on Parade – which featured dance, song, comedy and drama.

Sweepin' the Clouds Away – with Maurice Chevalier

Insurance – with Eddie Cantor

The admission was thirty-five cents. There were two shows each night. The Queen was between George Street and Water Street with its main entrance from Queen Street. Around 1939, it was connected by the construction of a long hallway to Duff's building on Water Street which became the main entrance to the movie theatre. It was renamed the "York Theatre."

In the 1960s, the York Theatre closed and was turned into a warehouse which was destroyed by fire around mid-May 1988.

City Archives of St. John's

Paramount Theatre on Military Road during WWII. Note light trim on bumper and fenders which were needed for driving during wartime blackouts.

THE PARAMOUNT

The Paramount Theatre was located on Harvey Road, west of The Rooms. It was opened on September 1, 1944, and was considered the most modern and plush theatre in all Newfoundland. It was closed down after its roof collapsed during February 1973. The movie showing at the time was *Mary Queen of Scots*. Nobody was injured in the mishap.

The Paramount was constructed by B.D. Parsons, the same man who constructed the Old Colony Club, Adelaide Motors and the King's Bridge Apartments.

Newspapers described the Paramount as the showplace of Newfoundland. The theatre had a seating capacity for 1200 people. It also had an air conditioning system which changed the air in the theatre every five minutes.

The Paramount was financed by a group of businessmen headed by W.R. Goobie. It was turned over to the Newfoundland Amusements Ltd., a subsidiary of Famous Players Theatre, which, in turn, was owned by Paramount Pictures of Hollywood.

The Paramount was built on the same scale as the York in Montreal and the Eglington in Toronto. It was managed by Nora Hogan who also managed the Capitol Theatre. The movie which was played at the opening of the Paramount was *Broadway Rhythm* starring George Murphy and Ginny Simms.

THE CORNWALL THEATRE

The Cornwall Theatre was on Lemarchant Road in a building used today as Smith Stockley Plumbing just opposite the West End Fire Hall. It opened on Friday, October 1948, and closed in 1955, and newspapers described it as, "A well-equipped modern theatre."

The Cornwall was designed by Messrs Luke, Little and Mace of Montreal and was constructed by Concrete Products. Each seat in the theatre was accurately positioned facing the screen, thus eliminating all awkward angles.

A gold coloured stage curtain was imported from New York and was supplied by Motion Picture Supplies Ltd. The movie equipment was made by Motiograph and was installed by C.H. Hutton & Sons of St. John's.

Alexander McKenzie of United Movies Ltd. supervised the outfitting of the theatre. Unlike other theatres in St. John's, the Cornwall hired usherettes instead of ushers. The manager of the Cornwall was Thomas Hibbs and many movies shown there were British produced films.

The first movie shown was *Sun Valley Serenade* starring Sonja Heini and John Payne. Matinees were twenty cents for adults and ten cents for children. Evening admissions were forty cents for adults and twenty cents for children.

RADIO CHILD STAR

Jack Fitzgerald collection
Singer Jimmy Linegar

The Kid Ranger – A famous child performer of the late 1940s and early 1950s throughout Newfoundland was *The Kid Ranger*. He was popular for his guitar playing and singing of country music, and was often described as a young 'Hank Snow.' By 1953, he became the youngest Newfoundlander to have his own radio show.

At twelve years old, Jimmy Linegar of Shea Heights, then known as *The Kid Ranger*, could be heard every weeknight on CJON radio at 7:15. He made many appearances on local stage and radio shows and was also known as Jimmy Linegar, *The Singing Ranger.*

Another popular CJON radio show was called 'House Party.' Hosted by John Nolan, the show was aired live nightly at 11:00 when Nolan, speaking over a musical background, suggested listeners to, "Let's have a party." The show was live and traveled to the many nightclubs around town where live brass bands performed. A popular spot for the show was the swank Old Colony Club.

CONNECTION TO BOSTON POPS

John Williams, who succeeded Arthur Fiedler in 1979 as conductor of the Boston Pops Orchestra, had Newfoundland connections. In 1953-54 Williams served at the U.S. Pepperrell Air Force Base in St. John's with the 596th Air Force Band.

As a member of that band, Mr. Williams, a pianist, performed with the stage band 'Sky Nights.' He shared the stage with Ralph Walker, another pianist; George (Buddy) Pennington, a drummer; and Tom Severino, who played bass, all of whom married Newfoundland girls.

Of the three, Ralph Walker, who married Millicent Vivian of St. John's, stayed in Newfoundland after completing his military service. Walker was well-known around Newfoundland and was a regular performer at the old Hotel Newfoundland.

Tom Severino married Joan Laite and George Pennington married Betty Cromwell, both ladies were from St. John's.

In addition to serving as conductor of the Boston Pops, John Williams has written the musical scores for movies including *Star Wars, Jaws,* the *Superman* series and the theme for NBCs nightly news on Channel 11 with Tom Brokaw.

JOHNNY BURKE'S OBITUARY

The famous Johnny Burke, the Bard of Prescott Street, entertained Newfoundlanders throughout his lifetime with his music, song, writings and plays. People in St. John's waited enthusiastically for his next song, play or his celebrated annual Regatta program which was filled with humour and anecdotes about the Royal St. John's Regatta. Burke was also noted for his annual St. Patrick's night plays. His operettas drew the rich and poor alike, and Sir William Whiteway commented after attending one of the Burke productions[7] that he never laughed so much in all his life.

Johnny Burke passed away on August 8, 1930, several days before the annual Regatta. He was buried in an unmarked grave in Belvedere Cemetery in St. John's. The late John White, who performed on stage as Johnny Burke, compiled Burke's songs in a book which is still available in Newfoundland libraries. H.F. Shortis, who recorded much of the offbeat St. John's history, wrote Burke's obituary in which he preserved some of John Burke's biographical information. He stated:

> There passed away on Saturday last, after a short illness, and fortified by the rites of the Catholic Church, Mr. John Burke, undoubtedly one of our most popular and highly respected citizens, in the 79th year of his age. Mr. Burke was born in St. John's and was the son of the famous seal-killer and master mariner, Captain John and Mrs. Burke. Few men were more favourably known in St. John's, in fact, over the whole country, than was the deceased gentleman. He was a man of unblemished reputation throughout his life, possessing the natural wit and humour of his Irish ancestors. He was a poet of considerable ability, and some of his effusions were literary gems, and at many a fireside throughout the country, families were made happy by the rendering and singing of his songs, which convulsed the company with laughter. Some of his operas were side-splitting such as *The Topsail Geisha*, *Cotton's Patch*, etc., and were greatly enjoyed by the large audiences which attended the performances in our various halls.

Even the great Chieftan Sir William V. Whiteway told me upon one occasion that he never enjoyed himself since he came to this country as much as he did one night while watching Topsail Geisha and that he was going to see the opera again.

The deceased was a type of the good old families who by the simplicity of his life, the generosity of his character, the zeal for his religion and true patriotism, by his self-respect, he was respected by all. He was a most devoted and faithful member of Holy Church. He died as he had lived, fortified by the rites of the Catholic Church, at peace with God and his neighbour, holding the respect of his fellow man of all classes. A man who rejoiced when you rejoiced and sympathized with your adversity – a friend to little children, an adviser to the middle-aged. It was always a pleasure for me to write up the heroes of the past, and the father of 'Johnnie' Burke was undoubtedly one of these. For years he was master of Hon. Laurence O'Brien's brigantine 'Hollyhock,' and was most successful at the seal fishery. When our great sealing fleet was almost destroyed during the terrible disaster of what is known as the Spring of the Wadhams, Captain Burke was one of the lucky ones, and not alone did he bring in a good trip of seals, but he also came across two vessels that were abandoned, one of them was the *Dash*, owned by the great Captain Joe Houlahan, put ten of his men on board each of them and they were brought safely into St. John's. Of course, Captain Burke remained on board his own ship – the *Hollyhock.*

Success followed Captain Burke for many years, but on the 1st day of January 1865, when in command of the brigantine *Nautilus*, he lost his life when the ship was lost at Petty Harbour Motion. He was on a passage from Sydney to St. John's. All but three were lost: Captain Burke, his son William, a Mr. Bell (the mate), John Seeley and James Lane. The following were saved: William Dwyer, James Cash and James Foran. The deceased gentleman (Johnny Burke) has left to mourn his sister, Annie, and several relatives, amongst them Professor Charles Hutton and W.S. Dunphy, of the Commissioner of the Poor Office, who are cousins, as was also the illustrious prelate Archbishop Howley. May he rest in peace.

[1] More on the life of Mickey Quinn, along with the largest collection of Mickey Quinn stories ever published in Newfoundland can be found in *Legacy of Laughter* by Jack Fitzgerald and published by Creative Publishers.

[2] The Star was partially destroyed by fire in 1932 and rebuilt the same year. The opera seats remained as part of the rebuilt theatre.

[3] Records do not show how the winner was chosen.

[4] By 1948, Turner was Lt. Colonel and had received the Order

of the British Empire and the Military Cross. He also served with
a Canadian Division in Russia on the side of the White Russian
Army during the Bolshevik Revolution. Under Commission of
Government he was in charge of the Government's Forestry
Division. *The Evening Telegram*, October 2, 1948.

[5] The leader of the NDP in Newfoundland, Lorraine Michael,
is the daughter of the famous Mickey Michael who became leg-
endary among entertainers of old St. John's.

[6] *The Best of the Barrelman (1938-1940) J.R. Smallwood as the
Barrelman* Edited by William Connors, published by Creative
Publishers, 1998.

[7] Likely a reference to Burke's most famous operettas *The
Topsail Geisha* performed at the Total Abstinence Hall on
Duckworth Street on February 2, 1881.

CHAPTER 13

NEWFOUNDLAND JOKES

COINCIDENCE

In the 1970s, Jack (John) Ford, who was a Japanese prisoner-of-war and present in Nagasaki when the atomic bomb was dropped in 1945, along with his wife Margaret, were on vacation with friends in New Orleans.

On a tour of a graveyard in the city, the Fords experienced a remarkable coincidence which despite the morbid surroundings sparked laughter among those present. They came upon the graves of a John and Margaret Ford. The epitaph read:

Here lies the body of Margaret Ford
I trust her soul is with the lord.
If for naught she left this life,
It's better to be dead
Than John Ford's wife.

Both Jack and Margaret still recall the epitaph with amusement, but Margaret relishes the anecdote far more than Jack.

MONTY'S BARGAIN

Monty Hanames pulled his car in front of Crotty's Store on Flower Hill and invited Tucker Crotty to come out and have a look at the car which he had just purchased.

"What do you think, Tucker? You'd never believe that this is a secondhand car, would ya?" asked Monty.

"Not in a lifetime!" said Tucker. "I thought you made it yourself?"

CAR THIEF ESCAPES POLICE

Soon after Confederation, the Constabulary was given new cars. One day, a fellow stole a car parked on Harvey Road and was making his getaway when two officers in one of the new police cars spotted the action and gave chase. With their siren sounding, they followed the stolen car across St. John's.

When they returned to headquarters, their Sergeant asked, "Well, did you catch the car thief?"

"Nearly! We got as far as Road de Luxe when we realized that our one thousand miles were up on the motor and we had to stop for an oil change," explained the officer.

Poor Night's Sleep

When old Mrs. Flynn went on her first vacation outside Newfoundland, her children arranged for her to have the best room in a Toronto hotel — one with a private adjoining bathroom.

The next morning, her daughter called and asked if she had a good night's sleep. "In that I did not," replied Mrs. Flynn, "I was afraid someone would want to use the toilet and the only way to it was through my room. The worry kept me awake all night."

The Fire Exit

In the late 1950s, Beth Kearsey, her sister, Rose Jackman, and sister-in-law, Jean Murphy, visited relatives in Toronto. Beth was more nervous than the others about staying in a hotel and worried about the possibility of fire. While the others unpacked, Beth went through the halls trying to locate the fire exit in case it had to be used.

She mistakenly opened the door to a public shower room, adjoining the indoor swimming pool, and came face to face with an elderly naked man taking a shower.

"I beg your pardon, sir, I'm looking for the fire escape," said Beth who quickly left, closing the door behind her.

She got a few yards down the hall when she heard a commotion behind her. When she turned to see what was happening, she saw the naked old man running down the hallway shouting, "Hey, lady, where's the fire?"

Torn Pants

Dickie Murphy asked his mother, "Mom, what would you rather see happen – that I fall off Abbott's roof, or that I tear the arse out of my pants?"

"I'd pray that you tore the arse out of your pants," replied his mom.

"Well, in that case, your prayers have been answered," Dickie bent over to show his mother.

TOWN AND COUNTRY

On Patricia Murphy's first day as a waitress at the Town and Country Restaurant on Water Street, she ran into her first problem customer.

After the customer had ordered and eaten a full course meal, he told Patricia, "I want you to put this meal on the cuff."

Patricia warned, "I'll throw the whole thing in your lap if you want it, but you'll bloody well pay for it."

•••

On another occasion, a customer, who felt he had been waiting too long for his meal, demanded to speak with the Manager.

"What for?" asked Patricia.

"We have complaints," answered the customer.

"Complaints?" questioned Patricia, "This is a restaurant, not a hospital."

SPEEDING EXPLANATION

Patricia Murphy was speeding in Waterford Bridge Road when a policeman pulled her in.

"What's wrong officer?" asked Patricia.

"Ma'm, you were going fifty miles an hour," the policeman politely explained.

"Good Lord, fifty miles an hour! That's impossible. I haven't been in the car an hour yet," commented Patricia as the policeman wrote her a traffic ticket.

FAMILIAR FACES

Doc Butler held all politicians in contempt, especially Billy Brown, who ran and was elected both provincially and federally for the Progressive Conservatives. During a federal election in St. John's West, Brown encountered Doc Butler as Doc was leaving Jim Fardy's Store on Flower Hill. Brown instantly seized Butler's hand and said, "My good fellow, I feel certain I have met you somewhere."

"No doubt, you have. I have been there many times," commented Doc who then walked on past Brown and up Flower Hill.

WHAT IF?

Jim Fardy asked Doc Butler, "What would your wife say if you bought a car?"

Doc considered the question for a moment, then replied, "She'd say, 'Watch it. Look out for the traffic light! Careful now! Don't hit that truck! Will you ever learn! Watch where you're going!' And she would certainly add a litany of curse words."

CANDIDATE WITH NO PRINCIPLES

Doc Butler was describing one of the political candidates speaking at a rally held in the CLB Armoury, St. John's, "He's the kind of fellow who would put wooden legs on chickens if he thought there were votes in doing it!"

FONCE THE CONSERVATIONIST

Fonce Howlett of the central area of old St. John's attended a Holy Cross Literary Society meeting in which the guest speaker gave an address dealing with the 'Forests of Newfoundland.'

At one point in the talk, the speaker asked, "Is there anyone in the audience who has done a single thing to conserve Newfoundland's timber resources?"

The question was met with a silent pause lasting for several seconds. Then Fonce stood up and proudly stated, "I once shot a woodpecker."

•••

On another occasion, it was Fonce's turn to act as chairman. Dr. Tolson Smith was speaking about the part human blood plays in the functioning of the body. After being introduced, Dr. Smith began, "Gentleman, I assume you all know what the inside of a corpuscle is like?"

Fonce, who was always ready to step in and interpret comments, stood beside Dr. Smith on stage and said, "Dr. Smith, I believe that most of us do, but you better explain it for the benefit of those who have never been inside one."

POW CLOTHING

Fonce Howlett recalled that things were very tough in the German prison camp where he was confined during part of WWII. He told his friends, "After several months there was very

216

little food and no clean clothing. The Sergeant turned up one morning claiming he had good news for us. When he told us that we would all be getting a change of clothing that day, there was instant cheering and clapping of hands among the POWs."

The Sergeant said, "Thank you, gentlemen. Now, Fonce, you change with Stan. Stan, you change with Bob. Bob, you change with Johnny.....etc. etc."

FONCE AND TOMMY TOE

Fonce Howlett told Tommy Toe, "There's a fellow at the Brownsdale Hotel who claims he is related to you and he can prove it."

"He's a complete fool," replied Tommy Toe.

"That is probably nothing more than a coincidence," commented Fonce.

FONCE AND SILK HAT

Fonce Howlett was telling his wife, Mary, about a meeting he attended at the Knights of Columbus the night before. He said, "The Grand Knight offered a silk hat to anyone who could stand up and honestly say that during his married life he had never kissed any woman but his own wife. And, Mary, would you believe it, not one man in the hall stood up. Not one!"

Mary asked, "Well, Fonce, why didn't you stand up?"

Fonce wasn't expecting Mary to question him. He hesitated and then replied, "Well, I gave it some thought, Mary, but I know I look like hell in a silk hat."

FONCE THE BAND LEADER

After looking over Fonce Howlett's application for the position to lead a swing orchestra in the late 1940s, the manager asked Fonce, "Are you sure you are qualified to lead a swing orchestra?"

Fonce answered, "Absolutely. No doubt about it. I have had two nervous breakdowns, was shell shocked in Italy, and I live in a flat above a family with ten noisy children, a dog and a cat."

NOT DEAD YET

Doc Butler commented, "Gee, Fonce, I thought you were dead."

Fonce replied, "That story is all around town, but it was another man. I knew it wasn't me as soon as I heard it."

BIG TESS AND THE WALSH PORTRAIT
Paddy decided to have Bill Walsh, a St. John's artist, paint a portrait of his wife, Big Tess. He asked Bill, "Do you think you can paint a lifelike portrait of Big Tess?"

"My friend, Paddy," answered Bill, " I can make it so lifelike that you will jump every time you see it."

PADDY'S LUCK
Paddy and Saltwater Bill agreed to meet on Casey Street for a fight. Paddy arrived on the scene first and was greeted by a neighbour who told him, "Paddy, Saltwater Bill is telling everyone that after he fights you, he is going to run away with Big Tess."

"Well, that takes the cake. The fight's off. I haven't got the heart to hit a friend," commented Paddy.

BIG TESS AT BEAUTY SHOP
Big Tess had never been inside a beauty salon. She always wore her hair in a bun covered with a red bandana which she tied around a flowery hat. Her physical appearance attracted much attention and was a factor in her becoming a town character in St. John's. One day, Lucy Left Leg persuaded Big Tess to go to Milady's Beauty Salon on New Gower Street.

Fonce Howlett, a neighbour of Big Tess, told his friends, "Big Tess went into Milady's alright. She went in looking like a little old woman and came out looking like a little old man."

BIG TESS GETS A HEADACHE
After spending a long evening visiting Big Tess and Paddy McGrath at their Clifford Street home, Bessie said, "Well, I must get on home."

"Don't let us keep you, if you really have to go," said Tess who was bored to the extreme.

"I really have to leave, but I did enjoy the evening. Do you know that when I came here earlier today I had a headache, but now I lost it," said Bessie.

"Oh, you haven't lost it," Tess commented. "I got it now."

NOT THAT DARK

Paddy asked Big Tess to go down to Mrs. Kavanagh's store on New Gower Street to buy him a bottle of Haig Ale. She replied, "No way am I walking down New Gower Street this hour in the night. Someone might drag me into a dark lane and rape me."

Paddy commented, "Don't worry Tessie, darling, it'll never get that dark."

DRESS MEASUREMENTS

Big Tess was being measured for a new dress at Ayre's Department Store on Water Street. Paddy watched as the saleslady struggled to get the tape around Tess's waist. She observed, "If a spruce tree measured that big around, it would be thirty feet tall."

GETTING OFF TRAIN

Big Tess asked the conductor on the *Newfie Bullet*, "Sir! Could you please help me get off the train?"

"Yes, ma'm," said the conductor as he approached Tess.

Tess explained, "It's because of my weight, sir, that I have to get off the train backwards. And that porter should be fired. He thinks I'm getting on and he shoves me back on again. I was supposed to get off at Clarenville and here I am now in Corner Brook."

BUYING A BOOK

Big Tess was browsing around Garland's Bookstore on Water Street when the clerk offered to help. "I want to buy a book," said Big Tess.

"You want to buy a book?" asked the clerk.

"Yes, my dear. Paddy bought me a lovely reading lamp for my birthday, and now I needs to buy myself a book," replied Tess.

BIG TESS'S NEIGHBOUR

Big Tess's friend and neighbour on Cuddihy Street operated a boarding house. When busy, she sometimes called upon Tess to work for her. She would always caution Tess, "Remember now, if you get any bad news for any of the boarders, wait and then tell them just before dinner. It makes a big difference in the food bill during the course of a year."

QUINN AT A DANCE

Just after being introduced to a young lady at a dance at the British Hall, Mickey Quinn, to make conversation, asked, "Who is that ugly man sitting across from us?"

"That's my brother," replied the young lady.

"Sorry, miss, I hadn't noticed the resemblance."

THE ELEVATOR

Mickey Quinn stepped into the elevator at the Atlantic Hotel and told the operator, "Stop at the tenth floor."

"There's only six floors in this hotel," said the operator.

"Then drop me off at the sixth. I will walk the rest of the way," commented Mickey.

QUINN AND THE PROFESSOR

Mickey Quinn was helping Professor Danielle move some of his antiques into the Octagon Castle.

"Be very careful, Quinn, that vase you're carrying is two hundred years old," cautioned the Professor.

"You can depend on me. I'll be just as careful with it as if it were spanking new," answered Quinn.

QUINN'S FIRST SHAKESPEAREAN PLAY

Professor Charles Danielle decided to introduce Mickey Quinn to a night of culture and took him along to watch the Shakespearean play *Hamlet* put off by the students of St. Patrick's Hall School. Outside the hall after the play, Danielle told Quinn, "It was most embarrassing to find myself in your presence here tonight. I shall never place myself in a similar situation again. Never!"

"Why are you so mad? I really enjoyed the play, as a matter of fact, I loved it," commented Quinn.

"You really don't know, do you? You poor simpleton," said the professor.

"No, I don't know why you are so angry, what's your problem?" Quinn asked.

"The very idea of you standing on your chair at the end of the play and bellowing 'Author! Author!' at a Shakespearean drama. Never again!" said the Professor.

The Introduction

Mickey Quinn was introducing Professor Danielle to a friend. He said, "This is my friend, Dr. Charles Danielle. He's not as stupid as he looks."

"Quinn's absolutely right. That's the big difference between me and him," quipped Danielle.

Quinn the Thinker

Mickey Quinn was sitting alone on the steps of St. Patrick's Church one day when Father Murphy came by and observed, "Mickey, my son, you look depressed. What are you thinking about?"

"My future," answered Mickey.

"What makes it so hopeless?" asked Father Murphy.

"My past," replied Mickey.

Quinn and the Old Sea Captain

Mickey Quinn was having a cup of tea with the Captain on his ship in the harbour. The vessel had just returned from a trip to South America, and the old Captain had many adventurous stories to tell.

"I was taking a swim in a very wide river when I spotted three gladiators heading straight for me. I'm telling you, Mickey, I had to swim for my life," said the Captain.

"You mean alligators," Quinn injected.

"Oh. Well, what are gladiators?" asked the Captain.

"Gladiators? Why, they're sort of flowers grown from bulbs," answered Quinn.

Quinn's Umbrella

Johnny Duff asked Mickey Quinn where he got the umbrella he was carrying. "It was a gift from my sister," replied Quinn.

"But you told me you had no sisters," commented Duff.

"I know, but that's what's engraved on the handle," said Quinn.

Deadly Statistics

Little Dickey Grey: "Do you know that every time I breathe, someone dies?"

Mickey Quinn: "Why don't you gargle your throat."

•••

Little Dickey Grey: "When you were talking to Slacker, I heard you use the word idiot several times. I hope you weren't talking about me."

Mickey Quinn: "Ah, don't be so conceited, Dickey, you're not the only idiot in St. John's."

ON IDIOTS!

WAITER AT EDWARDIAN RESTAURANT

In addition to its famous candy story, the Woods family operated a splendid Edwardian style restaurant on its second floor Water Street location. Mickey Quinn, who lived nearby at Furze's Boarding House on Queen Street at the time, was hired by Woods as a waiter.

When the manager noticed that a customer had tied the cloth napkin around his neck, he was shocked and called upon Quinn to handle it. He said, "Mr. Quinn, we cannot tolerate that here. This is not a greasy spoon. Please try to make him understand, as tactfully as possible, that his conduct is not proper etiquette."

Quinn assured the manager that he would handle the problem immediately. He approached the diner and said, "Pardon me, sir, do you want a shave or a haircut."

•••

On another occasion, Mickey dropped into Casey's Restaurant for a plate of fresh, fried fish. He was waiting a long time for his order. Finally, the waiter told him, "Mr. Quinn, your fish will be here in a few minutes."

"Is that right? What kind of bait are you using?" asked Quinn.

"No need to be sarcastic, sir, it won't be much longer," said the waiter.

"In that case bring me a pen and ink," Quinn asked.

"Whatever for?" asked the waiter.

"Well, judging by your idea of a short while, I have given up all hope of ever getting what I ordered, so I want to make a will leaving it to my brother Jack."

DINTY AND THE POLITICIAN

Billy Brown was a prominent politician of the 1950s. He served terms as a PC, MHA and a Member of Parliament and Cabinet Minister in the Diefenbaker Government. During a class visit to Holy Cross in 1955, he was asking Appy Murphy what he wanted to be when he grew up. The boy answered, "A pro soccer player."

Trying to inject some humour into the situation, Billy chuckled and said, "When I was your age I wanted to be a pirate."

From the rear of the class, Dinty Hearn shouted, "Congratulations."

BILLY BROWN

Billy Brown was tired of being interrupted while he was delivering a political speech at the CLB Armoury during a 1950s election campaign. Brown stopped his speech to comment, "We appear to have many fools here tonight. Wouldn't it be advisable to hear one at a time?"

"You are right, Billy," shouted Doc Butler from the front row, "get on with your speech."

WATER KILLS MORE

A clergyman was addressing a prayer meeting one evening on the subject of the need to abstain from consumption of alcohol. Tommy Toe and several friends had entered the hall to get in out of the winter's cold. Having heard the Reverend's admonition against alcohol, Tommy shouted, "Water has killed more people than liquor ever did."

The Reverend decided not to let the remark pass. He asked, "Can you defend that position, sir?"

Tommy answered, "Well, Reverend, there was the great flood!"

THE SIGHTS

Paddy from the Southern Shore turned up on the steps of Lucy Left Leg's house on Cuddihy Street one day.

"And what brought you to town, Paddy?" asked Lucy.

"Oh, well, I just came to see the sights, and I thought that I'd call on you first," replied Paddy.

THEY TOOK THE HINT

When Lucy Left Leg asked her neighbour Bridey Walsh if she was still being bothered by relatives from Bell Island who came to town every Sunday for the weekly pork and cabbage dinner and went home without ever offering to share in the expense of the meal, Bridey answered, "They finally took the hint."

"What did you say to them?" queried Lucy.

"Not a thing," explained Bridey, "but I served them sponge cake every time they came over."

DINTY'S INTERPRETATION

During a religion class at Holy Cross School, Brother Harry French was giving an example to reinforce a story he was telling. He said:

> He headed straight to his goal. He looked neither to the right nor to the left, but pressed forward, moved by a definite purpose. Neither friend nor foe could delay him nor turn him from his course. All who crossed his path did so at their own peril. What would you call such a man?

'A taxi driver,' shouted Dinty Hearn from the back of the classroom.

TAKING CENSUS IN TORBAY

During the 1940s, a census-taker approached a woman washing clothes in a galvanized tub outside the backdoor of her house in Torbay. He couldn't help but notice that there were many children going in and out of the house and playing around the garden.

"Excuse me, Ma'm, I'm the Government census-taker. How many children do you have?"

The lady stopped her washing, wiped her forehead and replied, "Now let me think. There's Alice, Bridget, Margaret, Betty Lou, Paddy, Mickey, Johnny, Jimmy and Frank. And there's-"

The census-taker interrupted, "Ma'm, if you could just give me the number–"

"Number!" exclaimed the lady indignantly. "Listen here, Mister, we ain't got to numberin 'em yet. We ain't run out of names!"

PATSY AND THE DOCTOR

When Patsy Muldane was a patient at the Waterford, she tried to commit suicide by hanging herself. A doctor entered the room and found Patsy standing on a table with a rope tied around her waist.

He asked, "What in God's name are you doing, Patsy?

"I'm going to kill myself, doctor," answered Patsy.

"Going to kill yourself! Why then did you tie the rope round your waist?" asked the doctor.

"Well, when I put it round my neck, it chokes," Patsy replied.

IT'S IN THE BOOK

Doris, an attractive brunette working at Ayre & Sons Department Store on Water Street, was approached by a Canadian soldier who asked, "If you'll give me your telephone number, I'll call you up Friday night."

Not at all impressed by the soldier, Doris replied, "My number is in the phone book."

"Fine," said the soldier. "What's your name?"

"That's in the book, too," answered Doris.

IDENTIFICATION VERIFIED

A man approached the bank teller to have a cheque cashed. The clerk asked the man if he had any identification. The customer removed a photograph of himself from his wallet and, as he passed it to the teller, said, "I think this should satisfy you as to who I am."

The teller examined the picture closely and took several glimpses at the customer, then said, "Yes, there is no doubt that is you." She then cashed the cheque.

FIRST TASTE OF BEER

Poor old Mrs. Snow of Flower Hill was given the first glass of beer she ever had in her life. A puzzled look came over her face after her first taste.

"Strange, very strange!" she said. "It tastes just like the medicine my husband Mike has been taking for the last twenty-five years."

TEMPERANCE MEETING

A new member of the Total Abstinence Society was addressing a meeting at the TA Hall on Duckworth Street. Stan Dooley listened attentively as the man told the gathering, "I have lived in St. John's all my life. In St. John's, there are sixty-eight taverns and another thirty hop beer stores, and I am proud to say that I have never been in one of them!"

Temporary silence greeted the ending of the speech until Stan asked, "Which one is that?"

HIMEY BROWN

Frank Jackman, a struggling artist from Conception Bay rented an apartment on Casey Street from a well-known city landlord named Himey Brown. When Jackman got behind a month in his rent, Himey paid him a visit.

Frank reminded his landlord, "Listen here, Mr. Brown, in a few more years people will look up at this dilapidated house and say, 'Jackman, the artist lived there.'"

Himey responded, "If I don't get the back rent by tonight, they'll be able to say it tomorrow!"

AMATEURS

The Courier, an old St. John's newspaper, printed one of the shortest musical criticisms of the nineteenth century in Newfoundland. It read, "An amateur string quartet played Brahms at the Pitts Memorial Hall last evening. Brahms lost."

BEN JACKMAN REMEMBERS

Ben Jackman at the West End Club in St. John's recalled his childhood days growing up in St. John's. "I overheard my father telling a neighbour, 'We always hide the Christmas presents from Ben, but he always finds them. This year we're going to hide Ben!'"

STOPS LEAK

The little boy went into the kitchen and told his father, "Dad, you can take your finger off the leak in the pipe now."

"Thank the good lord," said his father. "Is the plumber here at last?"

"No, the house is on fire," replied the boy.

THE LORD ANSWERS BESSIE

Bessie knelt down before the altar in her parish church. After praying for a list of favours, she asked, "Lord, I just don't understand your ways. I come to church every day, and I never ask for anything big or expensive, just little favours, things like jobs for my relatives, a cure for my lumbago or that I win the odd game of bingo. But it seems like you don't hear my prayers. They are never answered. Now Maudie McGrath, that auld hussey next door to me, is on her third husband and still seeing half the men in the neighbourhood. She never goes to church, she smokes, drinks and swears. Blessed Redeemer! She got a fine house, a new car, a cabin at Deer Park and she's never in want of a dollar. Why Lord? Why?"

Suddenly a thundering sound fills the church as God answers, "Bessie, Bessie, my child. The answer to your question is simple. Maudie don't bug me!"

BESSIE IN CONFESSION

Bessie never missed mass on Sunday nor the weekly confession at her parish church. She always sought out one particular priest to hear her confession. This prompted the priest to comment to a fellow priest, "I dread hearing Bessie's confession. It's like getting stoned to death with popcorn."

BLACK FLAG

"What does it mean when there is a black flag flying over the post office?"

"They're hiring."

DUNNE IN BOSTON

The little old gray-haired mother of Paddy Dunne asked Barney Sullivan, a neighbour, who was going "off to the Boston States," as the old folks would say, to seek his fame and fortune, if he would do her a favour. Mrs. Dunne told Barney that she had not heard from her son in ten years and asked, "Would you be kind enough to look him up when you get there and tell him to write his poor mother."

"I'll be happy to do it, ma'm, but how will I find him," asked Barney.

Mrs. Dunne answered, "Well, the last I heard, he was living in a little white house in Boston."

Off went Barney Sullivan to Boston. One day, while walking along a road, he noticed a small white house in a field off the road. He had no idea it was an outhouse. Barney walked right up and began banging on the door. The fellow inside asked, "What do you want?"

"Are you Dunne," asked Barney.

"Yes, I am," replied the occupant.

"Well, why in hell don't you write your poor old mother?" shouted Barney.

He Would Work for Nothing

Some weeks later, Barney Sullivan ran into some old friends from St. John's in a Boston pub. He had just found work and, to celebrate, he offered to buy a round of drinks.

"What kind of work are you doing?" asked Johnny Murphy.

"Well, that's what makes living in Boston so great. I'm a labourer helping to tear down a Protestant church, and guess what? I'm getting paid for it!" replied Barney.

Happy Compromise

"What a beautiful little baby he is!" exclaimed the neighbour who had called.

"He isn't six months old either, and he weighs over twenty pounds," said the proud young mother.

"What have you named him?"

"Well," hesitated the mother, "Henry and I differed a little about that. He wanted to give him one name, but we finally compromised and agreed to call him John Wesley."

"I see, you named him after the great founder of Meth–"

"No, indeed," quickly interrupted the mother. "That name, as I said, is a compromise."

"But how?"

"The John is for John Calvin and the Wesley is for John Wesley," explained the mother.

"Oh, I see."

The Irishman and the Priest

A priest, who was rather a pompous gentleman, visited the house of an Irish-born farmer on the outskirts of St. John's to baptize a child.

"Are you prepared?" he asked the fond parent.

"Oi am father, I've got a grand ham for tea."

"I mean spiritually prepared," thundered the cleric.

"Af carse I am, oh yes, I got two wonderful bottles of first-class whiskey from O'Rielley's Pub."

Wrong Again

Peter Cashin, speaking at a political rally in the west end of St. John's, was attacking the Government with more venom than reason. A man at the back of the hall at last cried out, "You're wrong, sir!"

A little nettled, Cashin continued and ignored the heckler.

In answer to another strong condemnation of the Government came again the assertion, "You're wrong, sir!"

Cashin looked angry, but continued on the warpath.

"You're wrong, sir!" again rang out.

Angrily addressing the persistent heckler, Cashin shouted, "Look here, I could tell this man something about this Government which would make his hair stand on end."

"You're wrong again, sir!" came exultantly from the critic, as he stood up and removed his hat. His head was as bald as the proverbial billiard ball.

The Other Side

Murphy, who is a vegetarian and of an argumentative turn of mind, was recently urging Hearn, who is fond of roast beef and pork chops, to join the ranks of those who shun meat.

"You'll feel so much better if you give up all that flesh diet," Murphy said complacently. "It's coarsening to the nature, too. Wasn't it some wise old German who said that a man becomes like what he eats? Think of what you may look like if you keep on eating pork!"

"Oh, yeah!" snorted the unconvinced Hearn, "I'd just as soon look like a lolly, comfortable pig as like a bunch of carrots. You're the one who should look out. You could become a cabbage head."

Chicken Homiletic

A country minister in the course of his dining out on the circuit came to a house where a roast chicken was served for dinner.

He had previously encountered a series of rib-corned beef dinners and chicken looked good to him.

"Well," he facetiously remarked, "here's where that chicken enters the ministry."

"I hope it does better there than in lay work," commented the small boy of the family.

How He Remembered

The absent-minded professor arrived home in a thoroughly soaked condition. "I forgot my umbrella, my dear," he exclaimed to his wife.

Surprised that he had even remembered about forgetting anything, his wife said, "When did you think of it?"

The man of genius smiled with satisfaction. "Why, dear," he remarked, "when the rain stopped, and I attempted to put it down."

Townie Thoughts

When the beer runs out...does it hop?

•••

City belles encase themselves in paper petticoats. Now, in case of a rain shower, could these belles be wrung out?

•••

Impressions of Greece. A pork chop dinner at Lucy Left Legs.

Waiter Encounters

"Hey, waiter, did you forget about me?"
"Certainly not, sir. You're the stuffed cod's head."

•••

"Hey, waiter, there's something wrong with the chicken."
"Don't tell me, buddy, I'm not a vet."

NEXT TRAIN

"When is the next train to Grand Falls?" asked Angus.

"At 1:00 p.m.," replied the ticket agent.

"What? Isn't there one before that?" asked Angus.

"No, sir, we never run one train before the next," answered the agent.

AS THE CROW FLIES

A motorist ran out of gas and asked a fisherman working nearby, "How far is it to the next town?"

"Well, it's about four miles as the crow flies," answered the fisherman.

"Well, how far is it if the damned crow has to walk and carry an empty gas can?" asked the motorist.

GALLOWS HUMOUR

The executioner of Wo Fen Game was a prisoner from Bell Island. During the procession to the gallows in the prison yard at HMP, he stumbled while attempting to walk up the steps to the gallows and exclaimed, "A man could be killed going up these steps." Fortunately, the condemned man could not speak English. The comment sparked muffled sounds of laughter among witnesses.

BEN JACKMAN

Ben Jackman was the old centre town's answer to Milton Berle, a real master of the one liners. One day, he met Gog Abbott on John Street. He told Gog that according to the day's newspaper, Ferg Snow was sent to jail for a month. Gog asked, "What was the charge?"

Ben replied, "No charge. Everything is free."

●●●

Whenever the boys talked about some of the stupid things a neighbourhood kid named Spuds used to do, Ben was usually ready with a few quips. He would ask, "You know, the only thing that stopped Spuds from going to University?"

"No, tell me," said Gog.

"High school," answered Ben.

•••

On another occasion when Dinty Hearn asked Spuds what he would be when he finished school, Ben interjected, "Forty."

•••

Ben noted that Spuds ran away from home once. "His parents never found him.....they never looked."

At this point Ben would take a sip of Blue Star and reminisce, "Spuds' father always said that Spuds could have been anything he wanted....and he wanted to be an idiot."

•••

Ben described a lazy downtown character called 'Saltwater Bill' who often said that he would rather die than work, Ben would say, "Don't condemn poor Saltwater Bill, the problem goes back to his youth. He swallowed a spoon when he was a baby and hasn't stirred since."

•••

A neighbour of Ben's on Pleasant Street was known for his stinginess. While discussing him, Ben used to say, "He keeps his wife's teeth in his pocket when he goes out so she can't eat between meals."

•••

Ben was telling his friend Gog Abbott that Jim Higgins was Newfoundland's most brilliant lawyer. "He can take one look at a contract and tell right away if its oral or written," said Ben.

Gog added, "Not only that, but Higgins can read blueprints."

"Yeah," said Ben, "he can read any colour print. Smart lawyer!"

•••

At the 1999 Flower Hill Reunion at the Knight's of Columbus, Ben upset his wife Pauline with one of his witty responses. Pauline had bought a new dress for the event. Before entering the banquet hall, she asked Ben if he felt the dress made her look big.

Ben replied, "No, its not the dress, its your fat arse that makes you look big."

Pauline got in the last jab. After Ben had to leave early on the first night of the Reunion, friends asked her what happened to him. Pauline said, "He was trying to impress the women and he held his stomach in so much, he threw out his back."

•••

Ben worked at Horwood Lumber Company for several years. He recalled the time a fellow from George Street came in and asked if Ben knew where he could buy some cockroaches. Ben asked, "Why would you want to buy cockroaches?"

The fellow answered, "My landlord just gave me my notice to get out and insisted that I leave the house in the same condition it was when he first rented it to me."

NIGHT PRAYERS

When Jean Baird was courtin' Frank Murphy, she was often called upon to babysit Frank's younger brothers and sisters. On one occasion, she asked baby Trish if she knew the Lord's Prayer. Trish proudly answered, "Yes."

"Well, it's past your bedtime so say your prayers and it's off to bed," Jean told Trish, who knelt down by her bed and prayed:

Now I lay me down to sleep
I pray the lord, my soul to keep.
And if he hollers, let him go,
Eenie, Meenie, Miney, Mo.

MAN OF PERCEPTION

Gosse's Tavern on New Gower Street was a popular watering hole for working class people for more than fifty years. On one occasion, a Trinity Bay man was having a drink at the bar when he noticed that the man beside him had only one leg. He looked down, and commented, "Hey, buddy, I see you've lost a leg."

The man looked down, then turned to the bartender and said, "Good Jasus, Tom, I think he's right."

DINT'S MECHANICAL PROBLEMS

There wasn't a car in St. John's that Doug King of McFarlane Street could not fix. On one occasion, he was called upon to fix Dinty Hearn's first car. Dinty explained the problems to Doug, "The engine makes a knocking sound, the battery is dead, the plugs are not working, the radiator is leaking and there is a humming sound from the rear end. Is there anything you can do for me?"

As Doug removes his hat and places his right hand on his heart, he says, "Sure, Dinty, repeat after me....Our father who art in Heaven..."

SCHOOL DAYS

Brian Healy remembers a fellow in his class at Holy Cross whose father walked him to school every day. Brian explained, "They were both in the same class."

JACK MURPHY'S FAVOURITE WITTICISMS FROM THE 1950S

"Don't worry about biting off more than you can chew. Your mouth is probably a whole lot bigger than you think."

•••

There was always keen competition between St. Pat's and Holy Cross during basketball season. Jack says, "One year St. Pat's had a 14 and 6 record, 14 arrests and 6 convictions."

IT'S A LIVING

"I think you would like my husband, he makes a living with his pen."

"Oh, so your husband is a writer."

"No, he raises pigs."

•••

"What's worse than eating hash at a restaurant when you don't know what's in it?"

"Eating it at home where you do know."

•••

234

Stan and Johnny talking military.
Stan: "How big is a battleship?"
Johnny: "What kind of a battleship?"
Stan: "A big one."
Johnny: "How big?"

LETTER TO SON IN BOSTON STATES

Many St. John's fellas went to work in the Boston States. The following is a letter one mother wrote to her son. It was first presented in Newfoundland through newspapers in the 1940s. There is another version which has an Irishman writing his mother but the content is very different.

Dear Tommy,

I am writing this slow because I know that you can't read fast. We don't live where we did when you left home. Your dad read in the paper that most accidents happen within twenty miles from home so we moved. I won't be able to send you the address, as the last family that lived here took the house numbers when they left so they wouldn't have to change their address.

This place is real nice. It even has a washing machine. I'm not sure if it works too well though. Last week I put a load in, pulled the chain and haven't seen them since. The weather isn't too bad here, it only rained twice last week. The first time it rained for three days and the second time for four days. John locked his keys in the car yesterday. We were worried because it took him two hours to get me and Harold out.

Uncle Ron fell in a whiskey vat last week. Other workers tried to save him, but he fought them off and drowned. We had him cremated and he burned for three days. Charlie, Bob and Frank went off a bridge in their pick-up truck. Bob was driving. He rolled down the window and swam to safety. Charlie and Frank were in the back. We think they drowned because they couldn't get the tailgate down. Write soon.

Love Mom

POETRY CONTEST

During an English class, the teacher challenged anyone in the class to compose a short poem in thirty seconds. The prize...no homework for a week. Jack Murphy got up and recited his:

Slowly across the desert sand
Trekked the dusty caravan
Men on camel, two by two
Destination–Timbuktu.

The class loved it. Not to be outdone Dinty Hearn stood up and recited his four lines:

Tim and I, a huntin' went
Met three whores in a pop up tent.
They was three, we was two
So, I bucked one and Timbuktu!!

BEAVER MURPHY

Beaver's father was nearsighted and required glasses. One day, Harry, his father, received a letter about Beaver which apparently pleased him. He boasted to his wife Mary, "Beaver is well behaved in school. Look at the letter he got today from Mother Teresa."

Mary knew Beaver better and said, "Here, let me read that letter." She glanced down the page then scoffed, "This is not from Mother Teresa...it's from Teresa's mother and she warns that if Beaver doesn't stay away from her daughter, she's going to complain to the principal."

•••

In the early 1960s when a long-haired, unkempt hippie with a ring in his nose stopped in front of Walsh's Bakery to ask directions, Beaver noticed the ring in his nose and asked, "If I pull the ring out, will your head blow up?"

CAPITOL THEATRE

Whenever there was a good movie at the Capitol Theatre on Henry Street, people arrived early in all kinds of weather and formed a long line-up outside to make sure of getting a good seat.

236

On the occasion of the first Goldfinger movie in St. John's, the line-up was long. Gus Neville slapped the guy in front of him on the back, and when the guy turned around, Gus said, "It's OK pal, I'm just going to the store to get some smokes."

The man replied," Well, that's no reason to slap me on the back."

Gus said, "I didn't slap you. I just made a big chalk mark on your back so I wouldn't forget my place."

FAMOUS NAME

A young writer, hoping to have his first book published, called the publishing company to inquire about the manuscript he had submitted.

The publisher told him, "Your book is quite good. It's well-written, but we only publish work by writers with well-known names."

"Then I'm very happy to hear that because my name is Murphy," said the aspiring author.

DOG ATTACK

A man was walking his dog over Livingstone Street when it suddenly attacked a woman. She managed to outrun the dog and called out for her husband to come out and deal with the problem.

The dog owner knew the man well and feared he was about to receive a beating. He pleaded with the man, "How about we settle this. Will twenty dollars do?"

"That will be number one," said the husband as he handed over a twenty dollar bill, "and if you drop back in a few days, I'll give you a few more dollars."

BINGO

What has one hundred legs and no teeth?
The front row at the weekly Bingo game.

EPITAPHS

A moose, a man, a loaded gun,
No moose, dead man, thy will be done.

•••

Here lies father and mother and sister and I,
We all died within the space of one short year.
They all be buried at Harbour Grace, except I,
And I be buried here.

•••

Little Willie from his mirror
Licked the mercury right off,
Thinking, in his childish error,
It would cure the whooping cough.
At the funeral his mother
Smartly said to Mrs. Brown,
"'Twas a chilly day for Willie
When the mercury went down."

Tough Meat

Overheard at a fashionable Water Street Restaurant when the second course of the day's special was being served:

A trucker asked, "What's this leathery stuff on my plate?"

"Filet of sole," answered the waitress.

"Take it away and get me a nice tender piece from the upper part of the boot," commented the trucker.

Help Is On the Way

Two fishermen stranded on a large piece of ice off the coast of Newfoundland suddenly became very excited when they saw a large boat approaching. They waved their hands, jumped and shouted with joy, "We're gonna be saved! We're gonna be saved! Here comes the *Titanic.*"

Let 'er Burn!

A man watching his house burn says to his neighbours, "Ah let 'er burn. I got enough wood in the attic to build another one."

She Ain't for He

A favorite story of Premier Joey Smallwood about the first campaign after Confederation was the following. He recalled that a woman stood in opposition to one of his candidates. Smallwood said, "The Newfoundlanders in that riding thought up a slogan which became their battle cry and that was typically Newfoundland in expression, 'Don't vote for She – She ain't for he!'"

NOT ALL OUTPORTS FOR JOEY IN 1949

Joey Smallwood always chose this story as the most humourous of the 1949 Confederation campaign:

A fisherman from a harbour near St. John's came to the offices of the Confederate Party. 'Is Mr. Smallwood here? We want him to come to our harbour,' inquired the fisherman.

Greg Power, who later became my Finance Minister, patiently explained to the fisherman that Mr. Smallwood could not, in the short time of the campaign, visit every one of Newfoundland's 1300 settlements. But that did not satisfy the fishermen who persisted.'We want Mr. Smallwood to come to our fishing harbour.'

Again, Greg patiently explained that it would be impossible for the Premier to visit every settlement personally.

'Well,' the fisherman drawled, 'we want him to come to ours so we can drown the bastard!'

SMALLWOOD VS. CASHIN

In April 1953, during a debate in the Newfoundland Legislature over a Fisheries' Loans' Bill, Premier Joseph R. Smallwood engaged in banter with his arch-rival, Peter Cashin, and the leader of the Opposition, Malcolm Hollett. It left the house in uproarious laughter.

Smallwood was explaining to the Legislature, "The Arctic Whaling Company is a small company and they handle only small whales – Potheads, out around Dildo in Trinity Bay."

"There's a few of them around here too, aren't there?" interjected Major Peter Cashin an arch-rival of Smallwood at the time.

Smallwood replied, "I'd use a stronger word than 'Potheads.' I would call them 'Dunderheads.'"

Amid the laughter that followed, Malcolm Hollett shouted, "There's collusion going on around here." After which the laughter got even louder.

But, always one to get in the last dig, Smallwood commented, "Yes, indeed! The Honourable and gallant member and I have been collaborating with beautiful and even touching co-operation ever since Newfoundland got back Responsible Government, of course, at times we have fallen out, but at other times we see eye to eye. This afternoon happens to be one of the latter."

JACK KIDNEY'S SHOE REPAIR SHOP

Frank Murphy was rummaging through a box of old papers he had hidden away in the attic and came across a ticket from Jack Kidney's Shoe Repair Store on Brazil Square. He asked his wife Jean to take a look at it and she noted that the date stamped on it was over eight years old. They were well aware of Jack often being carried away with his well-known 'hot stove debates' with old-timers in back of the store and letting his work slide behind. But they wondered who in the family had forgotten to pick up the shoes.

For pure devilment, Frank convinced Jean to go with him. With his best poker player face, Frank handed the ticket to Kidney and asked, "Are these ready yet."

"Let me take a look in back," said Jack. There was a lot of shuffling and movement and after a few minutes, Jack shouted, "Here they are, I found them."

"You got to be foolin," said Murphy.

Kidney walked calmly back to the counter empty-handed and drawled, "You'll have to come back, they won't be finished until Friday."

BARBERSHOP TALK

A vacation outside the country in the early 1950s was always a source of interesting barbershop talk. When Pop Finn returned to St. John's after visiting relatives in London, England, he was mesmerizing his barber, Tubby O'Brien, who had been cutting pop's hair for years, with anecdotes about the trip.

Tubby: "Did you actually get to see Buckingham Palace?"

Pop: "Of course I did, I had my picture taken at the gate and got a tour of the Palace."

Tubby: "You did? That's amazing! Did you get to see the Queen?"

Pop: "Get to see her! Why I was as close to her as I am to you right now."

Tubby: "That's incredible! You were that close to the Queen of England."

Pop: "As a matter of fact, there was quite a crowd of tourists there, but she stopped and spoke a few words to me."

Tubby: "Go way by! The Queen of England actually stopped to talk to you?"

Pop: "Well, she stopped right in front of me, stared right at me, then leaned over and whispered in my ear."

Tubby: "What did she say? What did she say?"

Pop: "She said, 'Where in the name of God did you get that stupid haircut?'"

DOCTOR! DOCTOR!

A man leaving St. Patrick's Church after Sunday mass fainted and fell to the ground. In no time, a crowd surrounded him. Fonce Howlett ran from across the street and pushed the crowd back. A man, kneeling on one knee, was trying to help the victim. Fonce tapped him on the shoulder and said, "Move out of the way, sir, I have first aid training." The man stood back and watched as Fonce took charge.

Fonce quickly loosened the victim's tie and took his pulse. The man Fonce had ordered aside then stepped forward and tapping Fonce on the shoulder said, "Sir, when you get to the part where you are supposed to call a doctor, I'm already here."

INSULTED

One night in late October,
When I was far from sober,
Returning with my load with manly pride,
My feet began to stutter,
So I lay down in the gutter,
And a pig came near and lay down
by my side.
A lady passing by was heard to say:
"You can tell a man who boozes,
By the company he chooses,"
And the pig got up and
slowly walked away.

TALKING WITH SPIRIT

An old fishermen communicating with the spirit of his departed wife asked, "Is that you 'Enrietta?"

"Yes, 'Arry', it's I."

"Are you 'appy, 'Enrietta?"

"Very 'appy," she answered.

"'Appier than you was with me?"

"Oh, much, much 'appier."

"Where are you, 'Enrietta?"

"In 'ell."

WHEN RADIO CAME TO NEWFOUNDLAND

Mrs. Snow: "The radio will never take the place of newspapers."

Mrs. Murphy: "Why?"

Mrs. Snow: "You can't wipe your arse with a radio."

IN THE DAYS OF THE HORSES

Old Mr. Power was very proud of his horse. He told his neighbour, Mrs. O'Neill, "I got a really smart horse." As he proudly patted the horse on the head, he added, "Yes, ma'm, this horse knows as much as I do."

"Well, don't tell anybody that. You might want to sell him some day."

AMBITION

Doc Butler chatting with Jim Fardy at the Flower Hill store:

Doc: "You know Jim, some men thirst after fame, some thirst after love and some thirst after money."

Jim: "I know, Doc, but I can tell you something that all men thirst after."

"What's that?" asked Doc.

"Salted peanuts," said Jim, adding, "We have lots of them and only five cents a bag."

GREAT MEMORY

Stan Dooley trying to impress Khaki Crotty:

"You know Khaki, I can recite all the names on five pages of our telephone book. Wanna hear me?"

Khaki says, "Well, go ahead."

Stan closes his eyes and begins, "Murphy, Murphy, Murphy, Murphy, Murphy."

DIFFERENCE IN VISION AND SIGHT

Paddy asks Fonce, "What's the difference between vision and sight?"

Fonce says, "See Big Tess and Helen Murphy sitting there on Fardy's steps?"

"Yes," says Paddy.

Fonce explains, "Well, Helen there is a vision of loveliness, but Big Tess – she's a sight."

ADVICE NOT WANTED

"Are you taking anything for your flu," Stan asks Fonce.

"Yes, I'm taking boxing lessons to beat the crap out of the next person who tells me what I should be taking," answered Fonce.

BE ALERT!

Michael "Dinty" Hearn was not paying attention during a Geometry class being conducted by Brother Harry French at Holy Cross School in St. John's. Brother French noted the behaviour and said, "Michael, be alert!"

Dinty's brother Pat seated in the next row commented, "That's all the class needs now – another lert."

Jack Fitzgerald has participated and contributed to several national and international television documentaries. He has appeared in *The Real Treasure Island* produced by adventurer and author Alex Capus and filmed by Monaco Films of Germany; two documentaries on Cocos Island by Dr. Ina Knobloch of City Television, Frankfurt, Germany; *The Knights of Columbus Fire*, by Partners in Motion, a Canadian production company; and *Legends and Lore of the North Atlantic*, hosted by Gordon Pinsent and produced by Pope Productions of St. John's, Newfoundland. He is currently researching for, and will be participating in, an international documentary related to the history and treasures of South America being produced by a group of filmmakers in Germany, France and Australia.